ASTROLOCALITY ASTROLOGY

In the course of his work as an engineer, business consultant and sportsman, Martin Davis has travelled widely and lived in many different countries. He is a well known lecturer and practitioner in this area of astrology and his energy and enthusiasm for it have encouraged many others to investigate the subject further. Martin is currently the European representative for Matrix astrological software.

Martin Davis may be contacted at:

The Library Wing
Abbey Saint Bathans House
Duns
Berwickshire TD11 3TX
Scotland

Email: earthsearch@astral.demon.co.uk
Website: www.astral.demon.co.uk

ASTROLOCALITY

ASTROLOGY

A Guide to What it is
and
How to use it

by

Martin Davis

First published in 1999 by
The Wessex Astrologer Ltd
PO Box 2751
Bournemouth
England
BH6 3ZJ
Tel/Fax +44 (0) 1202 424695

Martin Davis asserts the moral right to be recognised as the author of this work

Cover Design by Arbuckle and Co., Swindon, Wilts
Back cover photograph by John Behm

Printed and bound in England by Biddles Ltd., Guildford and King's Lynn

A catalogue record for this book is available at The British Library

ISBN 1902405056

Win*Star Plus Version 2 by Matrix Software, Big Rapids, MI. USA.
Win*Maps (a module of Win*Star Plus) by Matrix Software.
Solar Maps by Esoteric Technologies Pty. Ltd. Australia. Published by Astrolabe Inc.
MA.
Official A*C*G* maps by Equinox, The Astrology Shop, London.

Astro*Carto*Graphy (A*C*G) and Cyclo*Carto*Graphy (C*C*G) are registered
trademarks of Jim Lewis.
Local Space (LS) is a registered trademark of Matrix Software.
Solar Maps copyright Esoteric Technologies Pty. Ltd. and Astrolabe Inc.

TIME AND SPACE IN ASTROLOGY

An Introductory Comment by Nicholas Campion
President of The Astrological Association of Great Britain

Jung's oft-quoted dictum that 'whatever is born or done at this moment of time, has the quality of this moment of time'[1] is, perhaps, the presiding manifesto of modern astrology. But, we may ask, whatever happened to space? Jung had nothing to say about the quality of the place at which an event happens, at least not in relation to astrology.

Students of astrology are taught that the three items of data required for the calculation of any horoscope are time, date and place, and those concerned with astrology's advanced technicalities argue the pros and cons of different house systems, yet for these purposes space is treated as neutral, as a means merely of working out the ascendant and midheaven. But apart from this, spatial questions scarcely ever make an appearance in contemporary astrology. Yet it was not always so. The placing and construction of sacred sites from Megalithic circles to Egyptian, Greek, Mesoamerican and Hindu temples, reflect a concern with both the universe's metaphysical structure and observations of horizon phenomena. The beliefs of the architects and builders responsible for these monuments indicate a concern with space that equals that with time. And that this concern was once widespread is demonstrated in the evidence provided by the modern historical disciplines of archaeo-astronomy and ethno-astronomy. When we turn to astrology itself, we find that the Babylonian astrologers were deeply concerned with such questions as the direction in which a celestial omen was observed, the part of the sky in which it took place, or the quadrant of the Moon which was obscured during an eclipse. The Babylonians, armed with this knowledge, believed that it was possible to ascertain the region in which an omen's significance would be experienced. Ptolemy rationalised and simplified the Babylonian model, inventing a crude system in which the twelve zodiac signs corresponded to twelve regions and peoples. Medieval horoscopy retained the allocation of houses to different places, and horary astrology has preserved the link between the four angles and the cardinal directions. Yet ninety-nine percent of twentieth century western astrology has focused on the inner journey rather than the outer experience. The question that psychological, natal astrology has failed to answer, for all its perceived advantages, is why an individual might have an inner experience in one place rather than another. It has tended to ignore the ancient notion that place, space and direction might possess quality, reveal symbolic significance or indicate divine intent.

Astrocartography, so ably developed and popularised by the late and sorely missed Jim Lewis represents a major innovation in the field, and offers a substantial aid to answering the question of why, within the terms set by astrology, people experience diverse cultures and places in different ways. And in this respect Roy Firebrace, the first AA President, deserves an honourable mention for featuring ACG maps in Spica, his magazine, in the 1950s. Local Space is less known than Astrocartography, but equally capable of providing insights into the question of 'where?' rather than 'when?'. Together these two additions to the astrologers' tool kit restore the divinatory link between space and time. Martin Davis' eloquent exposition of both techniques provides a comprehensive and welcome account of one of the most significant developments in modern astrology.

NOTE
1. C.G. Jung, In Memory of Richard Wilhelm, memorial address delivered in Munich 1930.

FOREWORD

The material in this book was developed from the Astrolocality lectures and workshops I have been giving over the past years, mostly in Great Britain but also in places farther afield such as Athens, Dublin, Johannesburg, and Moscow. I have tried to present it in a way that addresses the many questions asked by students and to directly cover areas they felt needed clarification. Among other things, the reader will find a unique and detailed presentation of Local Space maps and charts, as well as examples of 'destiny points': an outcome of combining the perspectives of both Astro*Carto*Graphy and Local Space into one system [1].

My explorations with these techniques began over a decade ago when I purchased my first A*C*G map from the late Jim Lewis. In 1989 I was one of the first to receive Matrix Software's DOS program AstroMaps Hi Res [2], which allowed me to begin my own in-depth research and then to pass my insights on to others in articles, workshops and lectures.

Since I have lived and travelled in many locations around the world, the influences described by the maps were immediately apparent to me. With my natal Moon near its zenith position over Sao Paulo Brazil, for example, I could now understand why I had been greeted so emotionally there. Although I was only a minor figure participating in the 1963 Pan American games in that city, I had been begged for autographs and carried off triumphantly on the shoulders of a Brazilian sporting crowd.

I was fascinated by Astrolocality astrology at first sight and an interest in it has never left me. At first, just having the information about global locations was justification enough, but after the Uranus-Neptune conjunctions of 1993 my life landscape began to change. A new awareness emerged heightening my sensitivity to the past and to the earth itself. To my surprise, Astrolocality astrology became more than just a tool for locational information. Through it I was able to focus on Mother Earth in a fresh way, thereby revitalising my connection with her.

The language of Astrolocality astrology not only revealed new earth connections but it also inspired me to reconsider its ancient roots. Again to my surprise, I saw current Astrolocality astrology was one of the so-called 'archaic revivals' [3] that we see today. As with all archaic revivals, we reach back to the past to see what we had of substance years ago and then determine how it might be reinvented to make it useful today. Contemporary Astrolocality astrology fits right in with this revival. With it, we're bringing back a form of geomancy [4], the art and craft of determining appropriate, meaningful earth direction and earth location in our lives. Geomancy was practised by shamans and priest-astrologers of past ages who employed such things as omens and astronomical markers to gain their knowledge. Nowadays we're using modern tools such as computers and computer software[5] for *specific* and *personalised* information about these locations and directions, be it in our homes, our communities, or the wider world at large.

I would like to express my appreciation to those who have been important in the creation of this book and the field itself. Firstly to the late Jim Lewis and to Michael Erlewine, both of whom contributed the original and inspired work which remains the backbone of Astrolocality astrology today. Michael's important original articles on Local Space are reprinted in Appendix 4. They are a must-read for all serious students of the technique.

I have a big and appreciative thank-you to other astrologers who not only gave me their support and encouragement in this project, but who also contributed their work to it as a help to all future students. In alphabetical order they are:

- Ralph and Lonni DeAmicas, for the rich examples they share with us from their Local Space consultations.

- Jeff Jawer, for his ACG interpretations (in Appendix 1). Jeff's delineations are a welcome and important addition to the field. I'm sure they will become a major reference source for years to come.

- Angel Thompson, for her descriptions of Local Space planetary lines in our homes (see Appendix 3). They too will be a major reference source for us. Angel, it is noted, is at the very centre of Astrolocality, writing, lecturing and co-ordinating activities in both ACG and Local Space[6].

My gratitude to Robert Currey of the Equinox Astrology Shop in London for allowing the reprint of the obituary he wrote for Jim Lewis (see Appendix 7) and for his providing the 'official' ACG maps used in this book. Gratitude and thanks as well to Paul Newman, Kris Shapar, Anthony Blake and Jed Pemberton for their assistance with the manuscript.

A big thank-you to my friends and astrological colleagues, Ron Howland and Sean Lovatt; their sound advice is reflected in much of what is written here. And I wouldn't want to miss the opportunity of proclaiming my gratitude to Margaret Cahill, my publisher, who convinced me that now was the time and this was the place for me to sit down and finally write the textbook I had been promising for years.

NOTES

1. The proposal for combined use of the Astrolocality techniques was first published by Martin Davis in the November/December 1989 issue of the British Astrological Journal in the article titled 'Local Space Astrology'.

2. Designed and programmed by Michael Erlewine.

3. We note archaic revivals in many fields. We are seeing them happen in spiritual traditions, customs, medicines, and yes, in astrology as well. See 'The Archaic Revival: Speculations on Psychedelic Mushrooms, the Amazon, Virtual Reality, Evolution, Shamanism, the Rebirth of the Goddess, etc.', by Terence McKenna, Harper, 1992.

4. From the Greek, 'ge', the earth; 'manteia', divination by means of the observation of points on the earth.

5. I have used two excellent Windows computer programs in the preparation of this book. They are Matrix Software's Win*Star Plus, v.2 (for all charts and its Win*Maps module), and the Astrolabe/Esoteric Technology program, Solar Maps v..1.07. I found both necessary to gain all the features that were needed. An appreciative and hearty 'well done' to the companies and the programmers who created them. I also used the 'official' maps as generated by the Equinox Astrology Shop in Covent Garden, London. Their full-colour presentation is commended, as are the accompanying ACG and CCG booklets.

6. Angel is the director of Continuum, the organisation that trains and certifies astrologers in ACG. Continuum uses its earnings to provide grants, donations and scholarships to the astrological community.

PREFACE

This guide is primarily a tale of two techniques, Astro*Carto*Graphy (ACG) and Local Space (LS)[1]. One astrologer has figured prominently in the development of each method. Here is a brief summary about each of them:

Astro*Carto*Graphy

Most of us today know that the technique of ACG was developed by the late astrologer and author Jim Lewis. The names of his teacher, Donald A. Bradley, and others such as Dr Marc Edmund Jones and Gary Duncan may figure in the original conceptualisation of the technique, but put simply, Jim did a magnificent job developing the tool to what it is today. Jim began his work on ACG in the 1970's, introducing it to the public in 1976. We can say he completed a major part of it in 1982 when he launched Cyclo*Carto*Graphy (CCG), the mapping of one's transits and progressions. Jim was the world's recognised authority on ACG. His writing on planetary effects at earth locations was prolific and brilliant in both scope and detail. He lectured widely and was well known for his technique, which, more and more, is being used as a mainstream tool by astrologers around the world. Jim's works include *The Astro*Carto*Graphy Book of Maps* (Llewellyn Publications, 1989), which he co-authored with Ariel Guttman. His booklet on using and interpreting A*C*G maps still remains a great condensed reference work on his technique, though it was published back in 1976. His booklet on Cyclo*Carto*Graphy, published in 1982, is equally powerful.

Though Jim died in 1995, his colleague, Kenneth Irving, assembled and published much of Jim's later work along with his own insights in 1997. The book, *The Psychology of Astro*Carto*Graphy* (Arkana, 1997), is the definitive summary of Jim Lewis's work, including his astrological ideas combined with depth psychology.

Local Space

The development of LS must be considered a personal *tour de force* for astrologer Michael Erlewine. He envisioned the idea, conceived the technique to match his vision, and finished it up by programming the calculator routines necessary to employ it. Michael gave it the name of 'Local Space' and he identified the important causal relationships within it. A noted astrologer, teacher and pioneering astrological programmer for many years, he is the founder and head of Matrix Software. Michael is also known for his work in astronomy, heliocentric astrology and more recently his *All Music Guide* and networking collaboration with the Alliance Entertainment Corporation. Michael's books include *Astrophysical Directions* (1977), *The Sun is Shining* (1980) and *Manual of Computer Programming for Astrologers* (1980).

NOTE

1. The technique of Geodetics has also been included in this book as it is an important adjunct to ACG and LS.

FIGURES LIST   PAGE

The Koch house system has been used in all chart wheels.

CONTENTS

CHAPTER ONE

Introduction; Astrolocality astrology; ACG - the basics; Advanced ACG

AN INTRODUCTION

There is a new field of astrology today which is as innovative and exciting as it is contemporary and useful. It is different from other astrological branches in that its techniques have a predominantly *spatial* rather than *time* orientation. This field or type of astrology is so new that it doesn't yet even have a commonly accepted name. I find that the name *Astrolocality Astrology* fits it best and have therefore used it for this guide.

The techniques of Astrolocality astrology are based on sound, traditional astrological and astronomical principles, yet they have become accessible to us only because of the support of modern computers and astrological software. Hence, this field is a unique blend of the old and the new, perfectly reflecting the essence of today's reality and therefore a true need for our time.

Modern physics has shown us that we live in what is called a 'space-time continuum'. Einstein's work connected space and time for the first time, because before this people saw them as separate. He reaffirmed that not only is there a space-time continuum, but that you cannot separate time from space and space from time, in terms of events. Events in our lives unfold against a backdrop of both a 'where' (space or place) and a 'when' (time), which gives them meaning.

Traditional branches of astrology have always had a time-oriented view. Location is an ingredient of traditional astrological work, of course, as longitude and latitude are necessary inputs, but the emphasis or desired information has been on *when* an event or astrological 'hit' would transpire. The natal or event chart is itself of a moment in time in which we usually look for a potential unfolding (in time) using techniques such as transits, progressions and directions – all time-oriented techniques. The space factor hasn't played a very big role, and the space factor is really what Astrolocality astrology is about.

Until recently, a spatially oriented, earth-view astrology hadn't been available to us in a readily accessible form – though its need had become very apparent. Now, more than ever before, we live in a relatively affluent and mobile society that not only offers us opportunities to travel, but where daily life may even *demand* locational change. When faced with today's issues involving new jobs, new relationships, and family responsibilities, we require a contemporary astrology that will not only indicate when to act (time) but also will help us determine where or in what direction to move (space) to accomplish our life goals.

The idea behind space-oriented techniques is that they symbolically **connect the planetary energies and influences directly to the earth upon which we live.** Planetary energies are brought down to earth, so to speak: they are no longer an influence 'out there', but 'down here', right where we stand or to where we can travel[1].

Just as time-oriented astrological techniques help us give meaning to our life events from the nature of the astrological 'hits' we may be having (at that time), the space-oriented techniques of Astrolocality Astrology bring meaning according to the location and direction of these events. Space-oriented techniques not only tell us *what to expect on earth at certain locations or in particular directions* but also why the people or things embodying these events are *coming to us from specific points or directions on the earth.*

In the past, for example, astrology has been able to indicate when (time) a new relationship might come into our lives, but now with Astrolocality astrology we can also see where (place or space) on earth it is most likely to occur or from where that individual would enter our lives. And it may no longer even be necessary to simply wait, longing for that special transit to our natal charts. We may now be able to bring the same energy into our lives (or to escape from it) by moving about on the globe, thereby immediately creating a transit or progression for ourselves *in space* rather than in time!

The Two Techniques

Astrolocality astrology employs two major techniques: Astro*Carto*Graphy (ACG) and Local Space (LS). Each technique or method can and has been employed independently. Practitioners today tend to use one or the other. However, in this book we will introduce examples showing the possibility of using them together, like the right and left hands of one astrological body – the wholeness and integration bringing a more complete and deeper meaning than either could uncover alone.

In the chapters that follow I will explain each technique, sometimes in its own right, sometimes in comparison with the other, and sometimes together as a holistic pair.

Let our earth journey begin......

A DIFFERENT PERSPECTIVE

Surely the traditional birth/event chart, as shown in Figure 1, is invaluable to astrological analysis. It remains and must remain the cornerstone of astrology itself. Although this chart gives us a pictorial sky view, looking upwards from an earth perspective, it only approximates a true astronomical situation. The traditional astrological chart is, in fact, a pseudo sky map as viewed from the earth (geocentric) *looking up into the sky*. I say it is 'pseudo' in the sense that one could hardly ever use it as a navigational aid to fly to the Moon, for example. But it does display meaningful information on relative astronomical positions from which much can be deduced.

The maps used in Astrolocality astrology turn this upward-looking perspective on its head. An Astrolocality map begins with a sky view from beyond the planets, *looking down upon the earth*, the planets superimposed exactly as they are over the earth in their zenith positions (exactly overhead). This means that when employing Astrolocality techniques, we often use actual geographic maps of the earth or of regions on the earth with their usual equatorial orientation.

Figure 2 is the starting basis of either the ACG or LS Astrolocality map. It is a portrayal of the same moment in time as shown in Figure 1. Here, from a vantage point above the planets we look down to see where each of the planets appears in its zenith position over the earth.

• The true 3-dimensional, global perspective is flattened out here to correspond to a 2-dimensional, flat earth map. In reality we would have to be viewing the earth all around its girth at the same moment to see this. The diagram is however completely accurate in its portrayal of zenith positions.

• The concept of a planet in its zenith position is not one we have directly experienced in our northern latitudes. Those readers living closer to the equator will be familiar with the Sun, for example, being directly above them at noon. The zenith is defined as the point immediately overhead from any given point on earth. Technically speaking, it is the pole of the horizon at that point[2].

• It's true that if an observer is not directly above a planet when looking down at the earth, parallax error might make it appear as if its apparent projection onto the earth has shifted. What we are speaking of and showing here is a vantage point and orientation that is truly taken at the zenith, that is without parallax error.

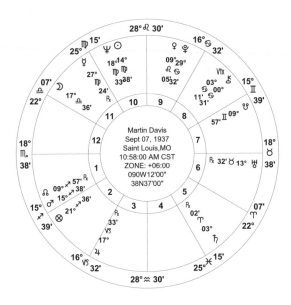

Figure 1

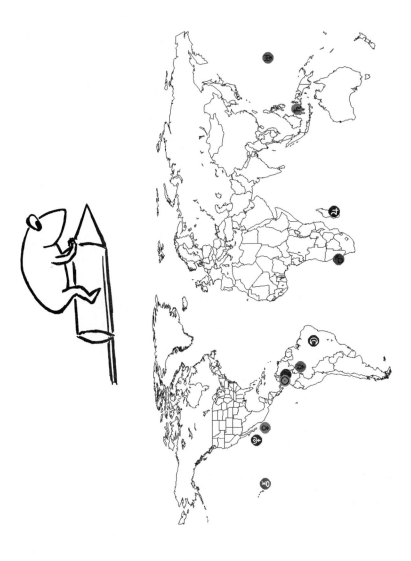

Figure 2

Spend a moment with Figure 2 and let its perspective sink in. This is the basic starting perspective for both the Astro*Carto*Graphy and Local Space techniques. *This simple picture may be the most important in the whole book as all else will follow from or be added to it.*

In summary:
It will be helpful to keep some points in mind about the techniques of ACG and LS as we begin to explore them:

• These techniques have primarily a spatial orientation rather than the more traditional time orientation.

• The techniques bring meaning to our life experience by relating planetary energies to locations and directions on earth.

In other words, with the development of Astrolocality astrology, we now have the astrological tools to explore the space that surrounds us. When this is blended with information from the traditional time-oriented techniques, we gain the more holistic space-time viewpoint of ourselves, giving us more informed life choices and a better understanding of our life experience.

ASTRO*CARTO*GRAPHY: THE BASICS

A*C*G maps: a tool to describe the effect of planetary angularity upon the earth. In its most condensed explanation, an ACG map is a diagram that shows where planets (I'm including the lights – the Sun and Moon – when I refer to 'planets') are angular at the moment under investigation. Let's now look at this more closely to gain a real understanding of what it all means.

Two ways to approach an ACG map:
In the literature of the field, ACG maps are often presented as either:

1. An indicator of angularity. This is especially so when the maps are employed as a tool in the field of mundane astrology[3], to study world or public events.

2. An overview diagram showing where individuals would have angular planets (on the ascendant, descendant, MC or IC) in their relocated charts.

Both viewpoints are correct! We will interweave both perspectives as we develop an ACG map. Firstly, let's look at the two perspectives in more detail:

1. As an (independent) indicator of angularity

ACG can be seen as a system in its own right, independent of any other techniques. This approach is based upon the well-noted effect that planets oriented to the earth in angularity pack the most power in terms of earthly effects or events. Angular positions are the rising, setting, high point (culminating), and low point (under foot or anticulminating) positions. The Sun, for example, at any given moment, will be simultaneously rising, setting, culminating and anticulminating at different points on earth, and in the 24-hour period of the earth's rotation all locations will experience each of the different angularities. John Muir, the Scottish-born naturalist, poetically expresses this as, "Eternal sunrise, eternal sunset, eternal dawn and gloaming, on sea and continents and islands, each in its turn, as the round earth rolls".

This simultaneity is the basis for the ACG map itself, which plots all the planets at once for their angular effects upon the earth.

As Lewis himself said of his A*C*G map, "I computer-generate a map on which lines are drawn that show where certain planets would occupy the *spotlight of angularity* [4]".

Seeing ACG this way is most useful in mundane astrological work, where we want to look at angular planetary effects on a specific country or geographic location.

2. As an individual's relocation map overview

Here we consider the ACG map as an overview of where we would find planets on the angles in our relocated charts.

What is a relocated chart?

Prior to the development of ACG and LS, astrologers had only one major technique to measure a client's relocation possibilities, the relocation chart. This chart is created by altering the natal co-ordinates of longitude and latitude to those of another location. Date and time remain while the locational information is changed [5]. *This gives us a picture of what the birth chart would have been had the native been born at the place of relocation (at the same universal time).* The planetary positions in Zodiacal degrees remain the same as in the natal chart, but the angles (ascendant, descendant, MH and IC) and house cusps of the chart are changed, moving the planets to different positions within the wheel itself.

In general, the movement of planets to angular positions in relocated charts is of greatest importance when evaluating them. A planet brought close to an angle can stand out from all the other chart factors and become a dominant theme in a person's life: Venus, for example, moving to the Midheaven (MC or MH) of a relocated chart, indicates that the individual might find a rush of friendly social activity at the new location, be able to create good relationships for business and perhaps, for the first time in their life, find opportunity in the entertainment industry, the arts, crafts or even in astrological relationship counselling!

When we use the ACG map with personal relocation in mind, the map becomes a grand overview of all earth locations where we would have planets on the angles of our relocated charts. ACG is then no longer a tool completely in its own right but rather is used co-operatively with our relocated charts.

Technical note
This co-operative use does bring up the issue of Pluto's exact position on the ACG map relative to its angularity on the corresponding relocated chart. Interested readers will find a discussion of this in Appendix 6.

In summary:
We can expect to see at least 40 lines on an A*C*G map: 10 planets, each represented by their four lines of angularity. Some maps may have more if we include Chiron, the Nodes, asteroids or even aspect lines to the angles [6]. This is so regardless of which of the two views of the technique we are using: planetary angularity in its own right, or as a grand relocation overview. In either case, with maps in hand, we can knowledgeably roam our 'global village', helped by an understanding of the type of life events that we can expect at its many different locations.

Building an ACG map

1. Culminating Lines (MC)
If you review Figure 2, you will see a picture of the planets in zenith position to the earth at the moment of my birth. Let's now examine Figure 3. Here a great circle meridian line has been drawn through each planet, with all the circles converging at the poles. Note that the Moon (in the centre) was over Brazil at my birth moment and that the Sun and Neptune were over Colombia, South America.

What justification for the meridian line through each planet?
Each planetary meridian line depicted here has a validity regardless of whether we are using the map as an independent mundane tool or as an individual's relocation overview.

a) Mundane perspective. From pole to pole, on the side of the earth which faces the planet, all the locations along the meridian line will experience the planet as culminating - i.e. being in its highest observed point in the sky that day. Though the actual sky position (altitude) of the high point would depend on an observer's geographic latitude, there would be the shared experience (of a culminating angular effect) for all people along that line.

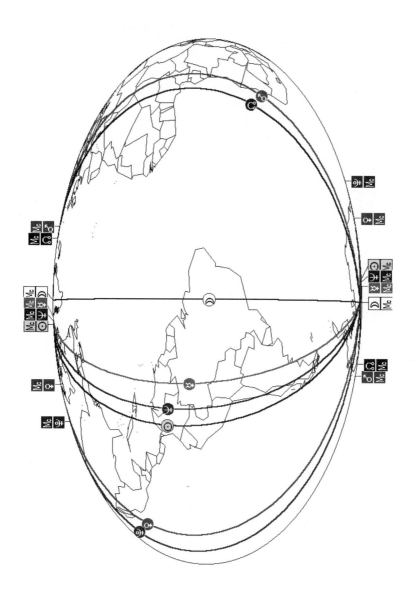

Figure 3

Perhaps this would be more clearly illustrated if we considered my natal Sun and its meridian line starting over Colombia and winding its way up and down from pole to pole. With the Sun over Colombia, it would be noon there (ignoring possible artificial clock time changes for the moment). Following the meridian line northward, we can see that it would also be noon near eastern Cuba as well as in Philadelphia at that same moment. Surely the noontime Sun would have been higher in the sky over Colombia and Cuba than at Philadelphia, but everyone living along the entire length of that solar meridian line was experiencing a culminating Sun at the moment of my birth – with that significance and meaning extending from pole to pole.

b) Relocation perspective. To see how this would relate to a relocation chart, let us look at Figure 4. It is my relocated chart for Philadelphia. Compared with my birth chart (Figure 1), note that my natal relocated Sun has now moved to almost perfect conjunction (alignment) with the Midheaven (MC). It could be shown that *all the locations*, from pole to pole, on that meridian line facing the Sun would result in relocated charts for me that would have the Sun on the MC.

What might this mean?
In my case I lived in Philadelphia for 12 years, rising in rank and success in my career in engineering and my sporting interests. I had a very public life

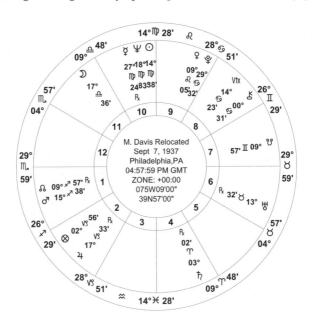

Figure 4

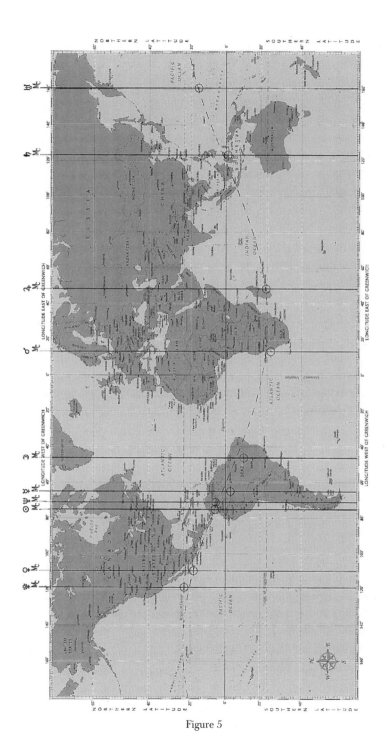

Figure 5

and was well known for my outer accomplishments. This fits very well with a Sun on the MC or in the 10th house. Jim Lewis said of Sun on the Midheaven, "Here, you rise and advance socially through career and vocational interests....". Jeff Jawer writes (see Appendix 1), "...It (this location) has to do with career, one's place in society and, to a certain degree, a place to which we are evolving...".

Figure 5 is a flattened earth view with all my MC lines shown at once. Each line was a curved meridian stretching from pole to pole on the globe depicted in Figure 3. So, thinking in terms of a dual view of ACG, here we have both a chart for culminating energy for me over the entire earth and, at the same time, an overview of all locations on earth where I'd find a planet on or near the MC in my relocated charts.

We have just constructed the first of the 4 types of lines found on the usual ACG map! Let's now discover how the other lines are created to show 'the spotlight of angularity'.

2. Anti-Culminating (IC) Lines

Figure 6 is an ACG flat map view with only my IC lines shown. These lines each represent the other half of the meridian circle that we drew on the earth for the planets in the previous illustrations. They differ from the last diagram inasmuch as they represent the lines drawn pole to pole that were *facing away* from the planets at my birth moment. These energies would be experienced as 'underfoot' for me or as the IC on my relocated charts.

What might this mean?

Let's look at an example of a visit to an IC location for me. Figure 7 is a detail of my South Asian map. From it we may note that my Mercury on the IC line runs through Brunei and down into Borneo but is less than 75 miles from the Malaysian city of Miri. Figure 8 is my relocation chart for Miri. Note that as we might expect, my natal Mercury has moved down to the bottom of this chart just a few degrees from a perfect conjunction with the IC.

What happened to me in Miri? I was invited there to be part of a business consulting team. I had never even heard of the place before, so had little sensitivity to its astrological potentials before being selected for the assignment. Once there, surprising to me, I felt very much at home. I felt a supportive environment both for body (warmth and good food) as well as for my career.

My first task in Miri was to conduct one-on-one interviews with about 25 employees from all strata of a local oil company. The ethnic variety was a surprise to me - every employee was different. Some were from Borneo, still involved with their native culture; some were Malaysians from Sarawak; others came from nearby China or Thailand. It was a friendly and varied cultural feast, yet as I made initial contact with each individual, I could feel their diversity as a sensation in my body. Many readers will recognise the mercurial

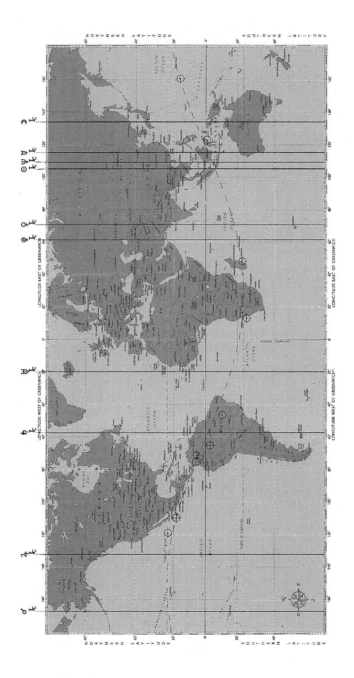

Figure 6

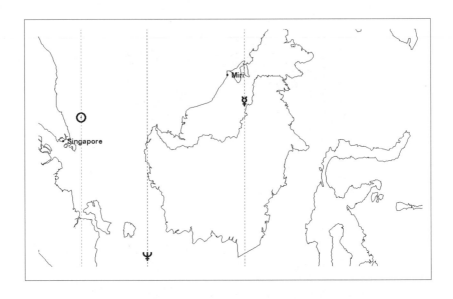

Figure 7

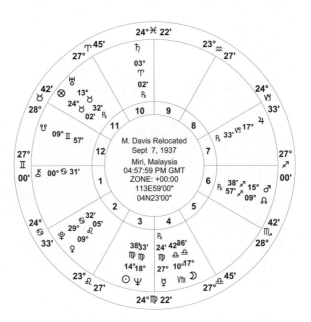

Figure 8

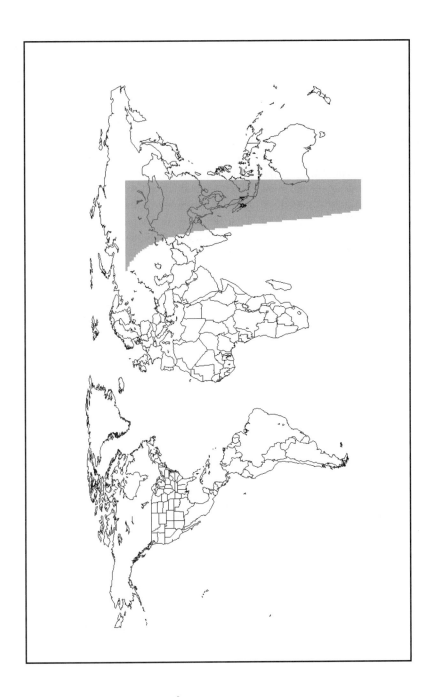

Figure 9

nature of my experience here: business travel, a communication project, diversity and the IC effect of a direct bodily experience that permeates to one's core. I left Miri with many new friends from our global family.

The shaded area on the world map of Figure 9 gives an overview of *all* of my global Mercury-IC possibilities, showing every world location that would have my natal Mercury in a relocated chart's 4th house[7] (for the Koch house system). Note that most of Malaysia is covered by this band, including Miri. Pottinger and Dobyns, in their book on relocation charts, *Planets on the Move* (ACS Publications, 1995), alert us that as wonderful as ACG maps are, they do not reveal the whole picture. They recommend a study of the entire relocated chart, because the new house positions for all the planets (not just those brought to angularity) will tell us even more about the experience there.

Returning to the example of my business trip to Malaysia, let's look again at my entire relocated chart for Miri, Figure 8, and briefly assess the new positions of all the planets in their relocated houses.

All relocated positions:

Saturn is in the 10th house	I was a business authority figure in Miri.
Uranus in the 11th house	New kinds of friends who, in their diversity, challenged and opened up my old views and limited cultural vistas.
Pluto in the 2nd house	A change in values; opening to cultural diversity.
Venus in the 2nd house	I was paid a lot more for that business trip than I'd earn from astrology!
Sun in 3rd house	Accelerated tempo and intense communication with my business associates.
Neptune in the 3rd house	Subtle insights but great care needed to keep communication clear across cultural boundaries and diverse systems of understanding.
Mercury near the IC but in the 4th house	Ease of expression of my innermost thoughts and feelings. Subjective, personal responses to events.

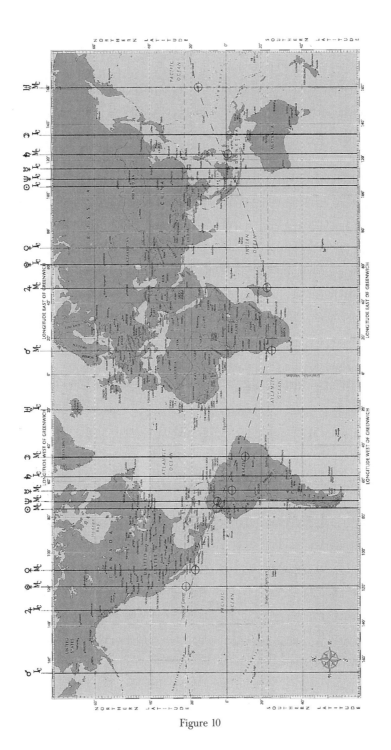

Figure 10

Moon in the 4th house	The time, place and situation for me to look inside at my attitudes, feelings and emotional orientation toward the cultural diversity around me.
North Node in the 6th house	Employed new computer-based techniques in my interviews, literally breaking new ground in the field of scenario planning.
Mars in the 6th house	Worked hard, mostly in a number of one-on-one situations in the work place. Assignment required individual initiative rather than that of a team player.
Jupiter in the 7th house	A classic! Partnerships. Intimate one-on-one encounters that showed me aspects of myself and the world around me.

We have now created two of the four angular groups of lines which an ACG map comprises. Figure 10 shows what we have looked at so far, the culminating (MC) and anticulminating (IC) lines. Let's move on to the rising (ascending) and setting (descending) ones to complete the map.

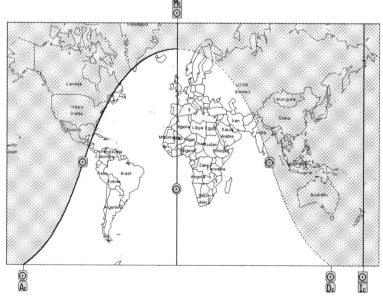

Figure 11

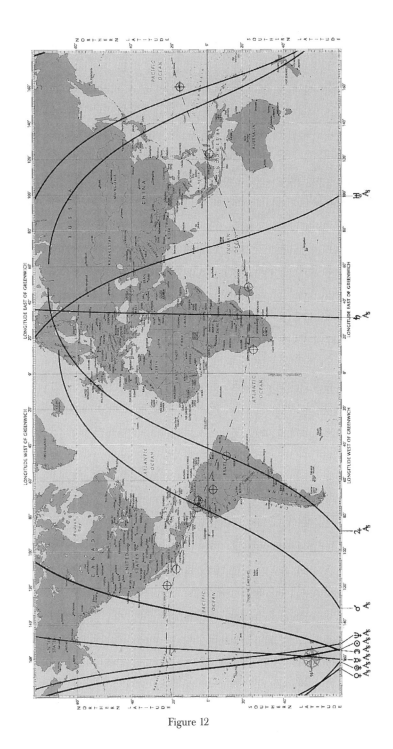

Figure 12

19

3. Rising (ascending) and Setting (descending)

To get a good understanding of the rising/setting components of the ACG map, it will be helpful to view Figure 11. Here I have isolated all the lines of the great light giver, the Sun, as it transits over my own home in Scotland, at noon. We can see that other areas of the world are experiencing a sunrise and sunset (and midnight too) at the same moment that I might be enjoying the midday sun. While I have my lunch, a small segment of the USA's East Coast is beginning to stir to the morning light of the sunrise. Also, at that same moment, many farmers have already left their fields for home as darkness descends over India. A commonality here is that everyone along the entire rising line (to the left of the diagram) is experiencing the sunrise of a new day dawning and those living under the entire descending line (to the right) are beginning to retire for the day. In astronomical terms, the rising and setting lines have zero altitude on their respective rising and setting earth locations. The earth itself is feeling the solar influence or information arriving or departing along those lines. For children born at this moment anywhere on earth, there would be an imprint, energy field or special quality that would connect them to those earth locations for their entire life.

Figure 12 shows the rising lines for all planets at my birth moment. This map represents the third component of the four found on a completed ACG map.

Figure 13 shows my relocated chart for Edinburgh, Scotland, near my current home. Note that on both Figures 12 and 13 it is clear that I have moved

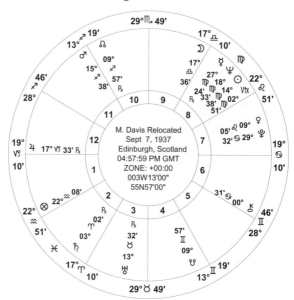

Figure 13

20

to an astrologically favourable location close to where Jupiter is rising. Perhaps this goes a way to explaining why I felt happy to move here before I had even considered information from my ACG map. And why not? Jim Lewis states about this line, "Here you exude self confidence, personal quality, and may have healing or religious power. Faith, optimism and hope are outwardly seen..." In the case with Jupiter lines he also warns that I might become pompous, self-important, oversized and lax. Jeff Jawer, in Appendix 1, adds an important point that rings so true. He states that I could expect to be guided by vision here but won't have patience for details and may feel as if I'm falling short of my expectations.

Figure 14 depicts my descending lines around the globe. Note that my Venus descending line goes straight through Paris. This correlates perfectly with my relocated chart for Paris, which has Venus smack on the descendant! What significance does this have for me? Well, for a starter, my wife was born in Paris – though we didn't meet there. This is an example of how we also draw people (and events) to us from sensitive earth regions without having to travel to them.

We have now discussed the major components of the ACG chart. Figure 15 is my full ACG chart of all 40 lines, the ten planets each with the four lines of angularity: rising, setting, culminating and anti-culminating.

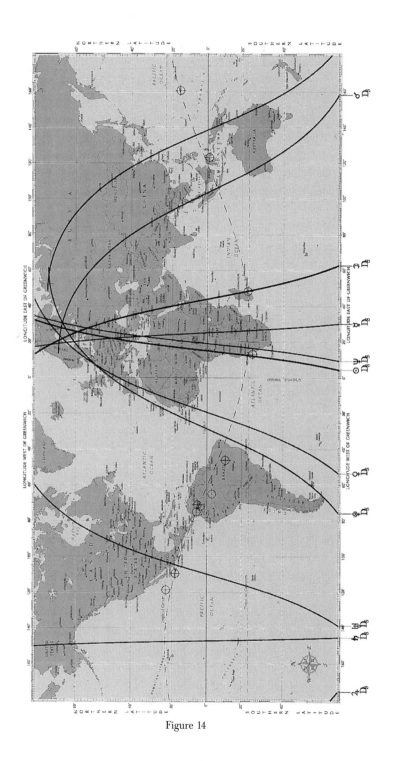

Figure 14

ADVANCED ASTRO*CARTO*GRAPHY
*Orbs of influence; Parans; Cyclo*Carto*Graphy; East or West of a line;*
Using the sidereal zodiac; Bringing it all together

Orbs of Influence

The closer a line is to one's location the more one would feel its corresponding planetary influence. But how close do we have to be to begin to feel it? It appears that Jim Lewis used various orbs in evaluating ACG maps. For some studies he used 300 to 400 miles as maximum distances for effectiveness and at other times up to 700 miles (1000 kilometres) were considered by him to be powerful enough to have an effect. He also felt that if one were investigating a location without any lines, the nearest lines would be the most activated, regardless of the distance. I think Robert Currey sums it up, "In any event, orbs depend on so many factors, and largely boil down to the astrologer's personal choice".

Parans

'Paran' is a term coined by astrologer Rob Hand from the Greek 'Paranatellonta', approximately meaning 'rising together' or 'rising side by side'. It is used in ACG to denote a crossing in space between a meridian (MC or IC line) and horizon (rising or setting) line. At this point we literally have a square in space and, as with squares in general, we are likely to be called upon to act or respond to events at these earth locations. The common usage of parans has been opened up to include all crossings on an ACG map (such as between the rising line of one planet and the setting line of another, for example). Paran lists are generated by computer programs or can be discerned approximately by eye from the maps. In addition to the exact point were the ACG lines come together, one notes the earth latitude where the crossing occurs and considers that specific combination of planets as potent for that latitude around the entire globe.

Why around the entire globe? Well, in 24 hours the earth will rotate below the crossing of the two planetary lines, imbuing that entire latitude with the influence of the planetary crossing (square in space). I feel the crossing point itself is most significant but that yes, the entire global latitude is affected (especially for slower moving planets, whose angular relationships to each other change very slowly). An orb of plus or minus one degree of latitude can be used for global parans when determining their range of potency. As with all of the other ACG lines, the tighter the orb, the greater the effect we can expect.

Let's look at an example to make this clearer. Reviewing my completed ACG map of Figure 15, it can be seen that I have a paran (crossing) of Moon on the MC and Jupiter rising over Brazil. This is, in effect, a square in space over Brazil for me. My relocated chart near that location should reflect this, with both planets being near the angles. Figure 16 is such a relocated chart for

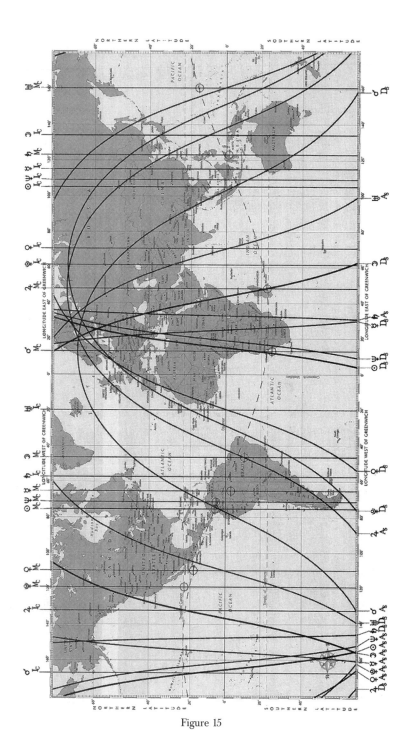

Figure 15

24

Sao Paulo, Brazil, which, though not exactly underneath the paran, is nearby. Note that on this chart the Moon is only 2 degrees wide from the MC and Jupiter is 5 degrees from the ascendant. Both are close enough to the angles to be felt.

Jim Lewis looked upon this planetary combination favourably. He states that Moon/Jupiter combinations are "One of the best places; this is where you are loved and admired... Here you are honoured by those in authority.."

In addition to that direct energy, I have a paran effect on Sao Paulo from around the globe over NW Australia. Here a paran (crossing) of Mercury on the IC and Mars descending affects the geographic latitude of 23 degrees south around the entire globe. Sao Paulo is at that latitude. Jim felt this combination gave a rougher edge than the Moon/Jupiter above. He said that daring and recklessness could manifest, it being a good latitude for active work, with mental and verbal abilities given force to accomplish goals. In analysing such a complex situation, I would give preference to the direct paran crossing nearby having the most power, with the distant paran latitude crossing acting as an additional, though secondary, factor.

What happened to me in Sao Paulo? In 1963 I was a member of a gold-medal sports team there (foil fencing, Pan American Games). I had been daring in the competition and it had paid off. I was given a tumultuous welcome by a sporting crowd - though I doubt anyone knew who I was or what I had accomplished. I was offered work by wealthy Brazilians to stay and teach foil

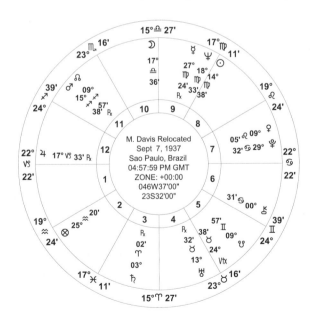

Figure 16

fencing at their country club as well as being quoted in the local newspapers. Here in Brazil, under my Moon/Jupiter paran, I was given more (undeserved) public adulation than I had ever received in my life. Surely the environment and events seemed to support the good auguries of the maps! As with any great location we might find in the world, another side always exists. Jim cautions us for example that Moon/Jupiter's good luck can result in slackened ambitions and diminishing demands on oneself at such a location. Yes, the choice is ours to make.

Cyclo*Carto*Graphy (CCG)

CCG is a mapping of our transits and progressions onto our basic ACG map. Once the ACG map has established the primary alignment of planets to the earth, our subsequent transits and progressions can be placed on it as well. Though the original ACG lines remain supreme and valid for our special earth locations, with this technique we can assess the secondary effect of moving planets upon the earth at specific time periods in our lives. This is similar to the way we approach transits and progressions for our natal charts.

When working with CCG information, we are looking at the *when* (time) that the *where* (place) will have temporary event-oriented possibilities for us. It might even be that a temporary effect can either mask or stimulate a permanent one just at the time we are visiting there.

CCG maps can be generated in some computer programs. CCG overlays to an 'official' ACG map can also be purchased from ACG sources [8]. The overlay is partially transparent, and when placed over the ACG map, it displays the CCG moving positions with the original ACG positions still visible below it. This allows a comparison of the new areas of the world that are influenced with those of the original birth (or event) moment.

The information that CCG maps yield is very useful. Normally, astrologers will closely watch the slower moving planets from Mars on out to Pluto for CCG transits (though I use the transiting Moon as a significator in an example that follows). The inner 'wanderers' of Sun, Moon, Mercury and Venus are most watched for CCG progressions. After a first reading of the CCG situation, subsequent reviews every year should be sufficient even for professional practitioners.

As examples, by progression, the Sun will move only about one degree eastward a year. This translates to about 55 miles on your earth map at temperate latitudes. The progressed Moon would move about the same eastward distance of 55 miles *monthly,* making it the most interesting progressed planet to follow over a period of time. Progressed Mars would move about 40 miles east in a year but it or any planets would be moving westward if they were retrograde.

As with the basic ACG map, CCG maps can supply us with information that sometimes seems astounding in its symbolism. Figures 17, 18 and 19

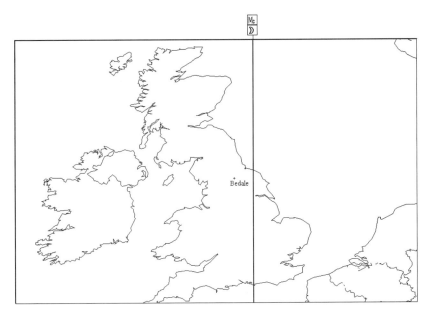

Figure 17

are CCG maps for me (aligned to my ACG birth map) at the moment of my daughter Simone's birth in Bedale, North Yorkshire in May 1988. I assisted in her home birth; it was truly a memorable time for me. Figure 17 is a CCG map of my transits. It shows that the transiting (CCG) Moon MC line was almost directly over the birth location at that moment[9]. That certainly speaks of emotional involvement and domestic concerns as well as the possibility of attention issues. Jeff Jawer writes of this configuration, "You become the mother of the world..."

Figure 18 is a map of my CCG secondary progressions at that moment showing Mars rising right over the birth location (not bad symbolism as my name is Martin – for Mars – and I was born on a Tuesday, the Mars day). And yes, I was physically energised there, feeling boisterous yet physically clumsy holding a new born infant in my arms.

Figure 19 is my CCG map for the tertiary progressions at that moment[10]. Here we see that both the tertiary Sun and Moon setting lines were very close to a perfect paran for the birth location/moment. Father (Sun) and daughter (Moon) in partnership (setting or descending). A perfect symbolism.

Which side of an ACG line is best?

Jim Lewis' material indicated that his clients sometimes found living on one side of an angular line was better for them than the other. Why might this be? The key idea is that the houses adjoining the angular lines can also be placed

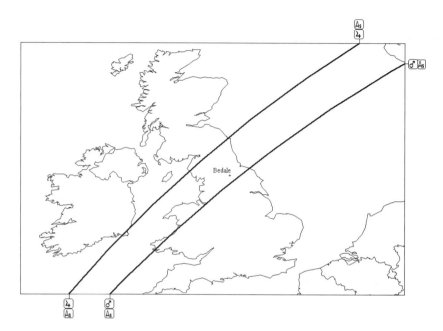

Figure 18

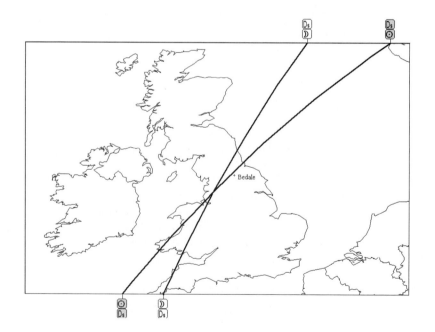

Figure 19

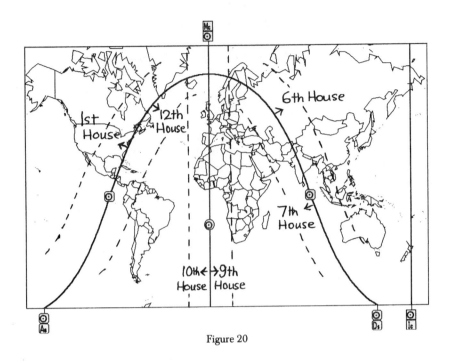

Figure 20

on the map. With that in mind, Figure 20 shows us the house positions located on each side of an ACG line. The angular lines of culminating (MC), anti-culminating (IC), rising (ascending) and setting (descending) can each be seen as the boundary lines (house cusps) between two houses [11]. Living on one side of a line versus living on the other brings this house division effect into play. As shown in Figure 20, locations to the right (east) of the MC line, for example, are in what can be considered the ninth house, approaching the MC itself. So here, for example, we would encounter an MC type of effect – but coloured with 9th house issues. On this side of the MC line your public role would be strongly influenced by the prevalent cultural, legal, educational or religious institutions. People from these institutions would have great effect in assisting you to establish yourself. One finds oneself moving towards taking on a public mantle. Living on the other (west) side of the MC line, however, would mean a prominent 10th house effect to the MC energy. Here you will find yourself more on your own, your public persona already in operation and dealing directly with the issues that are arising. It's a fine point to be sure but an issue to keep in mind when evaluating locations. Some guidelines on evaluating east-west positioning follow:

MC Line: social, career and reputation issues

Right of line (east) - 9th house influence. Legal issues may arise (caution!) but metaphysical ones too are possible. Moving towards your public role with the input from others, usually from diverse sources.

Left of line (west) - 10th house influence. Outward aspects of life are high-lighted. Dealings with parents come into focus. Personal authority and respon-sibility for activities and projects emerge.

IC Line: inner, intimate personal life and concerns

Right of line - 3rd house influence. Your personal issues are influenced by your immediate surroundings and your interactions with your friends, neighbours, relatives and business associates. Activity and an increased life tempo.

Left of line - 4th house influence. Much more inward focus on your personal life. Issues of home, family and parents become paramount. You might be required to confront issues of your origins and past history, necessitating a new personal narrative for yourself.

Rising Line: direct, outward personal expression

Right of line - 12th house influence. Events may force you to focus on the real intent or hidden agenda for your actions. You will be required to get in touch with your subconscious mind to prevent yourself acting against your own best interests.

Left of line - 1st house influence. Active projection of your personality and lots of subjective self expression. Events allow you to express and experience yourself strongly, but watch that relations with others don't suffer.

Setting Line: one-to-one encounters with others become the way you learn and function best

Right of line - 6th house influence. Your encounters focus mostly on day-to-day work, vocational and health issues. You may not be the one giving orders here but the experience will help you to manage your life.

Left of line - 7th house influence. You form working units with others for a variety of purposes and through them you will learn about the effects you have on others. A good location to receive business, vocational or personal coun-selling or input from others.

ACG and the Sidereal Zodiac

ACG is a specific and an observable technique. It can however side-step the tropical vs. sidereal debate among astrologers. Regardless of the zodiac that is employed, the angular positions of the planets over the earth and their rela-tionship to the angles in our relocated charts, both remain true. This means that both Western siderealists and practitioners of Eastern Vedic astrology[12] can bring the full depth of their crafts to astrolocality astrology.

Dennis Flaherty makes a case for employing the extra information when evaluating ACG maps from the Vedic perspective [13]. He has had success recommending locations to clients depending upon the ruling planets of their planetary periods (Dasa Bhuktis). Also, he uses Vedic principals to tell him more about the quality of the life experience they might have living near to or visiting various lines.

Let's have a look at this: planets in Vedic astrology actually have a preferred angle where they gain their greatest strength. This indicator is called *dik bala* or directional strength. It means that although all planets gain strength (significance of life events) at angular positions, they become even more powerful at specific ones. According to the sage Parasara, the following is appropriate:

Planetary Strength Positions

Mercury and Jupiter	rising (ascending)
Moon and Venus	anticulminating (IC)
Saturn	setting (descending)
Sun and Mars	culminating (MC)

So, Eastern or Western, tropical or sidereal, we can watch for enhanced operation of planets at these specific alignments.

Alas, Vedic astrology is a complex craft and positives can be overruled by other, debilitating factors. For example, although my home location here in Scotland is on the strong Jupiter rising line (see planetary strength above), it is weakened in Vedic terms because of the sidereal Libra ascendant of my natal chart (ruling inauspicious natal houses). This might mean that I can expect some of the more problematic characteristics of the position as well as the better things that Jupiter lines provide.

Bringing it all Together

There is an anecdotal story which, as I recall, goes something like this: a young man stops an older man, a stranger, on a street in central Manhattan, asking him for directions to a famous concert hall. The stranger just happens to be a noted performing violinist. The young man asks, "Sir, excuse me, do you know the way to Carnegie Hall?" The older man replies, "Practice, son, practice." And so it is with becoming proficient in employing ACG maps. Start with your own map if possible and those of your friends and loved ones. Notice the correlation between where you have travelled and what events actually transpired. Explore the world of other authors' writings about ACG. Books are available that are rich in examples and descriptive material. Listed randomly, here are some good sources:

*The Astro*Carto*Graphy Book of Maps* by Lewis & Guttman[14] (Llewellyn Publications, 1989). May be out of print; too good not to be reprinted one day.

*Where in the World with Astro*Carto*Graphy* by David Meadows (AFA, publication due to be published late 1999). An explanation of ACG and a varied and comprehensive listing of ACG examples.

*The Psychology of Astro*Carto*Graphy* by Lewis & Irving (Arkana, 1997). The definitive work of Lewis' approach and interpretations, with a strong psychological orientation.

Navigating by the Stars by Hathaway (Llewellyn Publications, 1991). Many good examples, maps fully explained.

Working With Astrology by Harding & Harvey, (Arkana, 1990). See Chapter 17; all major points covered in one comprehensive chapter.

ACG & CCG booklets that come with 'official' commercial maps. A fine source for Lewis' thinking about ACG and CCG.

Astrology on the Move by Sasha Fenton, (Zambezi Publishing, 1998). Insightful portrayal of ACG locations.

*Where in the World? Astro*Carto*Graphy and Relocation* by Erin Sullivan, CPA Press 1999. (Not reviewed but should be good for students and professionals.)

The Lewis and Irving book, *The Psychology of Astro*Carto*Graphy* (listed above), brings home the important point that we don't experience all of our lines equally, nor can their influence always be predicted in a standard cookbook fashion. This is discussed in Chapter 3, page 34, 'Shadowed Planets: Stages of Psychological Growth'. Also helpful is Table 1, found on page 39, 'Possible indicators of a shadowed planet', where the authors list eight possible planetary problems or shadows. They believe that shadowed planets will encounter more resistance from the ego, thereby making them more likely to manifest as difficult events at ACG, angular locations. This chapter is recommended reading, especially for those planning to approach ACG interpretations from a psychological perspective.

An unaspected (or least-aspected) planet is one possible indicator of a shadowed planet that might present difficulty in the expression of its energy. Robert Couteau believes these planets have 'transcendental' implications for individuals. He has done ACG research on this with the results, notable for their detail, presented on his web site[16]. The general principle is: *The experiences we have of specific planetary lines are influenced by the condition of the specific planets in our natal chart.*

One's Venus line, for example, isn't always a site for fun and beauty, but can be a location where we indulge to a degree that could later be regretted. Or moving to a Jupiter line might not result in any noticeable good luck. Or a Saturn line can be just what we need to get a difficult job done rather than it bringing delay or being an impediment.

If a planet has difficult aspects to it, the energies of the aspects are carried along to manifest at the earth location of the planet in question. My natal Mars squares my natal Sun, for example. When living on my Sun MC line in Philadelphia, I did truly advance in my business and sporting careers, but always with the problems, long hours and extra effort associated with the exhaustive assertion of a square from Mars. My Sun line locations will always carry the bite of that square from Mars, and I can expect that at my Mars line locations I will be challenged by solar, growth-type issues.

ACG gives us a measure of the type of experience that will transpire at various *locations* on earth. Next we will be looking at the fascinating astrological tool of Local Space for determining our personally sensitive earth *directions*. We shall then be able to see how both location and direction are considerations when finding our place as we roam planet Earth.

NOTES

1. Angel Thompson calls this process "taking planets from the sky". Michael Harding and Charles Harvey in their book *Working with Astrology* (Arkana 1990) note that the "image of the symbol of a planet somehow embedding itself in the surface of the earth" is so striking that it "demands its own language" to portray it. They choose James Joyce's word "geoglyphy" to describe this physical expression of planets in the world (see Chapter 17, titled Astro*Carto*Graphy, page 314).

2. The great astrologer Dane Rudhyar suggested that one day we should incorporate information about celestial bodies at the zenith of our birth moment/locations in our astrological analyses. This is because any such body would be beaming down on the top of our head – our crown chakra – at birth. The fixed star Ettanin (the gamma of Draco), for example, is almost at the zenith of Greenwich and is sometimes called the zenith Star.

3. Mundane comes from the Latin 'mundus' meaning 'world'. Therefore we use the term 'Mundane astrology' to study charts of countries, regions and public events.

4. From 'AstroMaps Hi Res' User's Guide, Matrix Software, 1989. Jim Lewis on Astro*Carto*Graphy, page 91.

5. It is usually necessary to first change the local time of the chart to the equivalent GMT (Greenwich Mean Time) to maintain the proper, universal, birth time-time zone combination, as the chart is relocated to new longitudes and latitudes. Computer programs will do this automatically in their calculations.

6. Astro Computing Services (ACS, San Diego, USA) provides quality maps with additional lines showing aspects to angles. I find it helpful to have this information, especially for square, trine and sextile lines to planetary midheaven (MH) positions, and therefore recommend them. I use Matrix Software's DOS program, Prima, for this. Though this feature may exist in a Windows program somewhere, I haven't found one that has it. Jim Lewis believed that these lines couldn't be as strong as angular ones. He and some practitioners today feel that they are 'incorrect' unless specifically calculated by ecliptic ascension (rather than equatorial ascension).

7. This useful planet-house feature for relocated planets can be found in the Win*Maps module of Matrix Software's Win*Star v.2, by programmer Stephen Erlewine, and in the DOS program Prima, by programmer Vladimir Bogdanov. An appreciative thank-you to both of them for this helpful new Astrolocality tool.

8. There are three official sources: in Great Britain: Equinox, at the Astrology Shop, Covent Garden, London; in the USA: Astro Numeric Services, Ashland Oregon; and in Continental Europe: Astro Data, Zurich, Switzerland. If and when an ACG or CCG map is purchased, be sure to include the ACG or CCG booklet in your order. The 55-page CCG booklet, for example, contains the fullest discussion on CCG transits and progressions that is published anywhere.

9. Note that because we are dealing with a CCG map (which is aligned to my birth ACG map), the Moon was not physically overhead at Simone's birth moment. (Astronomically it was over continental Europe at that time.) Rather, the Moon was overhead (or on the MC) of her birth location as seen from my ACG map . This isn't an easy concept to visualise but for now keep in mind that CCG information is aligned to the ACG map parameters.

10. A thank-you to programmer Graham Dawson of Esoteric Technologies (Australia) for including tertiary progressions in the CCG module of Solar Maps. As a result of this, tertiaries are another tool available in CCG investigations.

11. A few house-division systems don't hold to this rule. With Equal houses, the MC is not usually the 10th house cusp; and with the Meridian system, the ascendant is not the first-house cusp. But these and a few others are exceptions and their lines too could be plotted on an ACG map.

12. Called 'Jyotish', a Sanskrit word meaning 'the knowledge of light'.

13. See his article in The Mountain Astrologer magazine, Aug/Sept 1997 issue, 'Jyotish Locality'.

14. Jim Lewis and Arielle Guttman created what is probably the the best ACG data reference work available today in this collaborative work. Arielle is a leading ACG practitioner, teaching, lecturing and consulting on it in the USA and overseas. A full list of her services can be seen on her website http://www.arielle.com/

She can also be contacted at Astro Originals, PO Box 15006, Santa Fe, NM 87506.
15. Donna Cunningham is a relocation consulatant with a master's degree in social work from Columbia University. She brings over 30 years experience to her counselling and lecturing and is the author of 12 books. Her web site features her 'All Star Relocation Staion', with much information for effective relocation. The site address is http://www.integrityonline/smoothmove/

If you have decided on a region of the USA where you wish to move and are looking for just the right place, do check out her link to helpful books on relocation.

16. Robert's web site is: http://members.tripod.com/~astr_couteau/astro02.htm/
He presents about 80 'transcendental' biographies comprising ACG charts, a biographical synopsis for each individual and his explanation of their transcendental ACG lines. I leave it to the reader to decide upon the validity of his hypothesis as it is well explained. The web site is a valuable resource for data, short biographies and the ACG maps of notables and events.

CHAPTER TWO

Local Space; Using LS charts, chart maps and maps; Shifting aspect patterns

---

LOCAL SPACE

Local Space (LS) is a unique blend of the old and new. It is a technique in its own right, using both maps and charts, as well as a potent partner with ACG in giving us much Astrolocality information. The very fact that Local Space is available to us today is the result of the work of Michael and Margaret Erlewine, who formulated and developed the technique in a solo effort that compares with that of Jim Lewis' independent development of ACG.

Michael's interest in various co-ordinate systems (including the Heliocentric perspective) goes back to early in his career. In his book *Astrophysical Directions*, published in 1977, he alerts astrologers to the critical role played by the equatorial and horizon systems, which, along with the ecliptic, combine to give us the parameters of our natal and event charts. Michael credits the works of astrologer Edward Johndro in the early 1930's as an inspiration for a 'living-system' or separate-reality-view approach to understanding co-ordinate systems. He also cites astrologer Charles Jayne for his work on co-ordinate systems, dedicating *Astrophysical Directions* to him. It was Jayne who encouraged Michael to investigate the entire plane of the horizon system, for example, and not just the two points of it that intersect the ecliptic in the east and west, becoming the ascendant and descendant of our natal charts[1]. Michael and Margaret took up Jayne's challenge with much enthusiasm (and hard work), and the result is the technique of Local Space.

Local Space is based on a horizon system view rather than the usual ecliptic perspective and, as such, it points to the very heart of astrology itself. There is evidence that the horizon perspective is the most ancient of our astrological roots. In fact, it may have been the original system of astrology, working like this: the rising or setting of a certain star on the horizon in a specified direction would signal the commencement of communal activities and social rituals. In today's world it is our computers that allow us to employ the same system and to personalise this information for ourselves – then use it –

acting for our individual growth and satisfaction.

A startling characteristic of this system or orientation is that, uncoupled from the usual ecliptic view, absolutely any object that we can locate in the universe, be it in our homes or neighbourhoods or the planets and even out in deep space, has an equal and valid location. The important consideration is the object's direction in space relative to the observer, who at any moment remains the centre of the system. (In truth, isn't this the way we experience our world as either 'up and down' from where we are, as well as all around us?)

What is the Local Space, or Horizon system?

If we were to stand in a field (with our view unobstructed by hills or build-ings, and so on) and slowly turn completely about, we could perceive a circle around us where the earth appears to meet the sky. This 'small' circle is called the *visible* or *apparent horizon*. It would have a radius of about 7 miles [2].

Let us now imagine a smooth, flat plane connecting where we stand to the edges of the visible horizon. That plane is the fundamental plane of Local Space astrology. Directly above the observer is the zenith; directly below, the nadir. Where we stand is at the centre or anchor point of this system. Every-thing that then appears to us can be located relative to our horizon using the co-ordinates of azimuth and altitude. Though these terms may be new to us, they are not difficult to comprehend:

- **Azimuth** is this system's equivalent to our familiar zodiacal longitude. It is measured in 360-degree notation around the edge of our horizon. In astrological use we start in the east direction (similar to the usual ecliptic ascendant) 0 degrees, moving north and around the circle. Azimuth meas-urement proceeds therefore in the same direction in which we move through the signs and houses of our traditional astrological charts.

- **Altitude** is the measurement in degrees of location above or below the horizon. It is similar by analogy to ecliptic latitude. Altitude is measured from the horizon to the poles of this system, which are called the *zenith* for the point directly over the observer and the *nadir* for the point directly below (literally on the other side of the globe).

There are a few reference books available that explain the geometry of Local Space and/or the horizon system in some detail. Here are a some titles, listed at random:

Essentials of Intermediate Astrology, an NCGR publication, 1995, compiled by Alphee Lavoie and edited by Lorraine Welsh. Sixteen illustrated essays including two of interest here, Local Space by Cozzi & Munkasey and Astronomy for Astrologers by Munkasey.

Astrophysical Directions, by Michael & Margaret Erlewine, 1977, available from Matrix Software.

The Astrologer's Astronomical Handbook, by Jeff Mayo, 1982, L.N.Fowler& Co.

Planets in Locality, by Steve Cozzi, recently reprinted by AFA publications, 1997. Steve's book was the first and is still the only one available in English which is completely about Local Space. Many of his insights are reflected in this book.

De Astrologische Windoos, by Karen Hamaker-Zondag, 1993, Symbolon. This is in Dutch. Chapter 13, written by Hans Hamaker, is a complete explanation of Local Space geometry, including the mathematical formulae.

What does Local Space information tell us?
The Local Space (horizon) system perspective is unique in that it is specifically location centred. It gives us an idea of the 'what is' for us at a place. The view doesn't speak as much of future growth or potential as it does of the here-and-now of things; the existential situation we would find there and feel in our guts.

Michael Erlewine writes in detail about both the development and his view of the Local Space technique in two essential essays[3], both reprinted here in Appendix 4. He states, "The Local Space chart can show a concrete, measurable relationship of the individual to a place" and, "In a word, here is perhaps the most vulgar astrological system, where the obvious is enthroned and the subtle unnecessary[4]".

Steve Cozzi states that when using Local Space indicators, what you see is what you get[5] and Angel Thompson says of them, "You feel it. You live it".

Michael saw Local Space as an ideal response to the dynamic quality of modern life. He writes that our roaming "has to do with action and outreach on our part" .... "bringing out needed energies at one place and time, moving elsewhere for another life episode at another time". He observed that individuals tend to move toward cities that are in the directions representing the particular kind of energy required at the time, and that basically, "many people were concerned with where they might live in order to bring their self into some resonant and satisfying focus[6]".

A key point
Unlike ACG, which uses the same map to investigate all earth locations at once, we have a more subtle (and perhaps complex) approach in working with the Local Space technique: Yes, we always employ the natal Local Space data for its vital information; but alongside that, we relocate as well, *recalculating the Local Space charts and/or maps for each of the subject's new locations*[7]. A complete Local Space analysis, therefore, can be a combination of both natal and relocated

data. The use of either or both natal and relocated data will be illustrated in the examples to follow.

As this chapter develops, we shall see how Local Space becomes a tool to measure and guide our 'action and outreach' as we move about the globe, identifying those planets brought to the angles of cardinal direction and/or the horizon for each new location. We shall also investigate the direction of *all* lines (not just the angular ones) to determine the experiences expected from the paths we might be drawn to when entering or leaving our home, our city, our country, or locations around the whole planet.

LS astrology with our natal or event planets

Let us now see how we integrate the Local Space perspective with planetary positions in the sky:

If we were to walk outside at this or any moment, we might be aware that the Sun or Moon or various planets were all in specific directions from where we stood. We could then draw imaginary lines across the earth in the directions of each and all of them (ignoring their planetary altitude for the moment). These lines, when extended, would become great circles on our globe circling back to us. See Figure 21. They would pass through nearby and distant cities, expressing the type of energy we would encounter if we moved on them. This briefly is what Local Space astrology is all about, whether we are considering the planets or deep space objects or even specific terrestrial objects around us.

Local Space astrology is a mapping or representation of these directional alignments. In LS charts and maps we work with the lines of direction which connect the observer to the planets (or other objects) around him (her). Hence we may say that Local Space astrology is *directional* in its essence, while ACG is *locational*.

Our own Local Space natal *chart* is based on the directions of the planets around us at the moment of birth relative to the plane of the horizon. Local Space charts are valid for use up to about 50 miles, since the directional vectors are straight lines to that point. Local Space *maps* are a plotting of these same directional indicators on earth maps (as great circles) across significant distances. We use them for distances above 50 miles, since the lines of direction begin to curve on our 2-dimensional earth maps.

At this point it would be helpful to review Figure 2 of the previous chapter. I stated there that this illustration might be 'the most important in the whole book as all else will follow from or be added to it'.

It is a picture of the planetary alignments in zenith position looking down onto the earth at the moment of my birth. Keeping in mind how the ACG lines were added to it, let's now see what the LS perspective would be for the same moment in time.

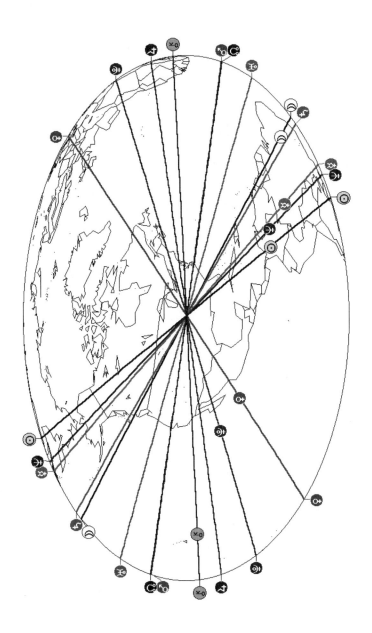

Figure 21

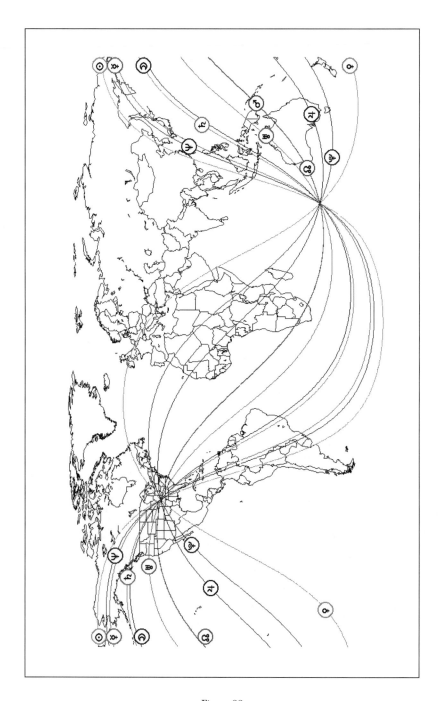

Figure 22

Figure 22 is the LS *map* for my birth moment corresponding to Figure 2. From it we can note the following:

- How all the lines originate from my birth location in St Louis, Missouri, such that there *must* be lines of direction there. This is not so in the ACG technique, where one's birth place or an event location may have no lines at all.

- How the lines radiate outward from my birth location toward and through each planet's zenith position on the earth. The lines themselves are great circles but are curved on the flat-map representation. (Figure 21 showed my LS lines on a globe as the great circles that they are.)

- Looking at Figure 22 again, note how the lines all come together for me in the Indian Ocean southwest of Australia. This location is my earth's natal nadir point. If I actually journeyed there, it would be the location where my most public and personal points (my relocated chart's MC and IC) would be reversed. Here I would experience the equivalent of a 'reverse flush', since my former public role, tendencies and issues (MC/10th house) would now become the most private ones in my life (IC/4th house) and vice versa.

Local Space Charts

Figure 23 shows my natal Local Space *chart*. The positions of the planets around the wheel are real representations of the directions of the planets that were around me (in degrees of azimuth) at the moment of my birth. Note that the chart itself is displayed with planetary positions in the style of a compass, though it could be shown more traditionally with houses and zodiacal notation as well (East would become 0 Aries)[8].

This chart is really appropriately named 'Local Space', for the directions are accurate within a radius of about 50 miles from my birth location. Figure 24 includes a box showing the altitude of my natal planets from my birth horizon. An altitude of or near 0 indicates that a planet was near the horizon. Not many planets were near it at my birth. Uranus was closest being just 4 degrees below. This corresponds with Uranus in the 6th house (just below the Descendant) of my natal chart.

A keen review of Figure 23 will show that in this LS (the horizon system) perspective, some of my natal aspects are now changed! Whereas in my natal (ecliptic) chart for St Louis, Saturn and Venus were in harmonious trine (within a 6-degree orb), from the LS perspective they are 89 degrees apart or in a tight, disharmonious square. That is, this angular relationship is different in Local Space, giving valuable information about the actual (difficult) quality

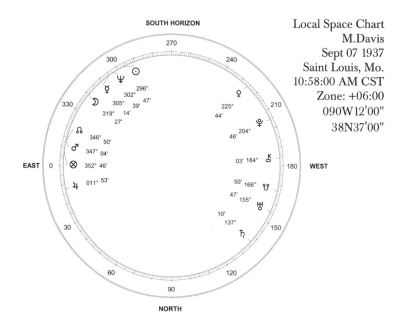

Figure 23

Local Space Chart
M.Davis
Sept 07 1937
Saint Louis, Mo.
10:58:00 AM CST
Zone: +06:00
090W12'00"
38N37'00"

Aspects:				
♂☌♌	♂☌⊗	♌☌⊗	♃☍⚷	☉□♀
☿☌♆	☉☌♆	☽☍♄	♀□♄	☽□♀

Closest	
♂☌♌	0°14's
♀□♄	1°26'a
☉□♀	2°01's
☽☍♄	2°16's
☿☌♆	2°35'a
☽□♀	3°42's
♂☌⊗	5°42's
☉☌♆	5°52'a
♌☌⊗	5°56's
♃☍⚷	7°49'a
♆□♀	7°53's

LMT:	10:57:12
UT:	16:58:00
UT-LMT:	06:00:48
ST:	10h02m36s
RAMC:	150°39'
DeltaT:	23.67"

Pl	Azimuth	Alt.
☽	319° 27'	+25° 57'
☉	296° 47'	+54° 39'
☿	305° 14'	+42° 23'
♀	225° 44'	+63° 27'
♂	347° 04'	- 25° 30'
♃	011° 53'	- 51° 17'
♄	137° 10'	- 41° 48'
♅	155° 47'	- 04° 48'
♆	302° 39'	+52° 34'
♇	204° 46'	+61° 13'
♌	346° 50'	- 19° 15'
⊗	352° 46'	- 29° 35'
⚷	184° 03'	+34° 07'

Figure 24

of events for me at that location. Furthermore, the possible *shifting of aspect patterns* is an important characteristic of Local Space charts, which I shall cover separately with examples. I will show how aspects change for us in Local Space as we move about the globe, our LS alignments readjusting for each new place. This powerful but unusual characteristic of LS charts is, unfortunately, little used in astrology today. I have enclosed an article by consulting astrologer Sean Lovatt in Appendix 5 which discusses this factor[9].

Chart Maps

Figure 25 is my natal LS chart *map*. Chart map? What's that about? This is the same chart as in Figure 23, but it has been turned upside down to give it a map's orientation. Now the north is truly pointing north or up, as it would on a map's representation. East is now as it would be on a map too, pointing to our right. This upside-down reversal is necessary for northern-hemisphere locations, where the MC's (the top) of our natal charts are actually pointing in the earth's southerly direction[10].

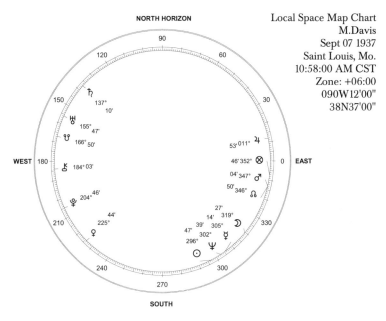

Figure 25

The need for this reversal can be a difficult concept for students of LS the first time they encounter it. A study of the various co-ordinate-system perspectives can clarify things, but for now let's see it as this: if a birth chart of a northern-hemisphere location has the Sun (or any planet) on the MC for example, that planet is actually geographically south of the observer. If we wished the LS perspective to correspond with a map's orientation, the chart would have to be reversed so that the MC were pointing down or south. If the chart were calculated for a southern-hemisphere location, the MC-IC orientation is correct as shown. That is, the Sun on the MC is already truly pointing north, as one would be looking northward to see it. (To get a southern-hemisphere LS chart completely in a map orientation, however, we would have to flip it around too, but left to right only, so that the east would point to the right as on a map.) Transformations from LS charts to LS chart maps can be handled by computer software for both northern- and southern-hemisphere charts, so this is less of a problem than it may seem to be.

Why do we utilise these turned-around, so-called chart maps? In a later section we will see how our LS chart maps can be used as directional guides in our homes, neighbourhoods and cities. When used together with LS maps, which are needed for broader regions and the world itself, they truly help us to 'think globally and act locally', a phrase one sees in today's ecological literature.

Let's not forget the Magic!

Astrology itself has been called 'the round art[11]', and this is especially pertinent for LS charts. LS circles offer us a view of the directions of planets (or other objects) around us. The directions are totally earth orientated to our immediate horizon and the earth's major directions: north, south, east and west. This Local Space view is strikingly similar to the circles created in the mystery traditions. The use of such circles can be found in native American vision quests and other important rituals. In fact, various systems of sorcery (enabling one's personal power), shamanism (healing and mediation with spirit beings), and alchemical magic (energy transformation) contain practices that have the subject sitting at the centre of a 'power' circle, carefully noting and responding to the direction from which animals, people and various natural phenomena manifest or come and go.

The philosophical and practical qualities of Local Space also seem to merge with those of another system, the Chinese directional art of Feng Shui. Feng Shui is practised and respected in parts of the East today. In Hong Kong, for example, Feng Shui practitioners are consulted and work with architects on building layout and design.

The directional information that we can acquire from Local Space bears a striking similarity to what one hopes to obtain from the systems mentioned above. Steve Cozzi, in his book *Local Space Astrology*, develops the theme that Local Space astrology is in fact a true and authentic form of Western geomancy in a personalised form.

The powerful correlation of Local Space with the magic traditions was quickly recognised by the Erlewines. Michael states this directly, "..the visible horizon being much like a magical circle..." and poetically, "I must confess, a somewhat magical view of our world begins to emerge: one in which every city and friend becomes a radiating centre of influence. Here for the first time the long history of magic, witchcraft and sorcery takes on a practical reality, where local deities and preferred directions become the rule, and we are thrust forever beyond the threshold of the just slightly remarkable...[12]"

What do we look for in Local Space charts?

In those pre-computer days of the 1970's, Michael worked with his calculator to create Local Space charts for himself, his family and clients. He noticed that:

- For a given location, those planets close to the major directions of north, south, east and west gave the corresponding planetary energies special, enhanced influence in his and his client's lives.

- Planets on or near to the visible horizon for a location brought their corresponding influence into 'focus'.

- He and his clients tended to travel or relocate exactly on the lines describing their planetary directions.

These insights proved to be major breakthroughs, as up to this point nobody had realised that:

Horizon system planetary positions were important as a relocation tool.

A planet's direction in azimuth degrees could be plotted as a line on a map of the earth's surface, connecting it to people and places.

USING LOCAL SPACE CHARTS, CHART MAPS AND MAPS

Local Space charts

These are best used to give us an idea of the quality of experience we might have at our natal and relocated locations. What should we look for in them?

Angularity
Shifting aspect patterns and
The altitude of the planets

Angularity

With our natal and/or relocated LS charts in hand, we first look for planets brought to the angles of north, south, east and west, just as we would for a regular natal or relocated ecliptic chart if we had planets on the MC-IC or ascendant-descendant axes. A planet near one of the cardinal directions of a LS chart (plus or minus 5 degrees is a usual orb, but I often use a bigger, 10-degree orb) will be of special importance in that locality. A planet's influence will be significantly increased. The qualities of that planet will be *substantiated* or *endowed with power* there. This empowerment means that either or both:

- Corresponding events, as well as talents, abilities and interests are likely to manifest.

- Corresponding objects and materials are likely to become available at that location when they are needed.

Now, let's develop the theme of what we should expect when planets in natal LS charts are found to be angular and/or planets in the relocated Local Space charts are brought to the angles at new locations. See Appendix 2, where I list and describe these planetary effects.

Note

In most instances, the east and west directions of Local Space will *not* be identical to rising/setting ACG lines or to the ascendant-descendant axis of the normal natal or event-based chart. *These east and west points usually represent completely new information and should therefore be carefully noted* [13]. Some examples should bring this idea of Local Space angularity (cardinal direction) into sharper focus.

Angularity in Local Space charts: four examples

1. A natal LS chart: Simone de Beauvoir

Figure 26 is Simone de Beauvoir's (1908-1986) birth chart. Born in Paris, she took a degree in philosophy at the Sorbonne in 1929, placing second to Jean-Paul Sartre. A novelist, essayist, and playwright, her work *The Second Sex* stands as the first landmark in the modern feminist wave that transformed perceptions of the relationship between men and women in our time. *The Second Sex* remains an outstanding work, combining anthropology, sociology, biology and psychoanalysis.

A quick reading of her chart shows a formidable grouping of Uranus, the South Node, Mercury and the Sun, all in Capricorn. This promises a unique talent, a desire for serious expression and well-crafted communicating skills. In the second house, this potent configuration indicates a need for her to express her values and concerns. As this conjunction is opposed by idealistic, mass-influencing Neptune, we see this expression directed to those issues which were affecting the entire culture. With her Jupiter in the ninth house she became the teacher and inspirer of the generation of feminists that were to follow. The Saturn square Pluto could indicate inner turmoil relating to the powerlessness she felt as a woman in French society and her resulting life decision to change this.

Figure 27 is the Local Space chart for her birth place and home in Paris. What does this chart add? Can we see from it how and why she was able to materialise her potential at this location?

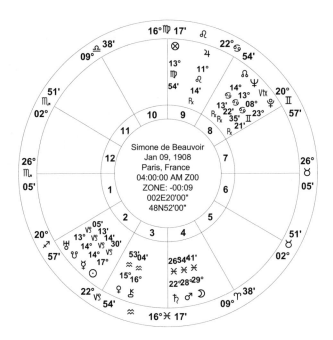

Figure 26

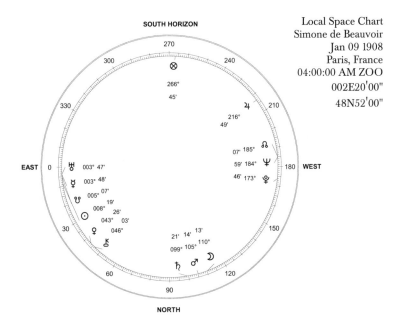

Figure 27

East power

Firstly we can note that her potent Uranus, Mercury, South Node, and Sun conjunction has *east* power. In her Local Space chart for Paris, they sit very closely to the earth's cardinal direction of east. Uranus and Mercury, though a degree apart in the normal radix, come together, conjoining by only 1 minute of arc in Local Space (increasing the potency of the combination), and both together are fewer than 4 degrees of azimuth from the east direction. This – with the Sun – is truly east power! That 'what is' for her Uranus, for example, would indicate that there in Paris she would find the will, courage and vision to be a reformer – or a trouble-maker, depending on your point of view. She would also have the mercurial language skills to express herself there. Cozzi writes of Mercury in the east that "circumstances continually prompt you to say what you feel and speak your mind[14]". South Node in the east might indicate that she was supported by many (she was actually the darling of the Parisian intellectuals and cafe society), and her eastern Sun (still in loose orb) might tell us that from Paris she naturally commanded a leadership role, which was important for her own personal development as well. Get the idea? The placement of those planets (and nodal point) in the east of her Local Space chart *empowered* her efforts there to call upon her talents and find the necessary tools (and audience) to accomplish her objectives.

What can we say about her **west power**?

Neptune (an orb of 5 degrees of azimuth). Her ability to tune into the collective mind was a fact of that 'what is' for her. Her relationships in Paris were idealistic and somewhat nebulous by any concrete standards. This was especially so with the philosopher Jean-Paul Sartre: she was 'entranced' by his ideas but found it difficult to maintain any normal cohabiting relationship.

Pluto (an orb of about 6 degrees of azimuth). She was able (empowered) here to achieve a deep level of self-analysis and understanding separate from the backdrop of the contemporary social conditioning. She was able to 'speak softly and carry a big stick'. Her life became tied up with the lives and destiny of all women.

North power

As with the placement of Saturn on the IC of our birth charts, we interpret this placement in Local Space as one where home-based responsibilities and duties begin to pile up. Home life wasn't really fetching for her and she spent as much time away from it as possible, in cafes with France's intellectuals and teaching in various academic situations. As Sartre became older and ill, she cared for him at home and, in Paris, she accepted more personal responsibility, adopting a young woman there as her grown daughter.

2. A relocated LS chart: Martin is offered his first job

Upon my graduation from New York University with an engineering degree, I was open to accept a position almost anywhere within or outside of the USA. In those early days of my career, when I had no work experience, only one job, but a promising appointment, was offered to me. It was in the city of Philadelphia, Pennsylvania. Let's now look at my relocated LS chart for that city, in Figure 28, to see why I might have been drawn to that location.

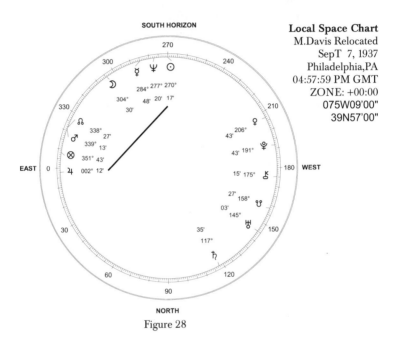

Figure 28

Even a quick review of it will show that two auspicious planets for employment and career growth are very empowered in that city for me. First we can see that the Sun is exactly in the south at 270 degrees of azimuth[15]. Sun in the South is *the* position for personal growth through a public role. The other point of note is Jupiter, almost exactly on the east at 2 degrees of azimuth. This placement is ideal for a location to find one's vocation or best training situation.

Almost immediately in Philadelphia, I was given supervisory duties and responsibility for a multimillion-dollar process. My career flourished and, at least for a time, I was satisfied with this situation.

3. LS event charts: Princess Diana

Astrologers commenting on Diana's death in Paris have noted her natal Mars-Pluto conjunction, in Virgo, within an orb of about 4 degrees, as being a significant piece of information in attempting to understand the events surrounding her violent end[16].

As in our work with any type of chart, once a possible theme is uncovered in a natal LS chart, its signature can often be discovered in subsequent LS event charts as well. Are there any threads that we can follow for this Mars and Pluto combination?

Figure 29 is the LS transiting chart for Paris at the reported moment of the crash itself, 12:25 A.M. local time. Note that Mars (a perfect symbol for a crash) is at 183 degrees of azimuth, or only 3 degrees from perfect alignment with the western direction (empowerment) at that moment[17]. *Note that this information is new and unique, since Mars is 37 degrees from angularity in the usual ecliptic chart for the same moment.* Pluto in the LS crash chart moves away from angularity at first (197 degrees of azimuth), but follows Mars to perfect western alignment 32 minutes after the crash at 12 hours, 57 minutes a.m. local time. Perhaps this indicates that some 32 minutes after the crash, and still without intensive medical intervention, her fate was sealed.

Figure 30 is another transiting LS chart (Paris location), this time for the exact moment of the eclipse two days after her death It is reasonable to assume this eclipse is significant for the event, since it occurred so soon after it. Note that Pluto, at 179 degrees, 32 minutes of azimuth, is only 28 minutes of arc from *exact* alignment with the west. This is a perfect symbolism for a death prior to a rebirth, perhaps for herself and the rest of humanity as well[18].

4. A relocated LS chart: Will Anna become a mother?

Anna is a single, dynamic, 38-year-old woman living in London. She met a Brazilian man vacationing in Great Britain and was immediately attracted to him. Prior to meeting him again, this time at his home in Rio de Janeiro, she consulted me about the astrolocality indicators of her journey. The first thing I noticed was that her Local Space Mars map line ran right to Brazil (these map lines will be explained later in this book). Not surprisingly, it is frequent for a woman to seek and/or find a male partner on her Mars line and for a male to find a female mate on his Venus line. On her relocated LS chart for Rio, another important indicator was evident. Her Moon came exactly to the east of the chart at 0 azimuth. What might this mean? I told her how the issues of motherhood, family and child-rearing could arise for her there. And that there might even be the opportunity (wanted or unwanted) of a pregnancy.

Upon her return she reported the following: "Motherhood issues arose almost immediately as my journey began. On the plane to Rio I sat next to some children of similar, fair complexion and the stewardesses, assuming they were mine, kept asking me for approval as to what and when to feed them." [My note: it is a known effect that while journeying to a destination with LS angularity, though still many miles away, you'll find that the qualities of that destination will begin to manifest.] Anna continued, "Upon my arrival in Rio, Carlos took me immediately to the home of his mother. There I was introduced to his three children, who, I must say, were adorable. Over the three weeks of

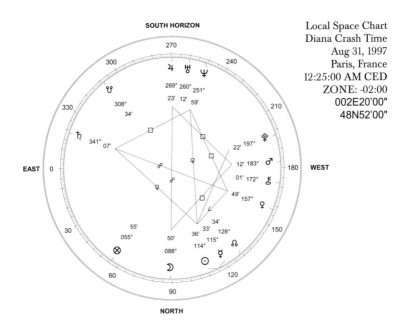

Figure 29

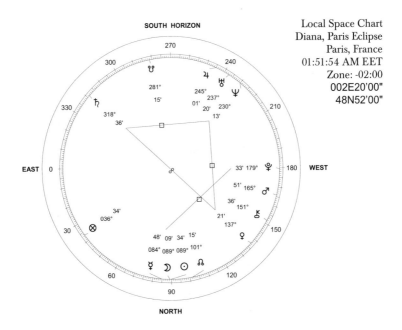

Figure 30

my stay I became a companion to them, all but being their surrogate mother. Carlos pressed me to remain in Rio, to live with him and the children, and yes, he wanted very much for me to have his baby. I could more accurately say that he pressured me on this. Even his mother joined in and asked me to remain. I must say that under the sway of that environment, I was tempted!"

Along with the other possible lunar issues, Sasha Fenton writes [19] of an eastern angular Moon, "Women may decide to become mothers here or you may suddenly take on someone else's child at this location.... Relationships with mother figures would become a strong feature in your life and such relationships may be marvellous, terrible or a mixture of both, but they would be pervasive... To sum up, you can feel as though you have come home ... but it can also bring you far too close to uncomfortable emotions..."

Anna returned to London, where her Local Space Moon moves safely back to its more public-oriented southerly position (10th house in her natal chart), hardly able to believe the sudden arising in Brazil of the motherhood issues she had never faced before. At this writing Anna has returned once again to be with Carlos and his family in Brazil. To be continued, I'm sure....

SHIFTING ASPECT PATTERNS
(A remarkable characteristic of Local Space)

An important feature of LS charts is that the angular separation (aspects) between planets can be different from those found in the equivalent radix (ecliptic) chart. This is due to the different perspective of each system. We shall see how this characteristic gives us even more information of the 'what is' for a subject at a given location. For me, however, the most remarkable characteristic of Local Space charts is that Local Space angular separations (aspects) may change as we shift from location to location! This is a new concept for astrologers in relocation work. We usually expect squares to remain squares, for example, in our relocated charts, even if planetary house positions change. But now we can observe if squares become trines (or vice versa) and what the implications of this might be for one's experience at a new location.

Figure 31 should help to clarify this phenomenon, which is inherent in the Local Space (horizon) perspective. It shows a figure on earth with the planets Mars and Saturn above, apparently in square to each other. By moving on the globe, however, the observer experiences a change: the two planets now appear to be only 45 degrees apart. The planets have not moved, just the observer and his/her perspective of them!

Very few of us have much experience in working with shifting aspect patterns, so let's take a closer look. In general, we will work as follows:

1. We obtain both a natal chart and the corresponding Local Space chart (for the natal location).

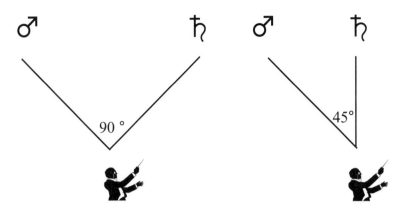

Figure 31

2. We note aspects in the LS chart that may differ from those in the natal chart. For example, a trine between two planets in the natal chart might became a square in the corresponding LS chart.

3. We will note that the subject's experience at the specific birth location will most likely be dominated by the LS configuration, in this example one of tension (the square) rather than the overall natal expectation of a harmonious flow (the trine). Even if our study stopped here, we would have valuable information on the subject's real experiential situation. And it is noted that we might find the opposite dynamic, i.e., a harsh natal aspect softened in the corresponding LS chart, resulting in a surprising ease of flow of events..

4. If and as we compute relocated LS charts for the individual, we may note that *some LS angular separations will continue to change at the different earth locations*. This will greatly assist us in finding favourable locations for the individual or in explaining their actual earthly experience (liking or disliking a location) as they move about.

5. If we are fortunate, we might even find a new site for a subject that would bring a difficult LS square back into trine, as will be shown below with my birth data. We might expect the subject to be drawn to such a location and to feel good about remaining there.

Let's look at two specific examples here to bring this new concept into focus:

Simone de Beauvoir - her frustration is channelled into writing
In her natal ecliptic chart (see Figure 26), we see that she has Saturn-Pluto in rather tight square aspect, within an orb of less than 1 degree (89 degrees, 5

minutes). This is admittedly a difficult configuration, indicating that she would experience frustration at being prevented or blocked in accomplishing her ambitions. Pluto rules breakdown and rebuilding, so one could surmise that this was a driving force in her attempt to expose – and change or rebuild – the inequity and attitude of society towards woman in her time [20].

When we look at her Local Space chart for the same location of Paris however, (see Figure 32), we can see that this angular separation (aspect) has changed: It has shifted from 89 degrees to 74 degrees, weakening the square and bringing it closer to one of a loose quintile. For her, in Paris, the expected blockage was eased and a way out became possible by a broad and profound philosophical expression through her writing.

There was a trade off in the quality of shifting aspects for her in Paris, however. Her natal Sun-Saturn sextile becomes a more difficult square with 91 degrees of angular separation between those planets. Though appreciated around the western world, in Paris her work was impeded by both traditional males and females, who felt threatened by it. This forced Simone to approach her work with a greater discipline and strategic sensitivity than she would have wished for, and it made it helpful for her to 'take breathers' away from the pressure cooker of Paris, either to the south of France with Sartre or to New York and Chicago for her liaisons with the American writer Nelson Algren.

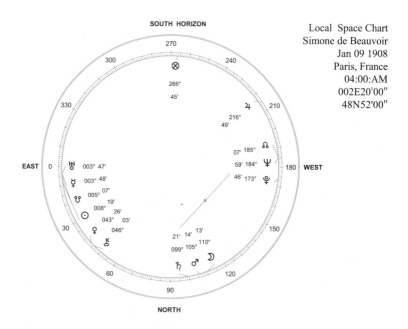

Figure 32

Martin moves to Scotland; an example of shifting aspect patterns at work:

Figure 33 is my natal (ecliptic) chart again. Note that by most standards my Saturn at 3 Aries and my Venus at 9 Leo are in a harmonious trine, 126 degrees apart, within an orb of 6 degrees. Both planets are also in trine by sign and house position. A review of my corresponding Local Space chart for my nativity location of St Louis reflects another story, however. Here, in Figure 34, it can be seen that the angular separation between these two planets is reduced to 88 degrees, only 2 degrees from an exact square! Not only that, but my weak natal Moon - Saturn opposition (14 degrees off from an exact 180-degree separation) becomes strong (too strong!) in LS, moving to become an almost perfect opposition – within a 2-degree orb. The square and strong opposition aspects indicate more tension and diminished parental attention in St Louis for me than a natal trine and loose opposition (from my birth chart) might lead us to expect. And it reflects the 'what is' or 'what was' for me there. Tensions between my parents absorbed most of their emotional energy, leaving less to concentrate on their children. This tension between them wasn't resolved until they separated, my mother, my sister and I moving away from St Louis to New York city, my father content to remain behind without us[21].

The Saturnian Local Space square (with Venus) and tight opposition (with the Moon) remained in effect on the east coast of the USA for me as I grew

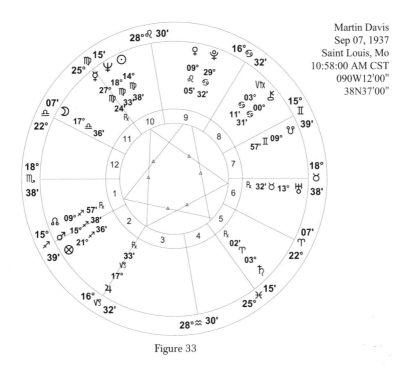

Martin Davis
Sep 07, 1937
Saint Louis, Mo
10:58:00 AM CST
090W12'00"
38N37'00"

Figure 33

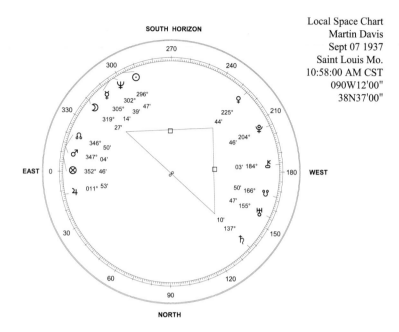

Figure 34

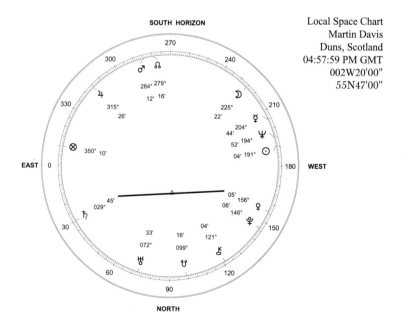

Figure 35

up and, continually finding myself lonely – even amongst many friends – I finally 'escaped' from it by moving to locations in Great Britain and continental Europe. Here in Scotland for example, my Local Space Venus/Saturn aspect realigns itself from a square to become a trine again with a 126-degree angular separation; just like it is in my natal ecliptic chart and the tight LS Moon - Saturn opposition eases considerably, opening to 206 degrees of separation or 26 degrees out of orb. I regained my birthright (as indicated by my natal chart) to experience Saturn's energies harmoniously, *and I did it by changing my earth location!* See Figure 35, my LS chart for Duns, Scotland. Note the separation of Venus and Saturn has returned to a trine as it is in my natal chart and that there isn't any apparent Moon - Saturn opposition anymore. In my mind this goes a way to explaining why I finally found satisfaction in business and personal relationships in Europe and the UK, away from the USA.

Planetary altitudes of LS charts

Michael Erlewine found that when people relocate, planets moving to the horizon (0 degrees of altitude) brought the issues represented by those planets into a 'focus'. They remain on the individual's mind and might even represent the background situation or issues there. Those planets aligned near the horizon of a LS chart will also be on or near the ascendant - descendant axis of the corresponding ecliptic chart. When this is so, it empowers them in both the LS and ecliptic systems. No wonder they represent issues that fill our consciousness at that locality!

Sean Lovatt points out that Local Space planets in parallel (the same degree of altitude) or contraparallel (the same degree of altitude but with one above the horizon or '+' and the other below the horizon or '-') are also related as aspects even if they are in different directions. This is exactly the way we would consider them in working with declinations in ecliptic charts [22].

Pl	Azimuth	Alt.
☽	225° 22'	+ 14° 17'
☉	191° 04'	+ 14° 42'
☿	204° 44'	+ 12° 30'
♀	156° 05'	+ 05° 38'
♂	284° 12'	+ 07° 53'
♃	315° 26'	+ 00° 34'
♄	029° 45'	- 19° 58'
♅	072° 33'	- 17° 15'
♆	194° 52'	+ 16° 27'
♇	146° 06'	+ 05° 21'
☊	279° 16'	+ 11° 49'
⊗	350° 10'	- 09° 50'
⚷	121° 04'	- 11° 41'

Figure 36

Figure 36 includes a list of the altitudes of my relocated LS chart for Duns, Scotland (Figure 35). Note, for example, that both the Sun and Moon have altitudes of + 14 degrees above the horizon. Though they are not in conjunction by azimuth (being about 34 degrees apart), they are in conjunction or relationship by altitude. This is a good indication for me of a location where I would be able to act with a natural inner harmony, both my will (Sun) and emotions (Moon) in accord with each other. A contraparallel of those same two planets would indicate that those factors would be at odds with each other and require my conscious efforts to bring them into a balanced polarity.

Technical points: Two special considerations in Local Space studies

1. Estimating Local Space angularity from the ecliptic chart

When reading a natal or event chart, we can see approximately what some of the angular LS planets might be without even calculating them. How is this possible?

When calculating the ecliptic chart, *include the vertex* as one of the points to be displayed[23]. Note if any planets are close to (in conjunction with) either the vertex or its opposite point, the anti-vertex. Planets close to the vertex will be seen to be in the west of the corresponding LS chart. Planets near the anti-vertex will fall onto the east in LS. Such planets may not appear to be of major influence in the ecliptic chart at first glance, but they can now be seen to be very important for the 'what is' of that location[24].

West power

Let's take Simone de Beauvoir's natal chart as an example. Please refer again to Figure 26. Note that both Neptune and the North Node are close to the vertex. This tells us immediately that she will have those power or manifestation potentials available at that location for her. This is confirmed in her LS chart as discussed previously. Our suspicions can also alert us that Pluto might be close to the west, though we can't be sure. On the ecliptic it is 15 degrees from the vertex, while on the actual Local Space chart it turns out to align more closely – within 7 degrees of azimuth – to the west direction, giving it west power too[25].

East power

Now let's see how we could have picked her east power points from her natal chart without even having calculated the corresponding Local Space wheel. Noting that her natal vertex is at 8 degrees, 35 minutes of Cancer, the corresponding point in the east (the anti-vertex) would be the opposite, 8 degrees, 35 minutes in Capricorn. Her chart shows that her 2nd house planets, Uranus and Mercury, are near the anti-vertex point with a possibility of the Sun too, if we use a wide 10-degree orb – as I usually do. A review of her Local Space chart, Figure 27, shows our 'guess' would have been a good one, with both Uranus and Mercury moving to the east and the Sun as well coming into an orb of 'east power', 8 degrees of azimuth from the east direction .

With this all in mind, perhaps we can begin to see a rationale for how the vertex-anti vertex axis is assessed in the growth-orientated ecliptic charts of astrology today. For the vertex, both Edward Johndro and Charles Jayne concluded that the points had to do with fateful and important encounters, either with people or circumstances. The vertex points to them seemed to be active in life's more dramatic and less ordinary moments. Could this be the same or similar to the 'empowerment' or 'substantiation' effects we read into our LS charts for east and west angularity at the same location? I think so.

North-South

The Local Space north-south alignments of planets are easier still to discern from the ecliptic chart. Generally stated: for northern hemisphere charts, planets on or near the chart's MC *usually* will be on the Local Space south direction and planets on the IC *usually* will be in the north. This is reversed for the southern hemisphere. Why the modifier 'usually'? The above rule is correct much of the time. However, as described in Footnote 10, the north-versus-south orientation of the MC-IC axis depends on both the observer's terrestrial latitude and the planet's declination If in doubt, then we must actually create a Local Space chart or a Local Space chart map from our computer program and see how it works out. The computer-generated chart or chart map should show the true orientations.

2. Local Space near or approaching equatorial latitudes

Local Space charts and maps give us less information if the 'anchor point' is near to the equator, the location's terrestrial latitude getting close to the declinations of the planets [26]. What then happens is that from the horizon perspective, most planets appear to move into two 'clumps', one in the east and one in the west, each in tight bunches [27]. On Local Space maps calculated for an equatorial or near-equatorial location, the pattern of planetary lines begins to look like a braid of hair lying east-west, not therefore showing us much about other earth locations [28].

Michael Erlewine discovered that when Local Space charts or maps became too bunched due to being calculated on or near equatorial latitudes, he could use another perspective that Charles Jayne had studied and recommended: that of *the prime vertical*. The prime vertical perspective is a view of planetary patterns from an east-west orientation rather than from the horizon. Michael found that it yielded information about what seemed like the more fated or passive characteristics of our lives – rather than the outreach type information we gain from Local Space. Prime vertical charts can be obtained from full-featured computer programs, but prime vertical maps can be found today in very few astrolocality-mapping programs [29].

NOTES

1. Astrologer David Perkins points out that one of the first modern systems for locational investigation was developed by Fredrich Sieggruen (1877-1951), who with Alfred Witte founded the famous Hamburg School of Astrology at the turn of the 20th century. Sieggruen introduced the Zenith Horoscope, in which planets were projected at angular distances along the horizon.

2. The true or rational horizon is called the 'great circle' It is parallel to the small circle but is expanded beyond the visible to divide the entire earth into an above and

below, with the observer located under the zenith. It too can play a role in an Astrolocality analysis of maps but perhaps it should then be called 'Global Space'.

3. *The Astrology of Local Space*, first published by Charles A. Jayne, Cosmecology Bulletin, number 6, 1977, and Local Space , Circle Books Astrological Calendar, 1978 edition. These 2 essays should be read by all serious students of Local Space.

4. From his essay, *The Astrology of Local Space.*

5. See his important book, *Planets in Locality*, AFA Publications, 1997.

6. See Michael's essays in Appendix 4.

7. The concept of a relocated chart was discussed in chapter 1. It is created by altering the natal co-ordinates of longitude and latitude to those of the new location. Date and (universal) time remain, just the locational information is changed. This gives us a picture not only of what the ecliptic birth chart would have been but also what the corresponding Local Space chart would be had the native been born at the place of relocation.

8. In normal navigational use, measurement of azimuth usually begins as 0 degrees in the north direction. Michael Erlewine took the decision to align the starting point with the east direction for use in Local Space. This corresponded with the usual astrological view of the (eastern) ascendant as the starting point of a chart, thus facilitating Local Space's integration with astrological practice.

9. Sean also uses the indicators of Local Space parallels and contraparallels in his consulting work. That means that Local Space planets at the same altitude (parallel), or opposing '+' or '-' altitudes (countraparallel) have a relationship regardless of their azimuth. He has also found that a Local Space planetary alignment becomes unmeasurable if we are located near a zenith position, below the planet.

10. Technical point: the above rule is correct much of the time. Technically however, the north versus south orientation of the MC-IC axis does depend on both the observer's terrestrial latitude and the planet's declination. When I speak of northern hemisphere charts I am assuming the observer's terrestrial latitude is greater than the planet's declination and vice versa for southern hemisphere locations. This is a reasonable assumption, but there can be cases where this may not be so, say for terrestrial latitudes below mid Florida for the northern hemisphere and above mid Australia for southern hemisphere charts. If in doubt then generate a Local Space chart or a Local Space chart map from a computer program and see how it works out. The computer-generated chart or chart map will show the true orientations.

11. *The Round Art*, by Tad Mann, Paper Tiger, 1979.

12. *The Astrology of Local Space*, 1977, Cosmecology Bulletin, and Appendix 4.

13. North and south Local Space angularity however will show a direct correlation with the culminating and anti-culminating lines of the ACG map.

14. In his book, *Planets in Locality.*

15. This is equivalent to the Sun on the midheaven in an ecliptic chart and it would mean that my Sun on the MC line would run through Philadelphia on my ACG chart. MC and IC lines show as south and north on Local Space charts but the east-west axis doesn't usually correspond to the ascendant-descendant axis, such that it is often new information for us.

16. The data used here and the crash data below are taken from Nicholas Campion's feature article in the Nov/Dec 1997 issue of the British Astrological Journal, titled: Diana, Princess of Wales. There is a discussion of the Mars-Pluto configuration in the article as well as other important factors. Recommended reading.

17. If one considers a time of 12:42 am or 17 minutes later, the Mars-west alignment becomes exact. This later time could have been a significant moment as events unfolded, perhaps the time she was pulled from the wreck, for example, as early reports stated it was about 20 minutes after the crash itself.

18. It is important to point out here that Pluto is not angular at all in the regular ecliptic chart for the eclipse moment, sitting in the 5th house over 30 degrees from the chart's descendant. That is, this information from the Local Space perspective is also new and unique.

19. *Astrology on the Move*, by Sasha Fenton, Zambezi Publishing, UK., 1998.

20. Even the title of her work was chosen from her frustration at the way things were and it was designed to jolt consciousness. '*The Second Sex*', was taken from a derogatory expression in France at that time which referred to gays as being 'the third sex'. She shifted this expression, identifying women in a similar oppressive light, such that it would impact upon the ear and therefore the understanding, of French society itself.

21. Astrologers will note that my Sun-Neptune natal conjunction could auger the loss of a father or the father figure in my life.

22. For a good explanation of this in ecliptic charts, the reader is referred to Robert Hand's book, *Horoscope Symbols,* Para Research, 1981, page 113, Parallels and Contraparallels. Another good reference, with examples, is: *Parallels, Their Hidden Meaning,* by Charles Jayne, Astrological Bureau, 1978.

23. The vertex is the intersection of the east-west meridian (called the Prime Vertical) with the ecliptic in the west, while the anti-vertex is this same intersection in the east. See *Horoscope Symbols* by Rob Hand, Para Research, 1981, pages 88-89 for information about these points.

24. Angel Thompson also recommends using the vertex, anti-vertex points, as what she calls the "eyeball" method, to turn an ecliptic chart into the west and east of a Local Space chart if/when a computer is not available.

25. See appendix 6 for a discussion of consequences due to Pluto's position so far off the ecliptic in our era.

26. The usefulness of the vertex-anti vertex axis as an informative point on the ecliptic chart also ceases when the terrestrial latitude of a location comes too close to planetary declination.

27. Even bunched up Local Space chart configurations can sometimes be useful, however. If one or more north-south planets stand out from the east -west planetary bunch, the standouts appear to be very important in a client's life. I call that type of Local Space chart pattern the 'butterfly effect', as the few north and south lines appear to be a head and tail, with the east-west planetary bunching representing the wings.

28. There is a similar type of problem, a breakdown at certain latitudes, on ACG maps where at extreme northern and southern latitudes many rising and setting lines cross each other. I consider those areas of an ACG map possible 'zones of confusion' for the native, where not too much specific information can be gathered.

29. I use Matrix Software's DOS program AstroMaps Hi Res to plot prime vertical maps. I haven't yet found a Windows mapping program that has this feature, though its inclusion is planned for Win*Maps.

CHAPTER THREE

LS Maps; Destiny Points

LOCAL SPACE MAPS

Local Space Maps can be seen as a necessary and useful extension of Local Space charts[1]. We have seen that LS maps, like ACG maps, are equatorial-oriented earth maps with the appropriate lines drawn on them. They are necessary to show LS directional influences over large distances. It has already been explained how LS lines are truly great circles emanating from the native's location or 'anchor point', with their directional influence in effect around the entire globe. When you plot these lines on a geographic map, they become curved after about 50 miles due to the perspective and geometry of representing them on a flat earth map.

With Local Space maps, we will now look at the significance of *all* directionality, not just the 4 cardinal angular ones. To begin with, and as a first principle, let's keep in mind Michael Erlewine's discovery that **he and his clients tended to travel or relocate exactly on the LS lines describing their planetary directions.** This can become important and very powerful information for us, either in explaining the directional outreach of our past actions or in helping us to plan our future activity.

We will soon see examples of how each planetary line describes a *directional* pathway for us on earth that reflects or radiates the qualities and attributes associated with the planet in question. The specific planetary energy becomes available as we travel on the line as well as describing the reason we may be moving to the new location. We may find also that it sends people and information *to us* from along its pathway. I have written a short description of what we might expect from each planetary line, as follows[2] :

Local Space Planetary Lines

> **The Sun** – Like the Sun itself, you'll be able to shine forth on this planetary line. You'll feel energised, confident and courageous as you travel

on it. It's an auspicious direction if you are journeying to a place where you'll be taking on leadership roles, positions of authority or taking creative risks. There is no need to be shy now; your personality can help you (but don't forget to listen to others as well). Follow your heart as you move in this direction, building a reality which includes growth and development for yourself.

The Moon – If you are looking to nurture someone or to be nurtured yourself, there can hardly be a better earth direction for you. A path to (or from) female relatives or friends is often found along this line. Issues requiring your sensitivity and response will pull you onto this pathway. On it, your intuition will flow easily and your emotional expression can be fulfilling, but be mindful of unconscious or habitual responses to things which can hold you in outdated situations.

Mercury – This earth pathway favours travel itself – especially journeys for business or to complete tasks. Movement in this direction supports projects in communication or those that require a high level of mental activity, study and/or writing. You may find yourself being very chatty as you travel along this line, while your mind is clear and insightful. Be careful not to get lost in details, possibly losing sight of the big picture.

Venus – This is a very good pathway on which to find a female love interest. You seem to look your best now, reflecting grace and charm. It's a fine direction, auguring success, if you are involved in an art project. You may also be drawn to it if you are travelling for the issues of love, beauty or relationship. You come to see the importance of these factors for your self-development. You must show maturity now, since compulsive attractions of appearance are possible to and from this earth direction. These attractions may not hold real substance or developmental potential for yourself.

Mars – Just do it! This is *the* direction to support you when initiative and action are required (but do make your actions meaningful and not merely impulsive). New challenges, even if risky, are highly favoured on this pathway. Women may find male partners either on this line itself or in new locations that are approached from its direction. Express yourself outwardly and actively so that anger doesn't build within and spoil your time.

Jupiter – This earth direction is about outreach and vision, all supported by an optimistic frame of mind on your part. It's a great pathway for travel itself, especially if you are moving towards situations where philosophy, teaching and general mental expansion are core issues. If you are willing to move beyond the safe and known in your life to an unknown realm of broader understanding, this is a line that will help you[3]. Do go for self-expansion now but bear in mind the Greek myth of Icarus: he flew too high to the Sun, melting his wings with disastrous[4] results!

Saturn – If you are moving on this earth pathway to a new situation where patience, diligence, discipline and/or maturity will be needed, this is the best direction for you to accomplish your goal. Your rewards (in time) will include new-found self-respect and inner development. Be patient, not pessimistic. People who dictate to you may appear from this direction. Be a real warrior now, consciously choosing when to comply with their demands or when to stand firm.

Uranus – Sudden career or relationship changes may find you travelling along this line. You feel an excitement in the air, and spontaneity will be necessary for you to deal with new conditions. If you have innovative projects to tackle, this line will support them. Your outlook on life is experimental and open. Surprises will come, so remember, 'surprises' mean just that, as a new and strange 'you' may manifest now. Do keep in mind that real creative change is more than mere restlessness, though restlessness may be one factor included in it.

Neptune – Neptune lines of all types present us with a dilemma, i.e., is this a place/direction of true inspiration, or is it one of illusion and perhaps deception[5]? Whatever the blend of these factors, if you are moving on this earth pathway in need of intuition and imagination, you will be amply supported. Don't expect a journey on this line to hold to logical planning choices; some form of spiritual guidance will be your best map. That guidance can come from within yourself as well as from others. You'll be successful if your intention includes service to others, compassion and/or a selfless type of love. Yes, there can be alluring yet cloudy issues facing you now, but you also have a priceless opportunity to nurture your soul.

Pluto – This earth direction will lead you to (or bring to you) intense situations which may become transformative to the point of changing your life. This is a great line if you are leaving an old situation behind or moving to a new one where deep security/power/desire issues within you are being exposed and must be dealt with. Events will push them upward to the surface mind for you to see. Travel on this line also supports worldly projects such as mining (extracting, digging deep and bringing to the surface) or tasks where you will have to deal with power over others and/or life and death issues in general. Your deep understanding and intensity can make you powerful on this pathway. If this turns to manipulation or ruthlessness on your part, you may find others blocking you, so do play your hand as lightly as possible to gain its benefits.

Let's start with the example of aviator Charles Lindbergh[6] and see how he was drawn towards specific Local Space lines (directions), *their energy helping him to accomplish his task.*

Charles A. Lindbergh captured the imagination and admiration of the Western world when on 20 May 1927 he took off from Roosevelt Field, NY and flew non-stop and solo across the Atlantic for 33 hours and 29 minutes, reaching his destination of Le Bourget airport, north of Paris, the next day. This event was considered a milestone for human courage as well for aviation at that time. A comparison in achievement with this era's Moon landing would be well founded. Let's not confuse Lindbergh's adventure at all with the ease we find today in catching a plane for Paris from our local airport. First of all, it was only a few decades after the very first flights, and planes were still under-powered and dangerous for such an adventure. Eighteen days before his flight, for example, Frenchmen Nungesser and Coli had disappeared attempting the same trip in the opposite direction, and in the following year, fourteen pilots – three of them women – perished trying to duplicate it[7].

There were no maps at all for an Atlantic crossing, so Lindbergh had

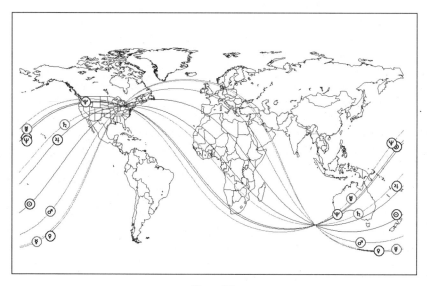

Figure 37

sought out fisherman who worked off the Newfoundland coast for weather and directional information. Even more astounding was that no one knew the exact location of his destination, Le Bourget airport! He was advised to search north of Paris and not to worry, as the airport would be well illuminated. In fact it wasn't. Airport authorities had turned off most of the lights so that the crowd could better catch sight of his approaching aircraft, The Spirit of St. Louis.

Lindbergh became an instant celebrity, with tumultuous and triumphant parades given in his honour in Paris, London and especially in New York, where he received a ticker-tape parade and a hero's welcome[8]. This event was the pinnacle of his public life, however, as his later years were marred by personal tragedy and his unpopular political views.

Figure 37 is Lindbergh's natal Local Space configuration (from Detroit) as seen on a world map. It is included here to illustrate how the LS lines seem to curve when represented on a map, though they actually cross the earth as great circles, returning at last to the starting point.

Figure 38 is a diagram of the route that Lindbergh took on his historic flight. It must be emphasised that his route was unique, as 91 other aviators had attempted the crossing before him, most on more northerly or southerly paths. Some had actually been successful in the crossing, but none had accomplished it as a solo and non-stop journey[9].

Figure 39 is the Atlantic detail of Lindbergh's natal LS map. It is quite startling to see what we discover here. His LS Mars line runs across the eastern Atlantic, over southern England and on to Paris, *almost perfectly duplicating the actual path of his adventurous, bold, pioneering journey!* What does this mean? From his birth moment, a direction, a path toward Paris would always be associated with initiative, assertiveness and courage for him. It is no surprise, therefore, that his pioneering journey would be planned just on that path and in that direction that would give him the very Martian qualities he would need to complete it. It seems to be a general principle that we are drawn towards our Local Space lines (directions) to fulfil the needs which require those specific energies. This may be what we can call our attunement or resonance with a situation[10].

The plot thickens! Although Lindbergh's natal LS map remains our primary source of information, let's also look for additional indicators from a relocated map. Relocating his LS information to the actual starting point of his specific journey – the airfield at Roosevelt Field, Nassau (NY) – we add the 'what is' for him from that specific location. Figure 40 is an Atlantic map of his planetary directional lines originating *from that airfield.* It is noteworthy to see that his Mars line has moved south and his Mercury and Venus lines (in LS conjunction) now become the ones that replace it, duplicating his flight path across the Atlantic and on to Paris, France.

What might this mean? Although the flight path for the pioneering flight itself is perfectly described by bold Mars (from his natal data), the location for

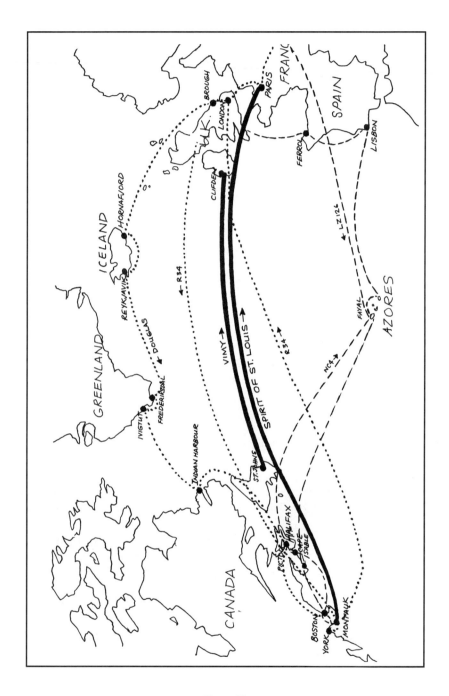

Figure 38

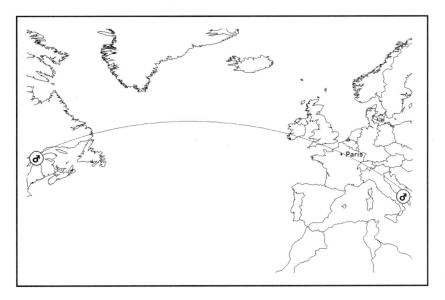

Figure 39

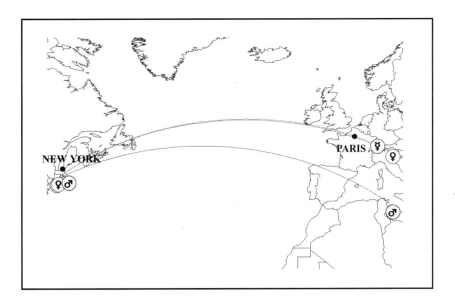

Figure 40

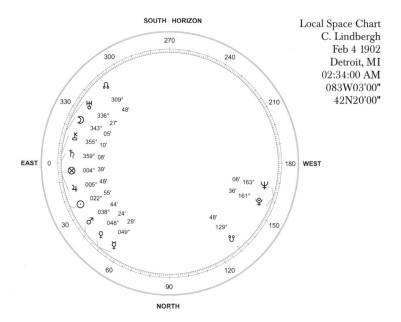

Figure 41

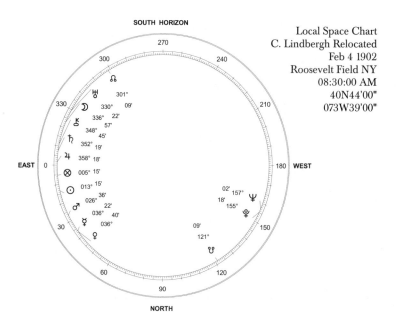

Figure 42

takeoff (relocated data) augured the journey's success, emphasising Lindbergh's professional skill and 'business travel' (Mercury) as well as his talents (Venus). And there is even more information to be had from those conjoined lines: Lindbergh's journey was in response to a $25,000 prize offered in 1926 by New York hotel owner Raymond Orteig for the first person to fly an aircraft directly across the Atlantic between New York and Paris. Lindbergh responded to this offer and within a year had made the journey and collected the prize. He was in fact journeying (Mercury) to gain his 'pot of gold' (Venus)!

Figures 41 and 42 are Lindbergh's LS charts for Detroit and Roosevelt Field, respectively. Note that for Detroit (in LS) he has Saturn almost perfectly in the east. Saturn power there indicates the ability to work hard and give form, shape and a concrete actualisation to his plans. This would be a perfect combination for the planning and implementation of his journey. The journey's starting location of Roosevelt Field, however, moves Saturn off of the LS east 'angle' and replaces it with Jupiter[11]. See Figure 42. He now has Jupiter power for his actual flight, or stated another way: plain good luck! Lindbergh himself recounted that he did doze off during the flight, but as the plane lost altitude, heading toward a crash into the sea, he had the good fortune to be awakened by the reflection of sunlight off of his instrument panel.

DESTINY POINTS; COMBINING ACG AND LS INFORMATION

In my work with both ACG and Local Space techniques I began to experiment using the information together as one system. Almost immediately I saw a valuable synergy could be obtained from the LS lines of direction with the intersections of the ACG lines of location. *Location* and *direction*: LS tells us the nature and meaning of the directional paths that we take, and ACG tells us what we could expect when we got there. I named these special crossings *bi-parans*, borrowing on the paran terminology of ACG and adding the 'bi' to identify that the data were coming from two systems. Later I came to use the term 'destiny point' to reflect how these crossings affected clients' lives[12].

Let's now go back to the Lindbergh saga and look for destiny points. Figure 43 is the European detail of his ACG map. This will help us to see how Paris played the important role of the destination of his historic flight. Paris can be seen as west of his Moon MC line. This certainly implies a possibility for him to become a focus of public attention there. This lunar quality may also explain the emotional but ultimately ephemeral nature of the adoration that he received. The ACG map shows us a lunar meridian which is, in effect, a line of possible locations where this type of public, emotional, lunar energy might manifest. But why Paris and not elsewhere - further north or south - on this Moon MC meridian? For an answer to this question let us look at Figure

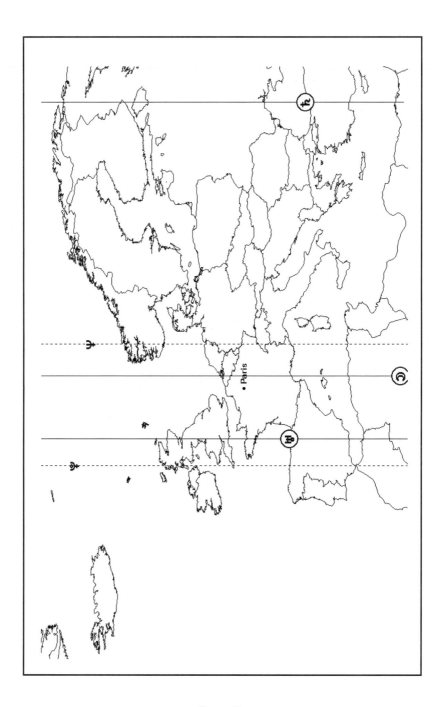

Figure 43

44, where both his ACG and LS lines are shown together. The LS direction of Mars and ACG location of Moon MC energy merge close to Paris. *This, therefore, is his Mars-Moon MC bi-paran or destiny point.* His pioneering, Mars directional line brought him lunar fame near the latitude and longitude of their crossing. In short we have a formula here:

The intersection of direction (LS) + location (ACG) = destiny point

Lindbergh did indeed land on the partially darkened airport at Le Bourget, and was immediately and energetically hailed by the crowd that assembled there. He was carried off on their shoulders as befitting his hero's status. Our pathways are active in both directions, so Lindbergh was raring to continue. He wanted to finish off his epic feat by flying the plane back to Roosevelt field, thereby accomplishing a world first round trip journey. He was refused permission to do this by the US president, Coolidge (In those days people heeded a president's wishes). Instead, the plane was flown to Portsmouth where it was disassembled and with Lindbergh accompanying it, both steamed back to the USA.

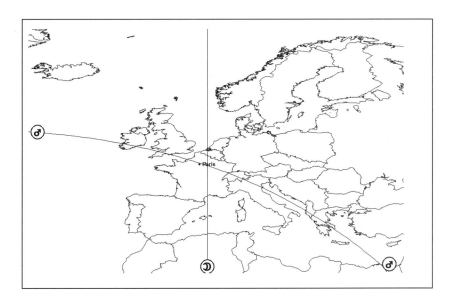

Figure 44

75

Using Local Space maps for natal, relocated and event moments

The underlying approach in working with the Local Space technique is to employ natal information first and then make use of relocated charts and maps for new locations[13]. As we have seen, for LS *charts,* relocating to new locations is very helpful, allowing us to ascertain what planets are brought to the angles of cardinal direction there (and the new horizon) or moved away from them. It may also tell us if any aspects have changed. For LS *maps,* relocating them will often give us important background information, especially of the intermediate journeys we must take in accomplishing our life tasks.

Experience has shown me that when you are looking for destiny points, it is most valuable to look first at the original natal lines to see where they fall across the earth. Often it is the natal LS lines, when combined with the ACG data, that give us the significant earth destiny points, regardless of the subject's current location[14]. Perhaps this means that from birth we have fated locations which will draw us to them regardless of where we may be residing at any time. In the Lindbergh example above, his natal LS Mars line from Detroit and his relocated Venus and Mercury lines from Roosevelt Field all impact with his Moon MC line in destiny points for him. But it is his natal Mars line, combining with the Moon meridian near Paris, that tells us the most about his remarkable pioneering achievement.

In the next example I will show how my natal astrolocality lines give me important destiny information. Following that we will see examples of Local Space lines on relocated maps and event moment maps as well.

1. Natal Lines: My date with destiny - the Munich Olympics, 1972

Here's an example of how natal directional lines from my birth location of St Louis, Missouri, helped to cast the light of meaning upon a period of big change in my life. Two events stand out:

In late August of 1972 I participated in the Munich Olympics as a member of the USA foil fencing team and only a few weeks later moved to Germany to live and work there for four years; an important period where my idea of 'home' was broadened beyond the boundaries of the USA.

Major transits and progressions were in effect for me, as might be expected. With transiting Pluto conjoining my natal Moon, many old patterns and situations were collapsing with new and unexpected ones arising from the ashes. In my Progressed Lunation cycle the Moon was making a waxing square to the Sun. Dane Rudhyar called this the 'crisis in action' life phase[15].

Let's look at the astrolocality map for this. Figure 45 is the European detail of my map. On it we can see my *natal* LS Venus line (from St Louis) intersecting two ACG (location) lines, Mars MC and my North Node MC[16] as well. Both of these destiny points occur in Germany and both directly correlated with what I consider major life events.

Taking the Mars MC-Venus bi-paran first, note that it is close to Munich, where the Olympic games were held. Destiny point it was, as many millions around the world saw me marching into the Olympic stadium on TV, although of course I was a faceless part of a large group and a very minor figure in the spectacle. No matter, as my Mars (combat sport) was being brought to public attention (MC meridian) in a pleasant scenario of enthusiasm and adulation by the spectators (Venus).

More on Mars: in spite of my ripe old age for an Olympian – at 35 the oldest man on the entire USA squad – I had never felt better or stronger in my life. Near my Mars line in Munich and with my natal Mars in Sagittarius, my legs were moving as if I were 10 years younger. And you may recall there was a terrorist attack during those games, with Israeli athletes, officials and German police officers killed. These tragic events happened nearby, perhaps expressing the dangerous side of Mars MC for me at that location. Might there have been a 'resonance' between that location and my surge of energy and good form relatively late in my sporting career? Did I make the Munich team (as I perceived it) or did my Munich destiny lines draw me to Munich for that Olympiad?

More on Venus: because of my age, I looked forward to the trip as an interesting and growth-orientated experience rather than with the nervousness and concern of a younger man. Perhaps it was the Venus energy that protected me from the martian danger of terrorism there, and Venus energy most likely explains the happy time I had after the events, going to concerts, visiting museums and travelling in the beautiful countryside.

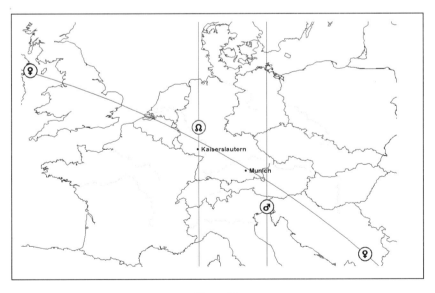

Figure 45

Let's now consider the LS with North Node MC - Venus destiny point: some weeks after returning to the USA from the Munich Olympics, I left the States again to take up a 4-year civilian employment contract with NATO in Kaiserslautern, Germany. I worked there as a quality-control engineer. What a delightful task for a Virgo: weeding out those imperfections! This destiny point falls less than 30 miles from Kaiserslautern. The Venus direction didn't let me down either. Almost immediately, a beautiful and secluded house in a nearby woods fell available (note that Venus rules the 12ᵗʰ house of secluded environments in my natal chart-as well as my 7ᵗʰ house). The house, with the surrounding natural beauty, was so perfect that it brought tears to my eyes when I first knew it would be mine. The North Node component of this destiny point was another, more difficult issue. New cultural experiences and issues came at me thick and fast. This had to be processed, along with the residual feeling of loss I felt for everything and everyone I had given up in the USA to get there (transiting Pluto on my natal Moon). My stay at this destiny location was associated with the most beautiful home environment I had ever known, as well another big change: becoming much more self-reliant in general (North Node in my natal first house).

2. Relocated Local Space lines show the way

Three examples follow: (a) on to Turkey, (b) I escape from my engineering career, and (c) a trip to India. Although my natal Local Space lines give me the most information when used for destiny points, it is important to note that my relocated LS maps from Germany (and later from Yorkshire, England) were important in describing significant life journeys to come. In general, relocated lines are useful for our investigations if the location has truly become our home for some time or if it is a an initiating location for a significant life event. I can't give any hard and fast rules on when to use relocated LS lines (or not), other than to note that after an analysis of natal lines, one's relocated lines should be considered for additional information.

Perhaps because I lived in the German village of Otterberg (near Kaiserslautern) as my true and only home for 4 years and because it was a destiny location itself, my relocated charts from that location were filled with important information. The lines of my relocated LS map from Germany projected outwards to locations that I would ultimately visit and even move to at later dates.

(a) **On to Turkey**. In 1976 my four-year contract expired and my job in Germany was finished. I was, however, able to extend my travels by taking a brief engineering assignment in Ankara, Turkey as a so-called "foreign national employee". How on earth did I ever even hear of an opening in Turkey, much less be selected for it? In retrospect, perhaps my relocated Local Space chart for Ankara gives us a hint. Figure 46 is my LS chart for that location. On it we

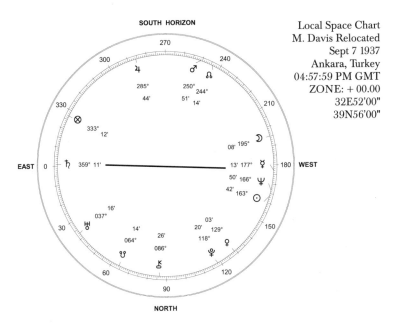

SOUTH HORIZON

Local Space Chart
M. Davis Relocated
Sept 7 1937
Ankara, Turkey
04:57:59 PM GMT
ZONE: + 00.00
32E52'00"
39N56'00"

Figure 46

can see that my Saturn is brought almost exactly to the east direction there –
within less than a degree of perfect alignment – and my Mercury is brought
to the west (within less than a 3-degree orb). Surprisingly for me, it turned out
to be an earth empowerment location, where things come to manifestation. I
had Saturn and Mercury power in Ankara, Turkey, pulling me there! (See
Appendix 2 for descriptions of Saturn in the east and Mercury in the west.)

In Figure 47 we see my relocated Local Space lines from Germany. There
are no direct lines to my next job in Ankara. *Note that we can't always expect to
find lines directly to everywhere we have been or may want to visit.* Ankara was an
important stepping stone for me, with empowerment energy, but it was just
one of the many places I have been, and a short-lived location of less than a
year. What *was* memorable was the journey I made to get there and, that said,
the LS directional lines from Germany do confirm this.

I travelled from Germany to Ankara by car and had arranged to have
some weeks free to do it. My Local Space lines from Germany provide us with
an example of how we can jump to different planetary directional lines (like
moving to different spokes of a wheel) as we travel, and therefore modify the
quality of our experience:

Mars and Node Lines: (See Figure 47, Line 'A'). Driving south from
Kaiserslautern, I set off first towards Switzerland, which turned out to be on
my Mars and Node lines. Although this was a life-changing trip, my energies
and confidence seemed very high and untroubled by the uncertainties I was

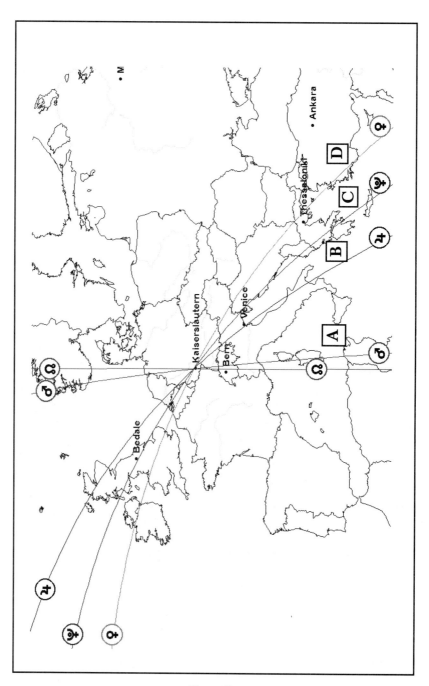

Figure 47

facing. My intention was to stop first for three days in Saanen (south of Bern) at a conference hosted by the philosopher J. Krishnamurti. The trip there was exhilarating. Near midnight, crossing the Swiss Alps, I experienced a full Moon that I can still recall. Travel, courage and good energy are positive manifestations of these lines.

Jupiter Line: (See Figure 47, line 'B'.) During the gathering, I enjoyed the conference itself with little contemplation of the deeper issues raised. When the conference ended I travelled southwest through Italy to Venice, and it was on this journey that the full impact of the teaching became clear. I felt elated at being able to spread my wings - so to speak - to travel and encounter a teacher and his teaching in such beautiful circumstances. I was now exactly on my Jupiter line (from Germany) as I approached Venice. Characteristically for a Jupiter direction, my attention had shifted to philosophy and I felt more optimistic about my life potential and future possibilities.

Pluto Line: (See Figure 47, line 'C'.) Driving east from Venice along the northern coast of the Adriatic Sea, I then turned south, crossing the border into Yugoslavia at Trieste. Unbeknown to me, I had now aligned with my Pluto LS line from Germany. My mood became more sombre. Now the reality hit home that I was leaving my old life behind forever (with the beautiful house in the woods) and going off alone into a new and unknown situation. It was an uncomfortable feeling, my psychological 'security props' of home, job and friends being kicked out from me once again. Bob Dylan's words drifted across my mind, "How does it feel.... like a rolling stone.... destination unknown.... How does it feel?"

The most noteworthy part of my trip was down the entire coast road of the former Yugoslavia, untroubled by the ethnic warfare which was to follow years later. It was a beautiful and even memorable journey, one I still recall. But the knowledge that nothing now remained of my past life in Germany brought a fear-tinged intensity to it.

With hindsight, another starting indicator emerges. The same LS Pluto line that led me down the coast road of the former Yugoslavia runs westward from Germany to Yorkshire (Bedale) in England. Then, in 1976, I wasn't to know that the same Yorkishire location would become my home one day in the 1980's. This relocated Pluto line, in its entirety (both directions), was providing me with information relevant to a new day that would dawn later in my life - rising from the ashes of the fields I had metaphorically burnt and was then leaving behind.

Venus line: (See Figure 47, line 'D'.) But now back to my journey to Ankara: as I drove around Albania and into Greece (and off my Pluto line), the intensity of my reverie suddenly seemed unnecessary. It was replaced by the happiness and appreciation for life that Greece can bring. Actually, I was now approaching my Venus line (from Germany) which lies just east of Thessalonika. Overcome with venusian feelings of beauty - and forgetting all my former plutonian misgivings, I interrupted my journey to experience Greece - and life. Parking the car at the airport, I took the next plane to a Greek island, where I drank wine, sat in the sun, and enjoyed the Aegean sea for a week. The intense, concerned 'me' had become a happy and thankful Zorba. Hooray for Venus! Flying back to the Greek mainland I picked up the car and completed my journey, finally arriving in Ankara ready to begin my new job, my new life.

There are some other considerations here worthy of mention: in using Local Space charts and maps, it must be kept in mind that the directions and directional lines don't work in isolation from the other astrological indicators, such as the transits, progressions and directions. At this time of travel I was approaching my so-called 'mid-life crisis', with change an absolute imperative for me. With my natal Uranus in my 6th house of workplace (being opposed by transiting Uranus in my 12th house), it's clear to see that my particular changes were associated with different jobs and changing work sites – which are typical 6th-house indicators.

Also, one can note the emphasis of Venus, Jupiter and Pluto lines in the travels I am describing. A review of my natal chart will show that Venus and Pluto are in my 9th house of long-distance foreign travel and 'outreach', along with my natal Jupiter on my travel-oriented 3rd house cusp (in most house systems), all excellent candidates to explain this period of my life

Another point to note is about aspects to a line we might be travelling on. The energy of any of our planetary lines is always affected in quality by the natal aspects we have to it. My natal Venus is squared by Uranus, for example, so that when encountering my Venus line in Greece, I would tend to manifest it with unusual, creative (or perhaps eccentric) Uranus-type actions (interrupting the journey and flying off to an island). For me, Venus lines will always carry a challenge from Uranus and Uranus lines, a challenge from Venus.

In the Lindbergh example, he has no 9th-house planets. However, those planets emphasised by the Local Space maps for his journey – Mars, Mercury and Venus – are all in his other house of travel, his 3rd. And his Mars, which is the major indicator of his pioneering journey, is in the path-making sign of Aquarius, a symbol and indication itself of unique, individual and forward-looking efforts.

(b). Escape from my engineering career. By 1977, living in Ankara, I had had enough of office work, so I resigned from my position as a quality-control engineer, scraping together enough money to keep me in a simple life-style for a few years more. After some 17 years in offices I was free. What to do next? I didn't know. (Note: in retrospect, how could I have known what to do? In addition to having transiting Uranus opposing its natal position at that

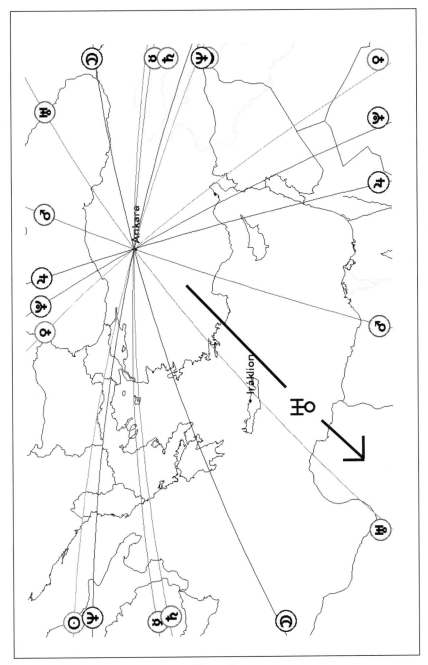

Figure 48

time (need to be free), I also had transiting Pluto conjunct my natal Moon and transiting Neptune on my natal Mars. In other words, all the outer planets were making major, once-in-a-lifetime hits. The cosmos was making - and working - me over.

I decided to travel to Crete, sit in the sunshine and ponder what to do next. Figure 48 is my relocated Local Space map from Ankara. Note that from that location, and at the time of my Uranus opposition, I was exactly (and unconsciously) following my Uranus line as I took my first steps toward what I saw as freedom from my former career. Again I repeat an important principle here:

We are drawn towards our Local Space lines (directions)
to fulfil the needs which require those specific energies.

(c). **A trip to India.** After Crete I had about 4 years more of adventure, living in European cities as well as some more offbeat Eastern locations. By 1982, I was living in Yorkshire most of the time. From this location I was able to arrange an eight month trip for myself to the Himalayan mountains of India and Nepal. This journey, really a pilgrimage, turned out to be the last and most significant expedition of my travelling, mid-life years. As it was a profound time for me, I would expect to find indications of it in my astrolocality astrology... and I do!

In my natal Local Space world map, there are no lines even near India from my birth location. It's as if I was never destined to visit India while I lived in the USA. But this destiny changes completely when I now move to Yorkshire, England, where the possibility becomes manifest. Figure 49 is my LS world map from my relocated position in Yorkshire. Note that two lines do now run over to northern India from my relocated home. Figure 50 is the Indian detail of the this world map. On it we can see that my Sun line direction (growth, creative expression) crosses northern India, almost exactly leading me to my arrival city there of New Delhi. My Neptune line (spiritual insights, as well as danger from polluted drinking water!) crosses the high Indian-Tibetan border region and on into Nepal, all areas of my most difficult – and rewarding – trekking. I had travelled on a journey (from England to India) where I had sought growth-orientated experiences (Sun line) as well as spiritual inputs (Neptune line). This trip worked best for me when originating from England, as I was (unconsciously) able to call on my Sun and Neptune energies to guide me from there, the perfect directional lines for me to complete my task successfully.

The Local Space chart for my relocated destination of New Delhi is unusual. It is shown in Figure 51. I have no planetary energy brought to the cardinal directions on this chart, but we can see that a less material symbol, my Part of Fortune, is brought exactly to the east at that location. My PF has

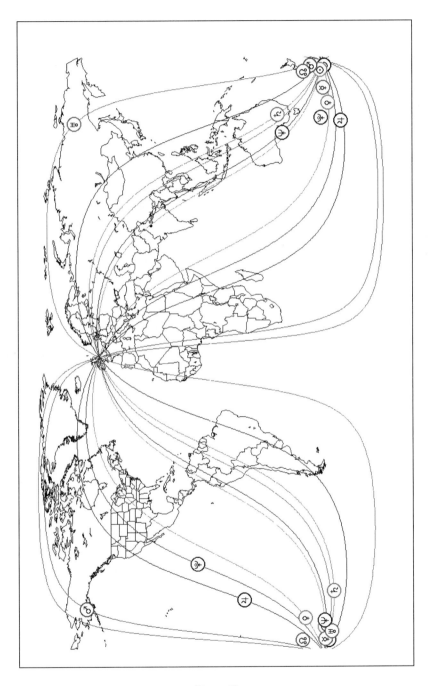

Figure 49

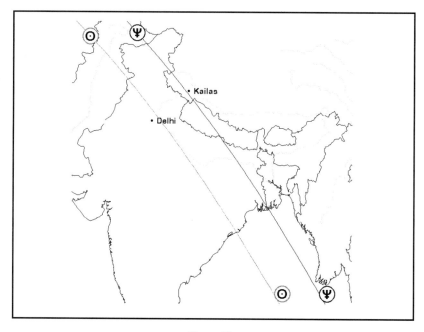

Figure 50

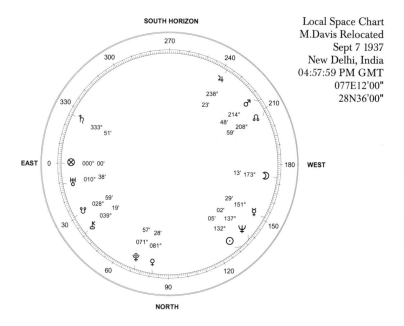

Figure 51

'east power' in New Delhi and northern India in general. Perhaps this is a sign of empowerment there for existential good luck; a place where the fortunes of destiny must smile on me, though not necessarily in a material way[17].

3. Using Local Space lines for event charts: Amelia Earhart, America's Sweetheart of the Air

One of the most famous and inspirational women in the early part of the 20th century was aviatrix Amelia Earhart. She stepped onto the world stage – and into people's hearts – in 1928, after becoming the first women to fly across the Atlantic. Flying made her famous, disappearing made her legendary[18].

Earhart disappeared as she was nearing the final legs of a record-breaking 29,000-mile journey, circumnavigating the globe near the equator. On the morning of 2 July 1937, at 10.00 AM local time, Earhart and her navigator Fred Noonan took off from Lae on the island of New Guinea, bound for a refuelling stop at Howland Island. At 2,556 miles away this was the longest leg of her journey. Howland Island itself is very tiny and flat and would be impossible to see until one was almost over it. Her dream never happened, however, as she and Noonan vanished in the Pacific without a trace.

Though various speculations abound about her disappearance,[19] historians still believe that she was lost because the US naval map she and Noonan were using was faulty, erroneously indicating a location miles away from the island's true position[20]. Researchers Elgen and Marie Long, who spent 25 years investigating Amelia's disappearance, wrote, "Her last words indicate that she was doing exactly what a lost pilot should have been doing: flying a search pattern, looking for the island." Noonan is thought to have brought them to where the island should have been according to the erroneous map, and there they began their search pattern. Final radio transmissions from Earhart indicate that she was running out of fuel and couldn't find the island. It is believed she ditched the aircraft somewhere northwest of Howland.

Astrologers will note that if we take the themes of 'lost' and 'lost at sea' and 'erroneous or deceptive information' and couple them with the fact that Noonan (possibly the most well-thought-of navigator of his era) had known alcoholic problems, we can begin to see Neptune as a planetary theme here. Perhaps her running out of fuel also alerts us to look for Saturn contacts, as this planet is associated with scarcity and lack of things. Let's have a look:

Figure 52 is a detail from Amelia Earhart's (natal) ACG map. On it we can see that her Neptune descending line runs right through Papua New Guinea, not too far from the embarkation point of her last flight. Taken negatively, this could mean the possibility here of poor communication as well as misrepresentations from others, as things wouldn't be as they seem.

Figure 53 is the combined *transiting* LS and ACG map for Lae at their moment of departure. True, this is a map for everyone there at that time, but only she and Noonan were departing then on a historic event, making it a valid

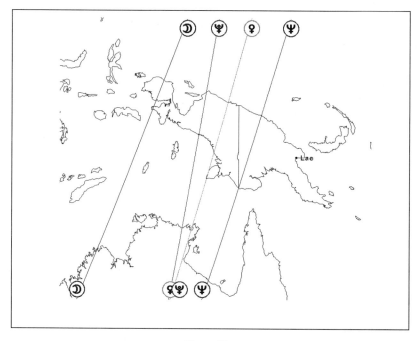

Figure 52

event, chart-of-the-moment for them. The first thing to note is that the Neptune line runs approximately in the direction of Howland Island. That itself, negatively taken, is a potential danger. This is compounded by the fact that the Saturn descending line (ACG) runs near to Howland, such that her target landing site is uncomfortably close to a Saturn-Neptune destiny point. This can be seen to be ominous, as Saturn and Neptune are not a happy combination, often associated with 'undermining circumstances'.

There is more. Figure 54 is the Local Space *chart* for their departure moment. On it we can see that the unwanted Saturn-Neptune combination is close to the east-west empowerment points, where those planetary energies might most likely manifest. Neptune is 5 degrees from due east (in orb) and Saturn is only about 3 degrees from the exact west direction. A possible dangerous combination in this case, 'empowered' or made more hazardous.

We might have hoped that the 'empowered' Part of Fortune, almost perfectly to the north direction of this chart, would have brought a more fortunate result. If we look at Rudhyar's Sabian symbol for this degree, however (10 degrees Gemini, from the ecliptic chart of the departure moment), we see that more transcendent forces may have been in effect. It reads, "An airplane performing a nose dive"; with the keynote, "A superior ability to challenge nature and play with danger." Rudhyar then goes on to comment, "By chal-

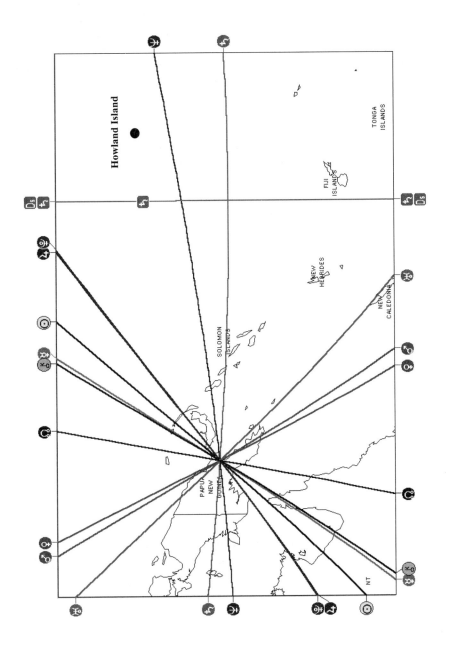

Figure 53

lenging it (nature) man prepares himself to pierce beyond the physical and to reach higher realms of existence. He may lose the struggle, but that prospect makes the effort more exciting. He may gain immortality."

With an exact Mars-Jupiter conjunction in the 5th house of her natal chart, Earhart was a spirited and creative law unto herself and perhaps the perfect candidate to "challenge nature and play with danger". She understood the difficulties she faced in pushing the aircraft and navigational capabilities of her day to their very edge. "When I go", she had told her husband, "I'd like to go in my plane. Quickly".

We should keep in mind that Amelia lived a full life, experiencing her dream of flying for sixteen years. She said, "The love of flying is the love of beauty. It was more beautiful up there than anything I had known".

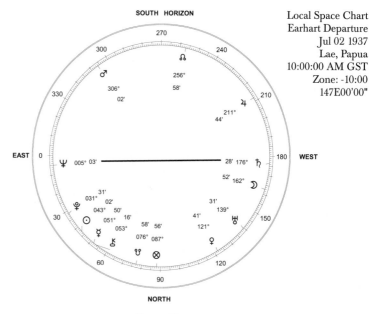

Figure 54

NOTES

1. Or more accurately stated, they are an extension of LS chart maps; that is, LS charts turned around so that north is 'up' and east is to the right as we would usually view a map.

2. Another source for this information can be found in Steve Cozzi's book, *Planets in Locality*, in the table entitled 'Travel and Relocation on Planetary Lines'.

3. Jeff Jawer says of the Jupiter Local Space line, "This is the direction to spread your wings, to move beyond old limits and live a life of high adventure".

4. An interesting word for astrologers: from 'disaster' [dis-aster], meaning against or counter to the stars.

5. Self-deception (idiomatically, the French 'mauvaise foi') is just as possible on Neptune lines and locations as is deception from others.

6. Thanks to Steve Cozzi for first suggesting that I investigate Lindbergh's maps.

7. This historical account (from Air France magazine, August 1998) of the first flight ever over the Andes in 1921 by French aviatrix Adrienne Bolland is so good and exemplary of the dangers of that era that I'll include it here:

"It was 1 April 1921, Adrienne was hunched over the controls in her tiny bath-tub like cockpit, an icy wind tossing the frail-looking plane about as if it were a toy. She was flying too high above the Andes. Her nose and mouth were full of blood. Bitter cold burned her hands and feet. Her vision was blurred. She felt dizzy and could hardly breathe in the rarefied atmosphere two-and-a-half miles above the earth. Adrienne was lost in the high-altitude wilderness. At times the plane was sucked down, and she gripped the throttle with all her might. The wings flapped and trembled... After ten hellish minutes, Adrienne spotted an oyster-shaped lake below. She had no idea where she was.

Shortly before her departure, a Brazilian woman who had read about the pilot in the papers walked into her hotel room. She left Adrienne some medals and a piece of advice: "When you're lost up there, you'll fly over an oyster-shaped lake. There'll be a valley to your right, which will look like the right way. It's not. Make a left toward a wall of solid rock that looks insurmountable".

Spitting blood, Adrienne turned left and headed straight toward the wall. She quickly discovered that when wind hits a mountain it is deflected skyward in the same way that the water in a stream flies into the air when it hits rocks in the rapids. She flew headlong into the blade of the wind, coming close to the wall. The wind lifted her aeroplane and carried it up, climbing the sheer rock face until a breach opened behind a peak. Adrienne steered the plane into the pass and suddenly found herself flying above peaceful valleys, with the Pacific straight ahead.

In Santiago, she was feted like no women before her. But the French consul was not there. He thought this business about a woman aviator who had conquered the Andes was an April Fool's joke!"

8. A recent biography of Lindbergh makes the point that he was the 20th century's first media hero because of the newly employed 'wireless', which instantly informed the whole world of his exploits.

9. *The 91 Before Lindbergh*, by Peter Allen. Airlife Books, UK. 1984.

10. There is a Sufi word for this, 'taqwa', being in the right place at the right time without knowing why.

11. Note that this Local Space information about Saturn and Jupiter in the east could have been surmised from the conjunctions of those planets with the anti-vertex in his natal (Detroit) and relocated (Roosevelt Field) charts respectively.

12. See my article in the British Astrological Journal, "Local Space Astrology", Nov/Dec 1989, page 324, for the introduction of the terms 'bi-paran' and 'destiny point" into astrological use.

13. This is the same as in 'traditional' astrological techniques, where natal data always contain unchanging and pertinent information, regardless of subsequent relocation.

14. Certainly don't rule out using relocated data for discovering destiny points, especially if the subject has lived at a relocated place for some time.

15. *The Lunation Cycle*, by Dane Rudhyar, Aurora Press, 1986

16. The diagram holds equally true for either my Mean or True Node. Separated by only 0 degrees 22 minutes of zodiacal degree, their slightly different alignments over the earth are hardly distinguishable from each other at this magnification.

17. It is interesting to note that the Sabian symbol for my PF (natally at 22 degrees Sagittarius) in both the Marc E Jones and D. Rudhyar interpretations refers to the ability of maintaining one's poise in unfamiliar or alien environments; certainly a helpful boost for me as a Westerner travelling in the Himalayas.

18. Quotes from article "Amelia Earhart" by Virginia Morell, National Geographic, January 1998

19. An Earhart cult has continued to thrive. A recent web search revealed at least 136 sites devoted to or concerning her.

20. The area of the Pacific around Howland was largely unknown and poorly charted at that time. Howland was placed in the wrong position on the map she had been sent by her navigational consultant. Ironically, in a survey conducted a year earlier, the discrepancy had been corrected, but the new information hadn't worked its way into

print. Howland Island was not where they expected it to be. Another factor might have been a radio problem or her lack of expertise in radio communications. The US ship Itasca was waiting at Howland to guide her in. They received one message from her stating she heard them but couldn't home in on their position. They transmitted continuously but didn't hear from Amelia again. Reasonable two-way communication might have saved her life. Excerpted from *The Sound of Wings*, by Mary S. Lovell. Hutchinson, London, 1991.

CHAPTER FOUR

The Local Space chart in the home, community and beyond;
Special studies in Local Space

THE LOCAL SPACE CHART IN THE HOME, COMMUNITY AND BEYOND

In my introduction to the Local Space technique (see Chapter 2) I pointed out that Michael Erlewine saw ".. the visible horizon being much like a magical circle" and that the use of such circles with directional power points is found in mystery traditions. I also stated that information from Local Space charts bears a striking similarity to what one hopes to obtain from the Chinese system of Feng Shui (which idiomatically means 'perfect placement').

This ancient art has guided the Chinese people for thousands of years in designing their cities, building their homes and even in burying their dead. The idea behind Feng Shui is to be able to read the patterns of the universe and live in harmony with them, especially as they relate to one's environment. In the past this powerful body of knowledge has focused on its general principles, not including individual directional patterns in its considerations. Utilising the Local Space charts[1] of today, however, we can refine this by adding our specific astrological information to the techniques of 'perfect placement'.

In short

The Local Space chart can be utilised as the individual's specific geomantic compass for determining arrangements in harmony with his/her immediate environment. In the discussion that follows, I will show how we can go about using our Local Space information in our home or office, in our community and then even beyond into the farthest reaches of the cosmos:

The Local Space Chart in the home or office

The Local Space technique is ideal for tuning into the situation and/or arrangements in our immediate environment. Cozzi[2] says it nicely: "Everything around you has a symbolic and literal meaning, and through the use of the Local Space chart you can begin to discover the vast interplay of the spiritual and material worlds".

Important points

• It must be stressed that – as with all the astrolocality techniques – a fairly accurate birth time is necessary. Hopefully, it will be accurate to within half an hour or better. The more vague you believe your birth time to be, the more tolerance or leeway you should give to the exactitude of your directional information.

• I recommend you use your natal data for this in-close work, even if like me, you now reside a great distance form your original birthplace[3]. If in doubt try both your natal and relocated data and decide for yourself.

The idea is to bring together a floor plan or diagram of your home, room or office with your planetary Local Space lines.

Here's how to do it:

1. Calculate (and print) your Local Space chart. If possible, choose a form that presents you with north at the top, otherwise you'll simply have to turn it around to use it. When the Local Space chart is used as a geomantic compass, planetary effect is represented by a two-way vector, a line which runs both towards and away from the planet (since it is truly the origin of a global great circle)[4]. Figure 55 illustrates what I mean. It shows a Local Space wheel turned into a geomantic compass by having the north at top and each planet represented by a line. If you have a wheel form that displays the lines this way, use it[5]. Otherwise, it is a straightforward procedure to turn a Local Space wheel into a compass. See Step 4 below to do this. I would include the 10 planetary lines as well as the node line. If health, healing or teaching issues are involved, you might want to include Chiron as well, although things can begin to get crowded with too many lines.

2. Draw a diagram of your living or office space if you can't obtain a floor plan. It would be very useful if you can add lots of detail to it. Delineate such things as the specific rooms, furniture, windows, important functional areas, and so on.

3. It's easiest to have a transparency of either your Local Space chart or the floor plan in order to overlay the information from both sources. If you are careful, it may also be adequate to simply draw your planetary lines on the floor plan[6].

4. As noted in Step 1 and Figure 55, planetary lines work in both directions. If you have a Local Space wheel and wish to create a compass, you will have to draw a line for each planet. To do this, find the centre point of your Local Space chart and, using a straight edge and marker pen, first draw a line from the centre to the planet and then extend that line from the centre to the other side of the circle. I would include the 10 planetary lines as well as the node

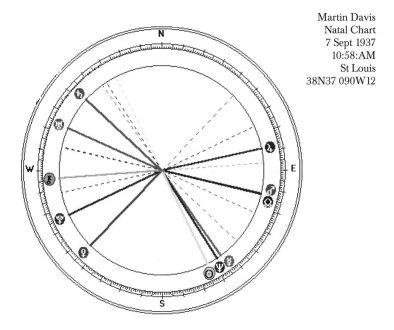

Martin Davis
Natal Chart
7 Sept 1937
10:58:AM
St Louis
38N37 090W12

Figure 55

line. Again, if health, healing or teaching issues are involved, you might want to include Chiron as well, although these extra lines can make your diagram crowded.

5. The next step is to determine where true north is on the diagram or floor plan of the home or office. One should have a general idea of north at a right angle from the approximate sunrise/sunset positions of the locality[7] A compass is helpful of course, but care has to be taken to obtain the proper correction from magnetic north to true north. Another way to get the northern alignment is to use a commercial map of your locality. Some very accurate maps actually show three north directions: true north (the one we want), magnetic north and map north.

6. One must now find the centre of the floor plan or diagram from which to align the Local Space compass. Finding the centre of a room in a home or office should be straightforward, with a satisfactory accuracy obtained by pacing it off. Determining the centre of a house (especially if it has patios) or a floor plan with adjoining rooms might be more difficult. Ideally one would want the true geometric centre of the area, but sometimes a functional centre is more appropriate. The only guide I can offer here is a general one: Locate the geometric centre first and use it, but in some cases try using other, functional centres.

97

7. Now you are ready to place your Local Space compass over/on the floor plan. Be sure to have the centres of both aligned as well as the directions. Figure 56 is floor plan of my large working and den space with some of the Local Space planetary lines superimposed on it.

8. Note that planetary energy works in both directions along each complete planetary line. Planetary conjunction and opposition lines will come together on the chart as one, indicating a blending of their energy over objects and direction on the floor plan.

9. Now comes the review and analysis of the lines! Think of the directional lines as making conjunctions with objects and living spaces as well as leading to things. Planetary lines have an attraction or repulsion to various objects and types of spaces. Perhaps it's more accurate to say they are in harmony with some and in disharmony with others. These correspondences are typical of astrology in general, and we can look to classical astrology to give us an idea what they may be. A Sun line for example would favour gold- or orange-coloured round objects, the metal gold itself, as well as objects that are personalised and important to the individual. Noting the Sun's obvious characteristics, we could see that stoves, fireplaces and warm parts of a house would be enhanced by a Sun line. William Lilley associated the Sun with dining rooms (as well as great halls), and generally we can see how creative areas of a house – such as play rooms – would be enhanced as well. For a female, lines leading to a husband or male partner's living space would be enhanced by the Sun direction, another obvious astrological correlation.

10. More specifically, let's review my personal lines again as shown in Figure 56. I arranged the room a few years ago without Local Space information, just by what seemed right for function and aesthetics. Note the Uranus line points right to my computer, an apt correspondence. My Sun, Mercury and Neptune lines, in Local Space conjunction, make hits in both directions. One way they lead me right out of the doorway to the rest of the house. The other way they cross over what I call my 'communication centre', shelves holding two telephones, a fax machine and my internet connection. I feel these are fortuitous alignments. The dreaded Saturn line falls on a table that holds stacked trays for incoming business requests as well as bills due. I often refer to the overflowing trays as 'the mess'. The Saturnian energy seems to appropriately describe it. The Venus line in one direction falls on shelves holding my music collection and in the other direction points to the wardrobe that holds my better clothes (not shown). Jupiter points in both directions to tables that hold items dear to me - like photos from my Himalayan journey. One such table is at the foot of my bed shown in the upper right of the floor plan.

Note that the use of the compass alone won't give us all the information we might need to study our living or working environments. For exam-

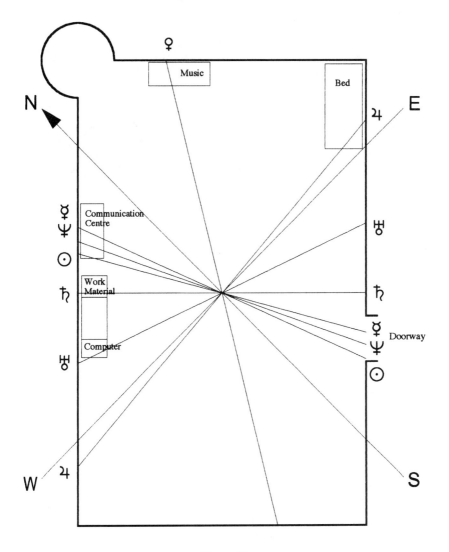

Figure 56

ple, I was told by a visiting Feng Shui expert that because my room was a mess, my affairs would be in a mess and that my rickety office furniture meant a rickety business for me. She cautioned that even my stuffed and overflowing trash bin was impacting negatively on my occupation. I corrected these things and found the results to be very satisfying. Experts can also advise on best placement of objects in the so-called 'money corner' of a room to improve one's income. In short, it's fascinating to see how the immediate arrangement and condition of our environment may affect us more broadly than imagined.

The Local Space compass in action

It may be helpful at this point to call upon the work of four experienced astrologers who actually have incorporated the Local Space techniques into their Feng Shui consultations. Let us now look at some input from Angel Thompson, Steve Cozzi, and Ralph and Lahni DeAmicis.

Angel Thompson[8] is noted for her writing and consulting in the field of Feng Shui, her endeavours in popularising Local Space and in directing the Continuum organisation, which furthers the field of Astro*Carto*Graphy. In appendix 3 she shares her insights with us on *Planetary Lines in Your House*. They will be very helpful for those exploring this geomantic use of Local Space. To them she adds important advice for us, which she has titled *Moving the Moon*:

> "Remember that all areas of the house are naturally ruled by one of these planets. Further, the directions run on a continuum: east will eventually turn to west; north will eventually run into south.
>
> If you are able to arrange your home to align with the natural meaning of the planets, for example, if by luck and coincidence, you are able to sleep on your Moon line, all the better. If your furniture is placed on unfavourable lines, you can modify the effect by using the colours and shapes of other planets you desire to modify the space. For example, using silvery blues, or other Moon related colours on or near your bed, you can 'move the Moon' to the bedroom. If you want to be alone in your office, emphasise Pluto colours; if you want to feel strong, use Mars objects. In this way, you can modify the effects of the lines through interior design and arrange your life to maximise the potential of your planets and your space."

Steve Cozzi[9] has some important and helpful tables in his book, *Planets in Locality*, on this subject. They are entitled *Planetary Lines in the Home, Planetary Intersections with Objects and Fixtures in and around the Home* and *Case Examples of Planetary Lines Throughout the Home*.

He found (perhaps not too surprisingly) that Saturn lines caused the most problems for his clients. In general, delicate objects didn't fare too well on Saturn's line. If a Sun item like a fireplace was hit by Saturn, he found that clients reported they couldn't keep the fire going effectively. Water pipes don't seem to be harmonious with Saturn lines either, as they lose pressure and freeze in the winter. Saturn lines were effective, however, when leading to darker, quieter or colder parts of a house or to pillars, doors and stairways. It's astrologically understandable that Mars, Pluto and Neptune lines are also problematical when hitting inharmonious objects.

Mars lines through a Mercury object like a telephone might mean it would need replacing several times and even that a preponderance of irritable and argumentative calls would result. Beautiful objects (Venus) can be damaged when met by a Pluto line, and leaky water taps seem impossible to fix when they are in a Neptune direction.

Ralph and Lahni DeAmicis[10] may be the most active American Feng Shui practitioners who blend Local Space into their consultations, using the 'compass' about fifty per cent of the time. They do caution us however that "Local Space by itself is not a substitute for a good grounding in ergonomic design, and a knowledge of the nature of energy pathways". In brief, here is a list of how Ralph and Lahni find each planetary energy can best be applied:

The Sun: Where you feel most centred, creative, warm; good for a bedroom, office, family room.

The Moon: Good activity area for nurturing, emotional connecting, sleeping. Beware, things move on a Moon line. This is the first place to look for your missing keys.

Mercury: The telephone, communications, working with the hands, consulting, parking your bicycle.

Venus: Social, artistic, loving, sleeping, harmonising diverse needs, conference and mediation rooms.

Mars: High physical activity, exercise, games, loving, but not necessarily sleeping. May be too ego centred to unwind.

Jupiter: Expansion, athletics, good for an exercise room, not good for the refrigerator (could expand your waistline!). Generally good sleeping line depending on the tone of the planet. Good home office line. Good for the health.

Saturn: Structured, ambitious, reserved. Good for an office if it relates to practical issues. Stiffening. Sleeping on a Saturn line tends to make a person feel mature, but sometimes oppressed.

Uranus: Computers, televisions, electronics gravitate to a Uranus line. Exciting, disruptive, inventive, not good for sleeping. The unexpected happens here.

Neptune: Dissolving, relaxing, meditative, intoxicating, illusionary. Great place to sleep or unwind. Things tend to disappear on a Neptune line. Second place to look for your keys.

Pluto: Secretive, powerful, sexual, transformational, great for a massage room, or any type of deep therapy. It can be very isolating, but people are drawn to sleep on a Pluto line when they feel the need for deep change.

Chiron: A good healing room, consulting, study, meditation.
Ceres: The kitchen, the studio.
Pallas: The work room, the weaving room, massage room.
Juno: The bedroom, family room, studio.
Vesta: The home office, the kitchen, the healing room.

More from the DeAmicis' broad experience:

"The hardest line to move off is Saturn's line. If a person is sleeping on that Saturn line, no matter how stiff their joints are upon awakening, they resist moving the bed. In that case the best thing to do is have them buy pieces of the crystal rose quartz and put them by the bed stand and between the mattress and bed springs. Saturn controls crystals, so this way you play the energy out and convert the energy over to one that is more loving and flexible. Sometimes it's helpful to put a picture of a large structure or building on the Saturn line to play the energy out.

The sign position of that planet has as much significance in the Local Space chart as it does in the classic horoscope, and the condition via rulership, exaltation, etc., will show how well that Local Space line will serve the person.

When people have lived in a house for a long time and have been able to decorate to their hearts content, if they are reasonably healthy people in an emotional way, they will literally play all of their lines out. It is the way in which a house completely becomes them because it is a true expression of their energies being projected by their aura.

When we consult we bring a Local Space Chart for each resident. What does it do for us? It will show the nature of a problem when there is no obvious reason in the Feng Shui design." Here are some examples:

• "The bed is placed well, commanding the door, not too much light, no oppressive features. The husband can't sleep there, and when he does it means nightmares. His Saturn line runs down his side of the bed. Saturn is representative of the father. From our discussions with him we find their relationship was horrific. Every time he lies down on that line he vibrates to that energy. But in the other bedroom we find his Jupiter line, related to generosity and good health. Change bedrooms!A couple is arguing, but always in the same two places in the kitchen, the table and the sink. The space design is harmonious, but the husband has parallel Mars and Mercury lines through the table, leading him to intense explosions of aggressive energy, that he soon gets over. By the sink he has parallel Pluto and Saturn lines. So when he gets mad there it's about deep seated power and father issues. The wife has a bundle of energies running near those locations, Sun, Moon and Venus, resulting in intense and emotional responses. So the angry kitchen scenario repeats and repeats: He gets mad, it challenges her identity and self worth, she digs in to defend herself, he doesn't understand why she can't just get over his outbursts. Her energy is fine there. The problem is his energy, so we need to play his energy out. The solution is simple, put some bright red apples in a silvery bowl to pay off that Mars-Mercury energy, and then eat in the dining room where the lines are more harmonious for both of them. It works!"

• "A woman can't sleep later than five in the morning in her bed. Her sleep patterns there tend to be unpredictable. However, her sexual experience in the space is positive, and in fact very exciting. There is nothing in the ergonomic design that explains that. In fact the bed is in the committed relationship section of the room and it's well centred against the wall. Yet she has a part time relationship that does not shout of commitment that yields a very entertaining, if somewhat sporadic love life. Well, running down the length of the bed is a Venus-Uranus in Leo line! Great for exciting and inventive romantic experiences, but that Uranus line is generally too stimulating for sleeping. After the client rejects the solution of moving the bed (big surprise!), we suggest that she hang a colourful mobile with lots of turquoise and silver over the bed. She hangs up an Indian medicine bag. This is perfect. These are colours and materials that relate to the Uranus energy. Out of the usual context, it comes from a different culture; its eccentric, like Uranus. By letting the vibration transmit itself through her interaction with this moving object, it does not need to express itself through her physical body. Part of the key here was that she needed to be able to see the expression of the energy. If it had been a turquoise bedspread it probably would not have been as effective. With a Uranus energy it is important that the interaction be visual, and preferably where it contacts that outer edges of the person's aura. Here we played out the Uranus energy, but not the Venus energy. What was the result? The very next day she slept to seven. The next day to nine. The next day she slept to ten, and had to buy an alarm clock. Then she began sleeping through the alarm. Why? Venus, the indulger, who had been sharing a bed with the eccentric Uranus, suddenly was free to express its self in true Leo nature, staying in bed late. When the energies have been stuck for a long time they sometimes come back with a roar."

• "A women had been sleeping on her Pluto (in Leo) line for ten years. In true Pluto fashion her life was always life or death extremes. She had a prominent Neptune and shared her bed periodically with her mysterious and deceptive boyfriend, but was unable to ever align her sleep patterns with his. She was a body worker, and her work room had her Neptune line running in it. We had them move their bed to the Neptune line. They were now able to sleep wonderfully at the same time. Problem was, they were used to being up early and out of the house on weekends. Now it was one o'clock in the afternoon and they were still trying to get out of the bedroom. Neptune is dreamy. She called us and said we should offer a precautionary warning before moving a person's bed onto the Neptune line! So we suggested that she start putting some Neptunian imagery in there. Fish, sea shells, dreamy images, and keep adding them until she got a good balance between sleeping well and getting out of the bed easily."

• "Kitchens are a natural place to hang out, but we had a client who had her Mercury in Gemini line running along the edge of her table by the door. Whenever she sat on that chair, and it was her favourite chair, (why? - because Mercury is in rulership), she basically half sat because she was always being called to jump up and run into the other room for something."

• "We have had many clients who were unable to use their family or living rooms because they had a Mars line running through it. They sat down and immediately felt the need to do something."

• "Transits set things off too. We had a client who had been sleeping well, then, at the time of her Uranus opposition, she moved her bed onto her Uranus line, and her sleep got very erratic. Of course since it was her Uranus opposition she didn't mind it. Sometimes clients at their Uranus opposition time will respond by moving all their stereo and TV electronics close to their bed. We had another client who was designing his house during his Uranus opposition, and he had set the floor plan up so that both he and his wife would be sleeping on their Uranus lines! Fortunately we were able to convince them to redesign. While the resulting sleep deprivation would seem normal during the heights of the transit, after Uranus had moved on it would become tiring and unhealthy for them."

• "When people come into a prospective apartment and immediately know that this is the one (that is they love it) you can bet that they have either Sun, Moon or Venus running through the front door. If Saturn is running through the front door they will see it as a good investment, and work like crazy to afford it. While in classical Feng Shui the belief is that a southern facing door is most beneficial, while generally true, it really depends upon the chart. For instance we had a client who had a poorly aspected and retrograde Saturn in Capricorn at the mid heaven of his chart. He had a house that had a southern facing front door, so that Saturn line went right through it. From the time he moved into the house his life was a disaster; the problems stemming from taking the wrong advice from an older and respected member of his community. He was close to losing everything, and only came through it because of his wife's support; she had a better line there. To give one an idea of how well Saturn can keep a person in a fixed reality, when he was looking to move to other houses after this one, he picked ones with the same southern facing front doors, and even more difficult environments in terms of negative Saturn qualities."

• "Another client had Mars and Vesta lines running through her kitchen. While both of these lines can mean ovens, we find Vesta often relates to Grand-parents. So what did she have in her kitchen? Two stoves, one new, and there on the Vesta line, another that was an antique."

The Local Space Chart in our communities, towns and cities

We have discussed how the straight directional lines (vectors) of the geomantic compass remain accurate up to about 50 map miles, after which we should begin to use Local Space maps. This makes the compass a valuable tool for looking at cities and towns that may be local to us. There are two approaches to this:

(a) **Using a personal geomantic compass**: In this, the most popular approach, take your geomantic compass (Local Space) and place it over the map of your local neighbourhood or city. The anchor point is your residence, such that all directional lines radiate outward from there. Be sure that the north of the compass aligns with the true north of the map and then observe where the lines fall on the map.

The energy of each planetary line should affect the quality of events for you in those directions and at the destinations as well. Here too Saturn lines often cause us the most trouble; one astrologer, for example, reported that it ran directly to a shop where she had been cheated by a butcher who was us-ing a fraudulent scale. Saturn may point to your work site if you don't like your job, but it can also indicate a path to a location where patience and diligence and ultimate success will be found. Cozzi gives us an interesting insight into work lines. He states,[11] "The line that runs from your home to where you work often describes the type of work you do, or it may reflect your attitude about your work". He goes on to suggest that the absence of a line here may indi-cate your job has no great meaning[12].

Here's another example: an individual recounted an incident of 'road rage' where he nearly came to blows with another driver. This event happened on his angry, conjoining Mars-Pluto directional line, which radiated outward to the North and South from his home.

Figure 57 shows my geomantic lines anchored from my residence in the Borders region of Scotland to other neighbouring cities within a radius of 50 miles. This map represents my local community, as journeys from my rural home require longer travel than if I lived in a city proper. A frequent journey for me (to the northwest) is to Edinburgh, where I still practice my sport of foil fencing. Note that this aligns with my conjoining Mars and node lines. Travelling for sport is surely well represented by a Mars line, and the accom-

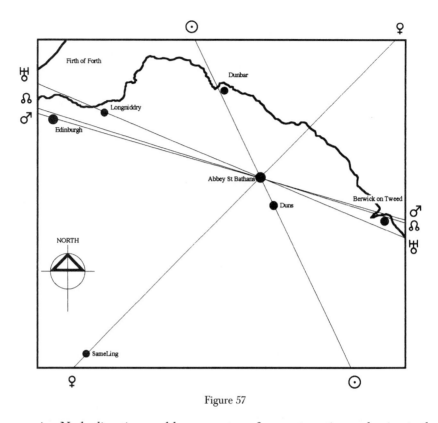

Figure 57

panying Node direction could represent my frequent coming and going to the Edinburgh airport, as well as the astrological contacts and alliances I have made there. That same line running in the opposite southeast direction takes me to the town of Berwick-on-Tweed, where I catch the train to London (Node line). I'm often late in getting to that station, speeding along while feeling hurried and pressured as I try to get there on time, a situation which reflects negative Mars qualities. The Uranus line points directly to another city, closer to home, where I occasionally practice as well. Sometimes I find that no adult fencers are present there, so I return home without a proper workout. Uranus seems to describe the uncertain nature of events I am faced with there. My Venus line runs southwest to within one mile of a prominent Buddhist community. Although I've never actually visited the site, I do maintain e-mail contact with their director of studies, who has provided me with information about books, videos and helpful contacts in general. And, last but not least, the Sun line runs to my nearest town of Duns, where I do chores like banking and shopping and make my contacts with the community. Perhaps the solar quality connecting me to Duns explains why I feel positive and confident on my trips there and why I usually return home having accomplished my objectives.

Important point

When a person changes residence in a city they are shifting the anchor point of their geomantic compass. If they now travel on new (different) directional lines to a destination (like a work site), would this actually alter the quality of their experience at the destination itself? In other words, might moving house change the nature of one's experience in that city? The answer to this seems to be yes from both my experience and Cozzi's as well. For example, over a 12-year period I lived in five different neighbourhoods in the city of Philadelphia. Each change of residence corresponded with an inner shift on my part, altering my view of work and the city itself. Cozzi agrees, stating[13], "It is my experience that if you change your residence within your community, your whole orientation can change along with it"[14].

(b) **Using a city's own geomantic compass**: A less used but informative technique is to create a geomantic compass from the founding or incorporation data of the town or city itself. This compass is placed over the city centre and the lines are used to give us information about how the city has developed. When giving a workshop in a city, I will try and obtain that city's

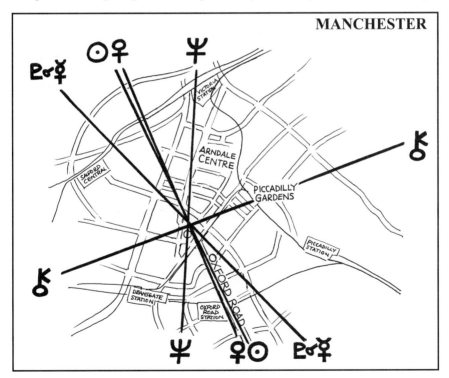

Figure 58

107

'birth' data. Using that information, I create a compass and overlay it upon the city's map. Figure 58 is just such an overlay for the city of Manchester in the UK[15]. The centre of the compass has been placed over the town hall. The first information of note is that the Neptune line, running northward, crosses the location where a bomb was placed in 1996. It blew up, almost completely destroying all of the Arndale shopping area. This is appropriate symbolism, as Neptune can represent loss and sorrow (as well as the dissolution of a situation); but with Neptune, things are not always as they seem. Although the blast resulted in the complete destruction of the seedy area, it became an opportunity for the city to rebuild it, constructing a bright new area. The Sun line of the Manchester compass runs southeast down Oxford Road, the busiest traffic thoroughfare in the city and one that leads to the city's universities. There are other correspondences; an interesting one is the Chiron line, which to the northeast crosses Piccadilly Gardens, the site of Manchester's famous mental hospital, which was bombed in WWII and not rebuilt.

The DeAmicis' have used city data in their work. They state, "Cities and towns have Local Space lines. Their prosperous main streets are typically on Sun lines, the fanciest shopping are on Venus lines, garages on Mercury lines, and due to the nature of duality both the Churches and the seediest bars will be found on the Neptune line. Look for the herbalist shops, healing centers and health food stores on the Chiron and Jupiter lines."

Steve Cozzi gives an example by using Denver, Colorado's geomantic compass superimposed over a map of the city[16]. He found some good correspondences: the Neptune line pointing to a polluted military area, the Moon line to a lake, the node line to an airport, Mars' line to military training centres, Saturn's line to a poor area of town and Jupiter's vector pointing to affluent neighbourhoods.

Cozzi and I have both had some misses with this technique as well. I think the problem is mostly due to uncertainties with city data. Often it is unclear as to what is the proper or best 'birth' time for a locality. Nevertheless, the use of the compass for this type of investigation can be informative, helpful and even fun. It is certainly one of the areas in Astrolocality astrology that needs more investigation, one day, perhaps, by a reader of this book!

The Horizon in outer space

Earlier in the book, it was explained how Local Space charts are calculated from the apparent or visible horizon[17]. The so-called 'true' horizon is a great circle parallel to this visible circle. It divides the earth equally into a top and bottom from where we stand. In their book *Astrophysical Directions* (1977)[18], the Erlewines alert us to its importance. They write, "The authors (Michael and Margaret Erlewine) have found that the entire horizon is sensitive and not only the points where it relates to the zodiac (such as the ascendant). The orientation of the horizon sphere provides a framework in which to examine our relationship

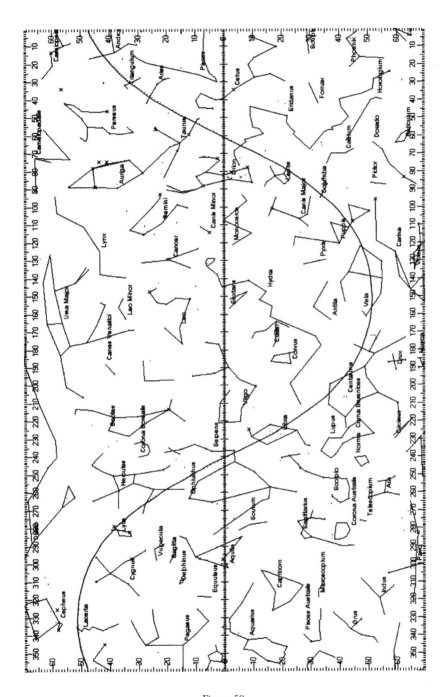

Figure 59

to all cosmic structure. For instance, the natal horizon passes through a particular band of constellations that becomes your own set of constellations".

Admittedly, this idea is as speculative as it is interesting. Today, however, with the aid of computer programs[19] we can view an overlay of our horizon upon the constellations and make up our own minds. Figure 59 will clarify this. Calculated for my birth moment and location, this diagram shows how the plane of my true horizon would be projected onto the fixed stars. It can be seen that it intersects the constellations Lacerta, Lyra, Hercules, Libra, Centaurus, Vela, Puppis, Lepus, Eridanus, Taurus, Aries, Triangulum and Andromeda. Myths surrounding these constellations would become indicators of my own personal unfolding at a deep, soul level. Let's look at my horizon's alignment with the constellation Lyra, for example. This constellation is associated with the myth of Orpheus and Euridice, Lyra representing the tragic musician's Lyre[20]. It could indicate I would need to experience an Orpheus-like journey in my life, perhaps into the underworld or shadow side of my psyche. The conjunction of my horizon with the fixed star Vega in that constellation might indicate I would be popular with my contemporaries (for a soul purpose) or from other myths, have an affinity with dolphins or even be taught by the Muses. It might also point to other, more esoteric possibilities for me, such as Vega's identification with the Babylonian Star Dilgan, the Messenger of Light, or its position as the Pole-star some fourteen millenniums ago. Might I be an ancient soul, or am I simply out of date?

Galactic Astrology and the Star Compass

In their work *Astrophysical Directions* the Erlewines proposed that we include an additional perspective in our astrological studies. It is a view which shifts us from the traditional role of placing fixed stars onto our personal charts to one where the essentials of our charts (and the earth itself) are seen in alignment with galactic parameters. In other words, it's about how we fit in with what's out there rather than how we squeeze 'out there' into our charts! This perspective offers us both an archaic revival of ancient astrological methods as well as a domain for contemporary astrologers to add the wisdom of current understanding.

In its revitalised form the field today is called Galactic Astrology. It is said to deal best with issues of both our personal enlightenment and the potentialities of global consciousness. Astrologer Raymond Mardyks[21] is at the forefront of this approach. Mardyks works with a variety of techniques, one of which he calls 'Star Wheels'. These wheels are a form of earth compass which identifies our star alignments. He says that by becoming aware of our star energies we gain the opportunity for an expanded level of consciousness.

Star Wheels are of interest to us for other reasons as well. Not only are they the ancestors of our contemporary Local Space wheels, their use going way back to ancient and indigenous cultures, but, perhaps more important, they remain pertinent today, providing us with new and powerful information.

Although a Star Wheel can be created for any location we wish, we will look at Ray's work in constructing a Star Wheel for a sacred site near Sedona, Arizona, as it offers us an excellent example of its use. A Star Wheel is similar to our usual Local Space compass insofar as we record celestial positions relative to the apparent horizon of our location. There are distinct differences, however:

• We are observing stars and constellations rather than planets.

• With a Star Wheel, we are watching the horizon to see where there will be a rising or setting star or constellation. In other words, we are only considering 'smack on', zero-altitude hits to the horizon.

• We include all rising and setting activity during a 24-hour period (not limited to a single moment in time, as with Local Space compasses derived from birth data).

This all works well, however, as fixed stars and constellations will rise and set in a constant pattern over time (for an Epoch), shifting slightly over the years from the astronomical effect of Precession (one degree every 72 years).

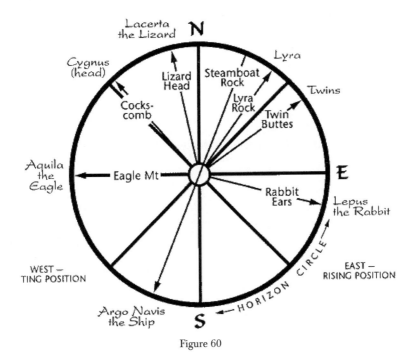

Figure 60

Quoting Ray directly from his article "Star Temples in Stone"[22], let's get his view of a Star Wheel and how it functions. "From the center of a Star Wheel, each star and constellation appears to rise and set in a specific direction. Each star and constellation rises and sets in this same location along the horizon once a day. If you imagine a line of light from one of these centers to the place along the horizon where each star rises and sets, you can begin to see the energy lines or spokes of the Star Wheel. The place where the stars cross the horizon is significant because this is the threshold between the visible and invisible and also between the conscious and the unconscious.......".

Figure 60 is Mardyks' Cathedral Rock Star Wheel, one of a number of sites he believes to be important near Sedona, Arizona, in the USA. Unlike ancient temples, which were constructed to align with stars, Ray found this site to contain natural alignments "formed without any human participation or awareness". Inside the wheel we find the directions from Cathedral Rock to various imposing natural sites nearby, such as Eagle Mount, Lyra Rock, and other sites. Quoting Mardyks again, let's see the astounding correlation he discovered. "From Cathedral Rock, if you looked toward the rock formation called Lizard Head, this aligns you with where the stars of the constellation of the Lizard, called Lacerta, sets every day. If you looked toward the Twin Buttes, and saw 'through' the rocks to the horizon, this is where the constellation of the Twins rises once a day". From Figure 60 the reader can note other correspondences he discovered, such as nearby Lyra Rock's direct alignment with the constellation Lyra[23]. Mardyks encourages us to employ Star Wheels to become aware of star energies, which he says are crucial for our personal development and for the earth's evolution as well.

SPECIAL STUDIES IN LOCAL SPACE

There are instances when Local Space is essential to make sense or give meaning to an Astrolocality study. In the examples that follow we will see how LS, used alone or with ACG, gives us valuable insight that we could not achieve from ACG alone:

Marjan Moves to Scotland

Marjan is a Dutch-born astrologer who now lives in Lockerbie, Scotland. I encountered her at a shop in Edinburgh where she was giving astrological consultations. Eavesdropping, I noticed her readings were lively and sensitive, emphasising Chiron and the Lunar Nodes along with other major chart placements. Marjan's life is notable for a variety of reasons, one of which was her completion of a 39-month retreat (3 years, 3 months and 3 days) at Samye Ling, the Buddhist centre in Scotland. Marjan took refuge in Buddhism and was in retreat there between 1993 and 1997. Her life story is one that is passion driven, filled with a yearning to find herself and the wish to help others. Marjan's natal chart is shown in Figure 61.

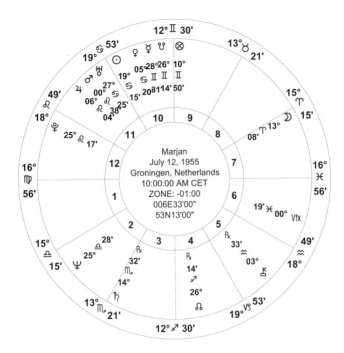

Figure 61

Marjan had investigated her ACG map but was disappointed, as it was devoid of any lines over Europe and Great Britain, the parts of the world where she spent most of her life. Not finding anything that corresponded with her life experience, she put Astrolocality astrology aside[24].

When we examine her LS map, however, helpful information emerges. Figure 62 is Marjan's map in European detail. We can note from it that her residence, Lockerbie, is exactly on her Uranus line, where she lives in a new-found psychological freedom and from where she centres her astrology practice as well. Further North, exactly on her Chiron line, is the site of her Buddhist retreat. It is here that her teacher, resides. Uranus and Chiron lines are fully compatible with these types of life situations.

Marjan's LS Sun line runs through Edinburgh. She occasionally visits Edinburgh to work and re-establish a public role for herself. She feels good there, since it brings a balance with her essentially secluded life in Lockerbie, where she lives quietly with her partner, does her astrology and serves others as a helper-carer for the disabled.

Her LS Moon line points just north of London. Her first visit there was on vacation with her older sister. It is there also, in North London, that she met and married a man whom she later divorced. She calls that episode in her

113

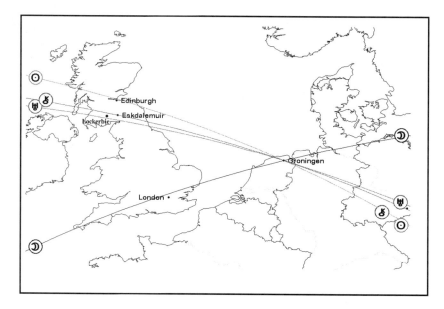

Figure 62

life an "unconscious" one. Both travel with (or to) a female relative and the manifestation of an unconscious pattern are possible Moon-line issues.

More: in Scotland, her relocated LS chart brings expansive, career-oriented Jupiter to the east, pushing aside the intense, psychological, easterly Pluto of the Netherlands LS chart. Her life in the Netherlands did have a psychological intensity about it, since she dealt with issues involving her often-absent father (whom she calls "an alcoholic genius") and where she studied and practised child psychology.

Upon review, Marjan's ACG map also gives us some interesting information, though nothing over areas where she lives. Some lines run through both Turkey and South Africa, for example, locations where two great loves in her life were born, but she has never visited either country. So, overall, it is the LS maps and charts that tell us the most about the 'what is' for her today.

A Love Story in Local Space; David and Martina fall in love

David Meadows is a certified ACG practitioner now residing in Munich, Germany[25]. He is active and well known in the field. In his important and comprehensive book, W *here in the World with Astro*Carto*Graphy* (AFA Publications, to be published late 1999), David recounts his meeting and marriage to Martina in Dresden, East Germany, as shown from their ACG maps. Notable in this love story is that, against all odds, they obtained official permission from the East German government to leave and move to Britain. At this time, before the fall of the Berlin Wall, such approval was an unlikely event. David

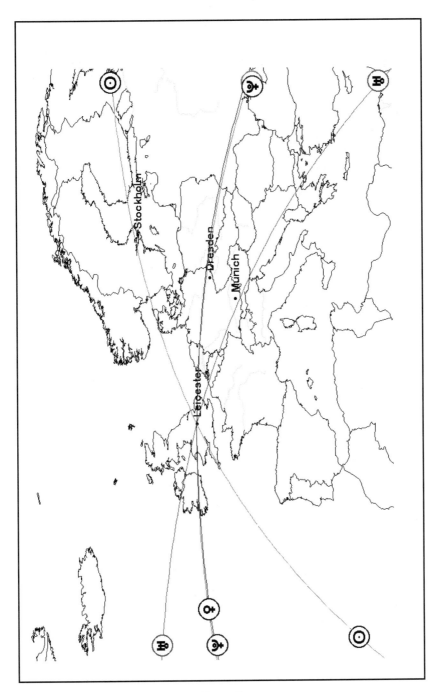

Figure 63

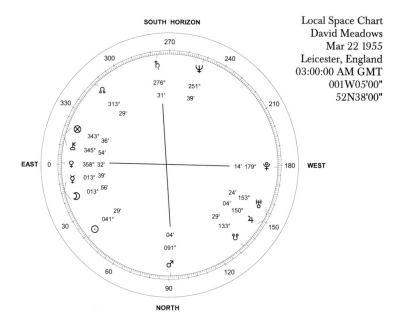

Figure 64

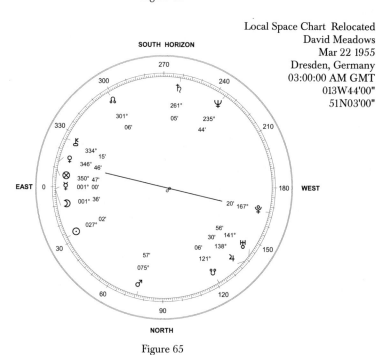

Figure 65

and Martina settled in Leicester, England, later moving to Munich, Germany (1991), where they reside today.

What does LS add to this story of love's conquest of official intolerance and political division ? Let's look at their LS maps and see. To start with, David's map in European detail is shown in Figure 63. On it we see that his Venus and Pluto lines, in LS conjunction, reach out from his home in Leicester and arc across Europe, running (through Amsterdam) to Dresden, within an orb of 35 miles from that city. What might this mean? David was empowered to find love (Venus) and take on the East German government (Pluto). It is most likely that if such a life scenario unfolded for him, it would be along those lines; and it did. Why might David even have dared to try and accomplish this? A look at his LS chart for Leicester, Figure 64, gives us a strong indicator. It shows Venus empowered in the east (personal love) and Pluto in the west (psychological understanding/power issues with others). In other words, David felt the power to accomplish this feat from its inception.

Once in Dresden, however, he no longer required the 'chutzpah' (brazenness) to accomplish his task, rather he needed to confront the East German authorities in just the right way, according to their own rules. And he was able to do just that, gaining the freedom for his bride and himself to move westward. What might his LS chart for Dresden tell us about this? Figure 65 is his LS chart relocated to Dresden. Note that the Moon and Mercury, in exact LS conjunction, are brought to within one degree (azimuth) of the east. He has Moon/Mercury power in Dresden or empowerment to successfully conclude legal or business actions concerning his wife. Also of note for this chart is that Jupiter and Uranus are both brought to less than 2 degrees of altitude from the horizon (not shown). Freedom was on his mind and in the air for him there in Dresden.

From his Leicester-based LS map (Figure 63), we can also note that his Uranus line runs close to Munich, the city where he would ultimately settle with Martina. Towards the north east his Sun line runs directly to Stockholm, Sweden, where he has had much professional success and prominence, speaking there on radio and television.

Now let's look at Martina's side of the story from the LS perspective. Figure 66 is her LS map in European detail. Most interesting is that her LS Chiron line from Dresden runs right to her destination in Leicester. Perhaps this indicates a teaching role for David in her life or that this first stop, out of totalitarian East Germany, had a healing potential for her. Some miles south of Leicester we find her Uranus line as well, alerting us that this was a likely direction for her dash to freedom. Looking at Figure 67, her relocated LS chart for Leicester, we see a reinforcement of the theme of freedom. Note that freedom-loving Uranus is brought *exactly* (0 azimuth) to the east there. This is a strong placement, with Uranus replacing the easterly Sun of her LS chart in Dresden. One imagines that at the time of her marriage she had had enough

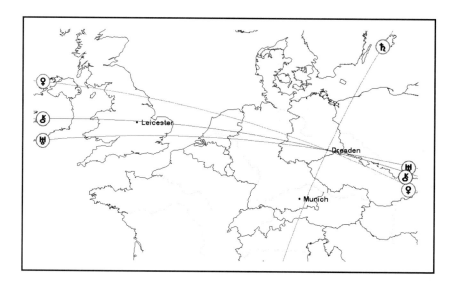

Figure 66

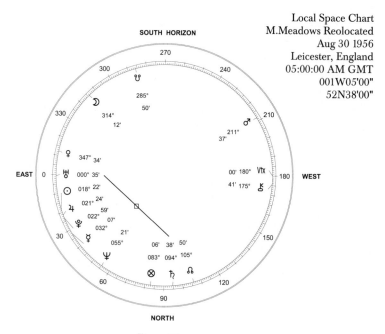

Figure 67

of Saturnian governmental restraint and restriction and that she was delighted to move in a healing (Chiron line) and freedom-loving (Uranus line) direction. But like it or not, fate determined that Saturn would remain in her life for a while longer. Figure 67 shows us that in Leicester, along with Uranus in the East, Saturn is brought uncomfortably close to the north. As explained earlier, this means Saturn was near the IC of her relocated ecliptic chart there, admittedly a difficult placement for one's residence[26].

Earlier in this book we also discussed the information obtained from shifting aspect patterns in LS charts. Let's have a look at this for Martina: when we compare all the locations where she and David lived – Dresden, Leicester and later Munich – it is noteworthy that in Leicester her Local Space Saturn and Uranus are brought most closely into an uncomfortable square aspect, 94 degrees of azimuth or only 4 degrees out of orb from an exact square. Ebertin in his work *The Combination of Stellar Influences* (AFA, 1972) calls this a challenging combination, often associated with irritability, inhibition and tension. This potential aspect is much less powerful, or out of orb, in her LS charts for Dresden (80 degrees azimuth separation) and Munich (79 degrees azimuth separation). As it is very much out of orb in her natal ecliptic chart (in square by sign but at 112 ecliptic degrees of separation), she would inherently find this a difficult energy to live with on a day-to-day basis.

With Martina becoming unhappy in Leicester, David and Martina reconsidered their living options once again. When she still resided in Dresden, Munich was in her LS Saturn direction, probably not making it an appealing possibility for her. From Leicester, however, Munich was now approximately in Martina's Venus path. Approaching Munich from this direction brought out its venusian possibilities for them, and it seemed to be the right move. They happily reside there today.

Local Space in Mundane astrology: the USA chart for Philadelphia, 11.00AM, 4th July 1776

A fertile area for Local Space analysis is in the field of mundane astrological research. LS maps, for example, indicate the directionality associated with the politically related events for a country or world region. This in turn can help us with rectification studies when a mundane birth time is unknown or in dispute.

There is currently a divergence of opinion as to the best chart for the birth of the USA or even if one chart alone can ever provide us a satisfactory amount of information. After many years of detailed research, British astrologer Ronald W. Howland proposed an American birth time of 11.00 AM on 4 July 1776, Philadelphia, PA. His well-researched work is presented in his book *A Chronology of American Charts* [27].

Is this chart a good one? A look at it from the Astrolocality perspective shows some startling correspondences that indicate that yes, it's certainly worthy of further serious study. Figure 68 is the chart itself. Astrologers will

Figure 68

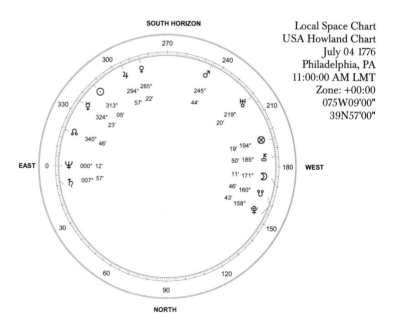

Figure 69

note the Virgo rising with Neptune prominent, the Gemini midheaven and the Aquarius Moon. Ron alerts us to the significance of the angular positions in the so-called 'late mutables' as well[28]. Certainly an Aquarian Moon could explain the USA population as the oft-quoted melting pot, and the Gemini MH could shed light on the development of its two-party system and its leading-edge communication systems.

The prominent Neptune, some 6 degrees from the chart's Virgo ascendant, may be what first captures one's eye, so let's look at the LS chart for further insights on this. Figure 69 is the corresponding LS chart. From it we can see that Neptune is tremendously empowered – exactly in the east at 0 degrees of azimuth.

What does this mean? With the Howland chart we get a confirmation of Neptune's influence over American actions and the American collective psyche, i.e., what's on the collective American mind[29]:

- Neptune is associated with dreams, images, fantasy and illusion. In the USA, the film industry has become the most potent dream-machine and image-making industry in the world. The techniques employed to create Disney world parks and the like are also unsurpassed.

- The possibility of actualising one's personal desires and vision in the USA is universally called the 'American Dream'.

- America has represented a haven for the poor and oppressed masses from other parts of the globe. Such representation of the masses is a Neptunian characteristic. The symbol for this is the Statue of Liberty, which sits in the water (another Neptunian symbol) in New York city's harbour.

- Idealism is another key concept associated with Neptune. In all of recorded history, the American rebuilding of its defeated adversaries after WW II may be unique.

- Neptune is also associated with deception and misleading information. The USA government's deceptive treaties with native American tribes over their land rights are fully documented historical facts.

But now let's move on to the telling Local Space maps. Figure 70 is a detail of the LS map for Howland's proposed USA chart. It shows the Uranus line, its origin in Philadelphia, running across the Atlantic and right over to London, England. This of course is a perfect representation of the radical and rebellious relationship that the Founding Fathers had with the English monarchy at the time of the Revolution.

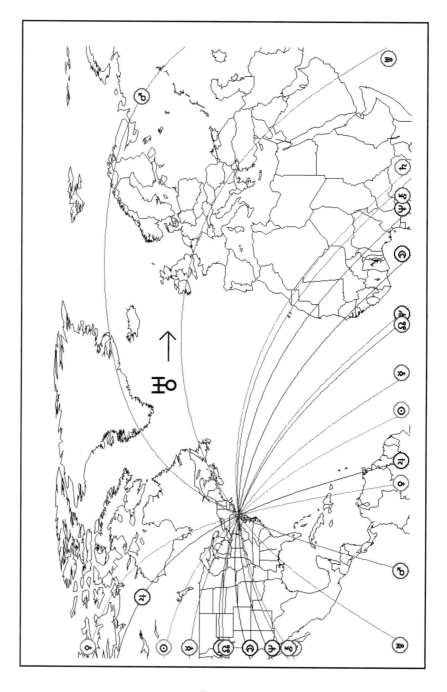

Figure 70

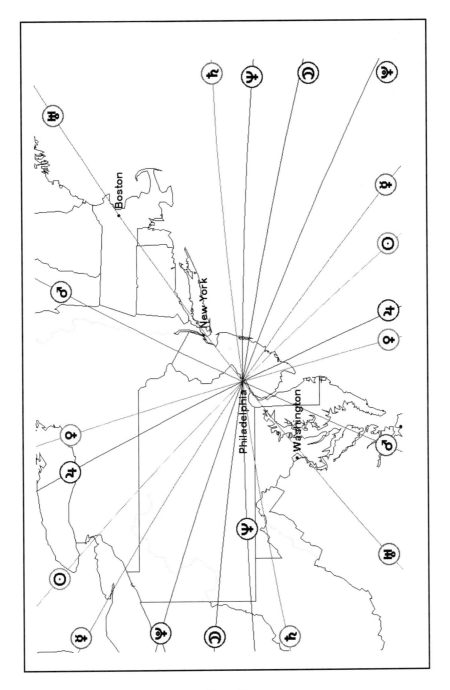

Figure 71

Figure 71 is the detail of the northeastern USA. Note that the Uranus line from Philadelphia curves upward, running exactly through Boston harbour before connecting with England. To those who know the history of the events of the colonial uprising this is truly amazing. The most important act of American defiance to British rule happened in Boston harbour in what has became known as the Boston Tea Party. The Local Space map for an 11.00 AM birth time confirms the historical connection of the events in Philadelphia, Boston and England. Uranus issues and Uranus lines seem to play a role in Anglo-American relations even today[30]:

- Boston (via the Irish-American community) remains the centre of anti-British feeling in the USA to this day.

- Americans acknowledge and appreciate the special relationship (another Uranian symbol) between their country and Great Britain.

- One can note the testimony of British visitors to the USA, who state they feel 'free' when travelling there.

There is more. Figure 72 shows that the same Uranus line running southwest from Philadelphia is fewer than 35 miles from Montgomery, Alabama. It was here that the Union experienced another act of rebellious defiance, less than 100 years later, when the Confederate states declared Montgomery to be their independent capital city; one of the acts that precipitated the US Civil War.

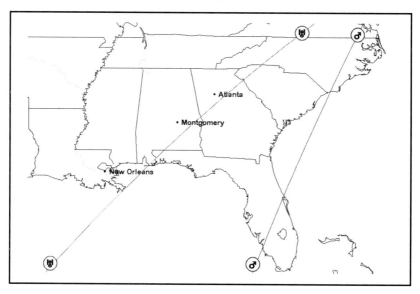

Figure 72

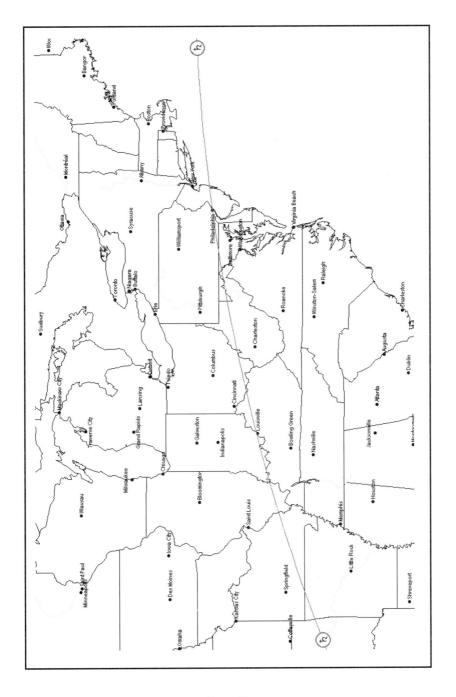

Figure 73

Figure 73 is another view of the eastern USA, with everything removed except the LS Saturn line. Note how it almost perfectly divides what were to become the warring Northern and Southern states of the Civil War, with much of the line right on the physical state boundaries themselves[31].

Mars too can give us insights about US relations. See Figure 74. Mars itself was almost directly overhead (zenith position) Havana, Cuba at the moment described by Howland's 11 AM USA chart. This obviously implies tension there. The map also shows the LS Mars line running very close to Havana and Managua, both locations where the USA had troops stationed in the past and where there are military undertones and tensions even today.

The interested reader is urged to review the corresponding ACG map for the 11.00 AM chart, as shown in Figure 75. In his book Howland points out[32] significant historical correspondences, such as:

• The Pluto-MC line crosses over southern Japan, aptly describing the atomic bombs dropped there in 1945. After the war, American influence regenerated Japan, helping its transformation into one of the great industrial nations of the 20th century.

• The Saturn-MC line near Moscow describes the USA's chilly (inhibited) relations with Russia and her 'Iron Curtain'.

• The Moon-Descending line runs alongside the most seismically active part of the US mainland, the San Andreas fault in California. Howland reminds us that the Moon's connection with seismic phenomena is well known to both astrologers and seismologists.

I can add here that Uranus-MC runs within 70 miles from Oklahoma city, OK, the site of a devastating bomb blast which was directed by anarchists against a US government building. That same Uranus-MC line is only 35 miles from Dallas, Texas, where US president John Kennedy was assassinated.

Whatever one's preferred USA chart (11.00AM or not), note how useful Astrolocality indicators can be when working with mundane data.

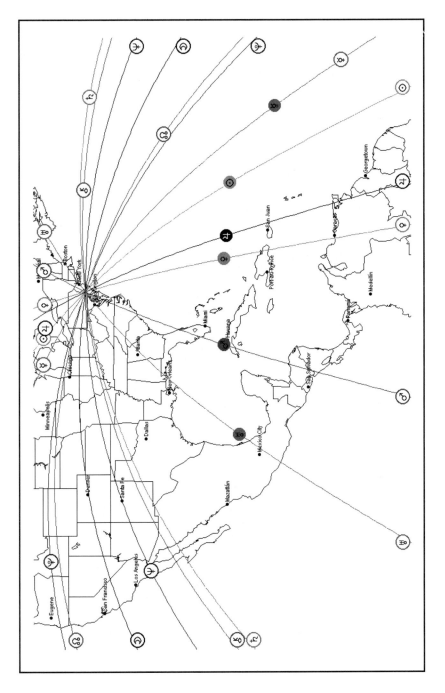

Figure 74

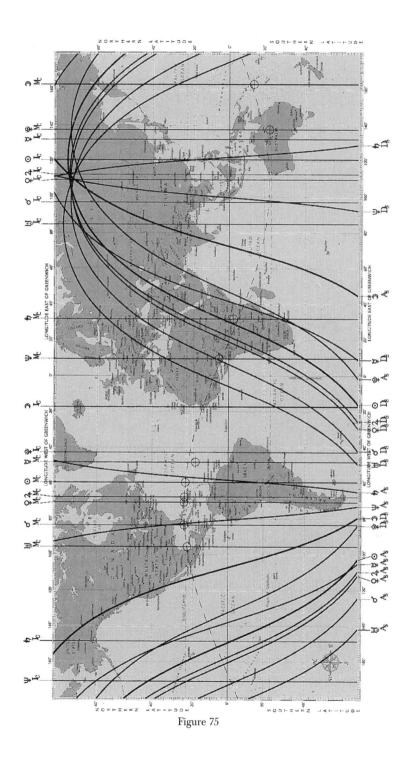

Figure 75

128

NOTES

1. Really the chart map. Remember: the chart map is simply the chart turned about so that its cardinal directions line up with a map's north, south, east, and west orientation.

2. From his important book on the Local Space technique, *Planets in Locality*, 1988, recently republished by AFA, Tempe, AZ.

3. My own natal information tells me much more about the 'what is' when I use it for in-close work as a geomantic compass. Experienced Feng Shui professionals Ralph and Lahni DeAmicis (USA) confirm this. Addressing this issue in e-mail correspondence to me, they state this:
   "When a person is living far from their birth place we still use the natal Local Space information. We believe that their electromagnetic patterning is still imprinted in the same way, and it paints the environment in the same pattern generally. There is probably some drift for a person who is recently relocated because the way their field is interacting with the earth's planetary field is resetting, and there is some resulting fuzziness. But after enough lunations the pattern reasserts itself."

4. My experience has confirmed that the planetary effects work just as strongly whether we move toward or away from the planet's zenith location. An early case history clarified this for me. A man was selected and accepted a job editing an astrological/occult magazine here in the UK. To take up the position, he had to move northwest of his current location, a journey which was exactly on his conjoined Jupiter-Uranus Local Space lines to the new city. Astrologers will note that these planetary energies would perfectly fit his new duties – and dare I suggest that they might be the reason he was hired over other candidates with less fortunate directional lines? By happily moving north-westward, he was travelling away from the zenith planetary positions of Jupiter and Uranus over the earth, but he was moving on their lines to his new career.

5. The Local Horizon Chart in the Solar Maps computer program (Astrolabe & Computer Technologies, Ltd.) will display the completed lines. Thanks again to those involved for including this useful tool.

6. Note that for both laser and ink printers today, transparency masters can be purchased so that a transparent copy of your Local Space chart (or chart map) can be obtained directly from your computer (that's the way I do it) without having to go to a photocopy shop to get one made.

7. Sunrise and sunset positions will be best aligned to a true east and west near equinox times of the year.

8. Angel Thompson can be reached at: 1809 Washington Way, Venice, California 90291, USA. Phone: (310) 821-2527. E-mail: ForCntnuum@aol.com.

9. Steve Cozzi has been studying and teaching astrology for over 30 years. He has been active in Local Space astrology from the early days of 1979, when Michael

Erlewine first developed it. Steve is credited with being the inventor of the West's first geomantic compass.

10. Ralph and Lahni DeAmicis can be reached at Space & Time Designing, Inc, 321 Avon St., Philadelphia, PA. 19116, USA. E-mail: Jupiter@comcat.com. Their web site at http:// www.spaceandtime.com has a complete listing of the services they offer Their next book will be published soon under the title *Feng Shui and The Tango in Twelve Easy Lessons.*

11. *Planets in Locality*; see the sub chapter and Table 6, both titled "Planetary Lines In The Community".

12. Today's recent trend of teleworking from home means that work lines outside the home are less relevant than they used to be.

13. *Planets in Locality.*

14. We can ponder what comes first: the move, which gives us new lines in a city and therefore different experiences, or a shift in oneself, which prompts the move and brings the new experiences. A third possibility is that everything unfolds together: the imperative or desire to move, the new lines and the corresponding experiences. This third possibility is not really a causal process but rather a 'wholeness' according to which everything happens at once as synchronous inner and outer events.

15. Manchester's data: 29 March 1853, 10 30am, LMT. The data was provided by Gary Parkinson, Chairman of the Manchester Astrology group. Gary states that there are several possible charts but this one has worked well and has been adopted by him. Gary can be reached by e-mail at gary.parkinson@mcr1.poptel.org.uk

16. *Planets in Locality.*

17. Also referred to as the 'sensible' or physical horizon, since we might actually be able to observe its boundary.

18. Page 16, *Astrophysical Directions.*

19. This feature is available in the Win*Maps module of WinStar (for Windows) and AstroMaps Hi Res (for DOS), both programs from Matrix Software.

20. See *The Living Stars*, by Eric Morse, Amethyst Books, 1988. Interested readers may want to review the work on star mythology by astrologer Diana K. Rosenberg, identified by Rob Hand as the foremost authority on fixed stars. Her Web site is: http://pw1.netcom.com/~ye stars/

I have found Anne Wright's work very helpful as well. Her Web site is a great resource: http://www.winshop.com.au/annew/

21. Mardyks is very active. He is the director of the Star School of Sedona, which offers e-mail correspondence courses. He is the author of *Sedona Starseed, A Galactic Initia-*

tion and he also offers personal reports, a newsletter and conferences in the USA, all with this galactic perspective. His web site is recommended: http://www.geocities.com/area51/nebula/9172/ He can be reached at: Raymond Mardyks, PO box 2841, Sedona, AZ 86339, USA.

22. See his article, Star temples in the Stones: Sedona Decoded, available from his web site: http://www.geocities.com/area51/nebula/9172/sedona1.html

23. For very interesting information about Lyra, see this page on Raymond's Web site: http://www.geocities.com/area51/nebula/9172/mes.html

24. Note in Figure 61 that her chart has 6 planets in the 10th and 11th houses. This tight bunching of planets yields an ACG map with similarly bunched lines. This leaves large regions of the globe not covered by ACG lines.

25. Certified in ACG by Jim Lewis in 1986, David is the most experienced locational practitioner in Europe today. He can be reached at Nabburgerstr. 3/111, 81737 Munich, Germany. E-mail: astrowelt@aol.com

26. This, in turn, means that Leicester would be near the Saturn-IC line on her ACG map, a topic covered thoroughly in David's book, *Where in the World with Astro*Carto*Graphy.*

27. Poz Publications (1998), PO Box 3104, Brighton BN1 5SP, UK. With over 500 charts, Howland's book is a feast of American charts and historical information. Recommended. Ron can be reached at the Poz Publications PO Box address above.

28. See his article "The Late Mutables, 1066, and the US Chart", NCGR Journal, Fall 1997.

29. An entire book has been written proposing Neptune's significance in America's history; see *The Sign of the Times,* by Stan Barker. Llewellyn Publications, 1986.

30. Interested readers will note that the LS Uranus line continues eastward from London near to Paris (the French supported the US in its War of Independence) , then it runs on between Jerusalem and Baghdad, two cities with a different 'special relationship' with the US to this very day.

31. Timothy Leary and revisionist historians have postulated that the real cause of America's Civil War was not the issue of slavery but the conflicting reality viewpoints of the industrial (the North) vs. the agricultural (the South) society. Looking at the core issue of the war in this light also makes the Saturn line meaningful because it truly separates the industrial and agricultural sections of the country. Note that Saturn runs along the very southern (bottom) boundaries of the industrial states of (west to east: Illinois, Indiana, Ohio, and Pennsylvania, separating them from the more rural and agricultural states below them.

32. See his book A Chronology of American Charts*, Poz Publications (1998), pages xiv-xviii.*

CHAPTER FIVE

Geodetics: the Geodetic world map; the Geodetic chart: what it is and what it tells us

GEODETICS: THE GEODETIC WORLD MAP

Geodetic mapping is a result of the yearning of astrologers over the centuries to associate earth locations with the qualities of the zodiacal signs. The signs are so to speak 'taken' from the heavens and wrapped around the earth. This gives us an earth horoscope of communal influences and it may even correlate with the rise of the globe's varied cultures.

An early attempt at this that survives was by Claudius Ptolemy in the first to second centuries AD and published in his work, the *Tetrabiblos*.[1] The system I will draw from here – and the one most used today – is usually attributed to the noted astrologer Sepharial (Dr. Walter Gorn-Old, 1864-1929).[2]

Geodetic practitioners believe that this technique yields valuable information in areas of mundane application such as political upheavals, wars, earthquakes, volcanic eruptions, fires, storms, and so on. Geodetic charts are also used by contemporary astrologers as a relocation tool and as a starting point if no event time is available. In this chapter I shall introduce an extension of its potential, *the Resonant chart*.

Creating the geodetic map

Taking a global perspective, we place the zodiac upon the earth's equator, with the starting point of 0 degrees Aries fixed (anchored) at the Greenwich meridian of 0 longitude. As we move eastward, every degree of zodiacal longitude equates to a degree of terrestrial longitude. See Figure 76[3]. This divides the globe into twelve equal 'slices', with the meridians from 0 to 30 degrees of terrestrial longitude east of Greenwich defining an Aries influence upon the Earth, the next 30 degrees defining a Taurus influence and so on through the zodiac and around the 360 degrees of the globe. This earth division can be seen more clearly on the next diagram, Figure 77. Here we have a flat earth map with the defining meridians drawn from top to bottom, north to south. This creates the possibility of identifying 360 individual geodetic meridians,

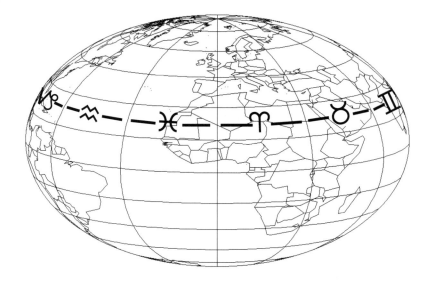

Figure 76

each in effect a midheaven for the location underneath it. We then view the map with the following in mind: *each area of earth between the defining meridians has or reflects the energy and characteristics of the sign superimposed on it.* It's important at this point to spend a few moments with this map to test this hypothesis. Let me take you through a few points, I expect you will soon be able to add your own:

• Since I lived in Turkey, the first thing that catches my eye is that the zero Taurus line (30 degrees east of Greenwich) defines the start of the Taurus mountains there!

• We note that the sign of Aries covers much of central Europe and a large part of Africa. Aries is often associated with war and, certainly, militant acts. Though, unfortunately, war can be found around the entire globe, it seems that an unusually high proportion of global conflicts originate in this area. Of course in the 20th century we had two world wars centred there. Also, if we consider military campaigns that had the express aim of world conquest, we find Nazi Germany in this band, as well as the home base of the Roman legions and even of the Macedonian conqueror Alexander the Great[4].Currently for Africa we can note that Rwanda (with its mass killings) is just inside the Aries band, as are violent regions of Angola and Nigeria. And let us not forget the turbulent

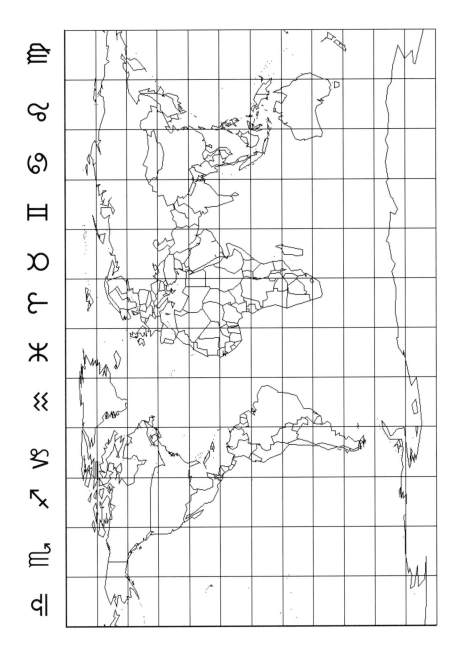

Figure 77

and angry Balkan region in south-east Europe which has been a flash point for violence throughout history, called by historians of our era, 'a volatile ethnic powder keg'. This is certainly apt for a region with a geodetic signature of Aries midheaven (and we shall soon see, of Leo rising).

• Aries is also associated with initiative. Four of the major industrialised nations in the G7 are found in this band, as well as many of the colonising nations.

• Now let's shift attention to the USA. Note that the eastern third of the country is covered by Capricorn meridians, which represent government and the establishment. The middle of the USA through most of the west is imbued with Sagittarian energy (meridians), appropriately reflecting the themes of independence (don't fence me in), large ranches and farms, cattle and horses (large animals) and cowboys on the move! And the most western bit of California is covered with Scorpio. Could this be the reason for the proliferation of therapists there?

The Geodetic Earth map - Earth Signatures

But there is more, much more. In the maps above we have defined the geodetic midheaven degrees around the world. If we also consider the latitude of a specific location, then by using a table of houses (or even better, computer programs that calculate geodetic charts[5]), we can come to see that geodetically, *every earth location has a specific rising sign along with its midheaven sign, and this combination is its geodetic signature. This signature is unchanging and unique for every specific earth location.*

With this in mind, let us now review the full earth geodetic map shown in Figure 78. It is hand drawn. I constructed it by calculating many different individual geodetic charts, getting the approximate ascendant bands by trial and error[6]. In a way it is analogous to a world ACG map. However, here we are looking at signs rather than planets and fixed, unchanging earthly signatures. Note the curved bands representing regions that share a common rising sign. From it we get the overview of all the earth's geodetic signatures for their rising and midheaven signs.

Later in this chapter we'll look at specific geodetic charts for pinpointed locations, but for now let's take some general examples directly from this map to make things clearer. Remember, the areas between the vertical lines define midheavens by sign and the areas within the curved bands show us rising (ascending) signs for the location in question:

• Look at the Capricorn (on the midheaven) ruled east coast of the USA. Again we note a significant division of geodetic ascendant or rising signs depending on location. Going north and east from Delaware – including Wash-

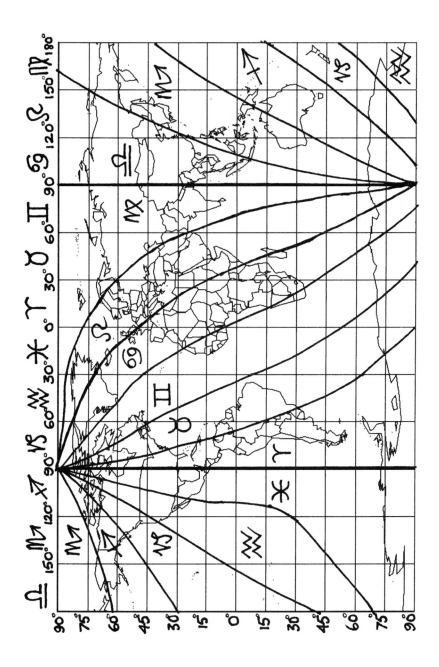

Figure 78

ington, DC, Philadelphia, New York City and Boston – we would have Taurus rising. What might this mean? Well, it could indicate that the wealth of the country would really be controlled or accumulated from there. This group of cities forming what has been called a 'megalopolis' may be the real power and cultural base of the nation.

• Below the region of Taurus rising, extending westward to New Orleans, we find an Aries geodetic ascendant. This area includes turbulent Miami as well as two countries where the USA has had troops in the past, Cuba and Nicaragua. From the meridian through New Orleans to the west we can see a Pisces ascendant. Associated with water, this area includes most of the Mississippi as well as the Missouri, Arkansas and Red rivers. Further west from there we find Aquarius ascending. This may describe the mystique of individualism for which states like Montana, Wyoming and Colorado are noted. California too is under Aquarius rising. Should we be surprised at this, considering the famous variety of life-styles found there?

• Notice that Japan, the land of the rising Sun, has a Sun-ruled, Leo geodetic midheaven. Even today it is considered a closed society, with its real social dynamic hidden from the view of foreigners. This speaks of a strong correlation with its secretive Scorpio geodetic ascendant. Japan, therefore, has a Leo midheaven, Scorpio rising geodetic signature.

• Two dangerous armies intending destruction and world conquest (the Nazis and Alexander's Macedonians) originated in a region with geodetic Aries on the midheaven, and now you can see that their geodetic signature has fiery Leo rising as well (as noted above, the Balkan countries have this signature too). France, Britain, Portugal and Spain have home-loving geodetic Cancer rising. Perhaps this explains their different approach to expansion: colonising and integrating outlying regions, turning them into models of their own culture. Rome (and therefore the Roman legions) is very close to Leo rising but just inside the Cancer rising band, with a geodetic ascendant of 29 degrees Cancer[7]. Perhaps this explains the somewhat Cancer-Leo dual nature of their world conquest, colonising some places according to a Roman model but ruthlessly suppressing and destroying almost everywhere else. Sicily, by the way, is just inside the Cancer rising band. Perhaps this helps explain the nature of their crime syndicates, organised as 'families'.

Before launching into a discussion and examples of geodetic charts, a few more points should be clarified:

• Some astrologers have questioned the validity of the Greenwich meridian as the 0 degree Aries starting point for the world map and the subsequent calculations deduced from it. The so-called 'pyramid chart', for example, shifts the starting point from the Greenwich meridian to the longitude of the Great Pyramid in Egypt, 31 degrees, 9 minutes east. In other words, that earth longitude would become 0 degrees Aries on the geodetic world map. My experience supports that the Greenwich meridian does work best and I believe it can be justified by its world-wide acceptance as a special location on earth maps[8]. I therefore use it exclusively in the examples that follow.

• Other significant Earth longitudes for a geodetic starting point have been proposed, but with no strong proof of their effectiveness to my knowledge. Some have suggested that superimposing the Zodiac on the Earth's equator in a westerly direction would work just as well. I can't substantiate this procedure, though it would be similar to the technique of converse transits or progressions found effective in usual astrology.

• Another system of interest was developed by the Canadian astrologer L.E. Johndro. It may be the most personal of the geodetic charts, since its calculation includes the position of the Sun. Though there is some historical evidence that Johndro himself dropped his system for the Greenwich chart for much of his career[9], no matter, because his work was invaluable in shifting the focus of geodetics away from earth calamities and towards use with personal charts. A really important insight gained from his work is that we can use a location's geodetic chart in the absence of timed data! Examples of this will follow later in the chapter.

• Astrologer Marc Penfield proposes what he calls a 'Modified' Johndro Chart. He finds it better for personal charts than both the Sepharial (Greenwich) and Pyramid methods[10]. Marc too, like Johndro, points us to the effective use of geodetics in our personal lives and as a great solution when you don't have a time of birth.

THE GEODETIC CHART: WHAT IS IT AND WHAT IT TELLS US

What it is
The geodetic chart is a mix of information from two zodiacs, the one in the heavens and one wrapped around the earth. First: for a given location the geodetic chart utilises the specific earth signature of geodetic midheaven and rising sign (as well as intermediate house cusps) defining the outer chart wheel itself. Second: inside these geodetic parameters we place the planets according to their positions in the sky's zodiac for our natal or other event data.

What it tells us

Fundamentally the geodetic chart tells us what the earth does to us at a given location. It's a measure of how we fit into the culture there. I see it as an indicator of how we resonate with the spirit of place and will use that word to define a new possibility, the Resonant Chart.

As this concept of mixing information from earth and sky may be quite strange to us, let's now create some geodetic charts to see if they add meaning to my change of earth location from St Louis to Scotland:

1. First we should review my natal chart again, calculated in the usual way according to a combination of parameters of both time and place. See Figure 79. Note the ascendant-descendant axis is 18+ degrees of Scorpio and Taurus and that the MC-IC axis falls at 28+ degrees of Leo and Aquarius, respectively. The intermediate house cusps are determined by a function of the MC and my birth latitude at St Louis.

2. Now we will review my geodetic (birth) chart for the same location. See Figure 80. The first thing to note is that there has been a significant shifting of the ascendant-descendant and MC-IC axes, along with the intermediate house cusps. In late degrees geodetically, I now have a Pisces-Virgo ascendant-descendant axis with Sagittarius and Gemini defining the MC and IC. Now this is important: since these are geodetic parameters, that is, the unique geodetic signature of St Louis, everyone ever born there would have the same outer wheel or defining axes.

The next thing to note is that the planets inside the wheel are in exactly the same degrees as found in my natal chart (Figure 79). Their positions in the geodetic wheel have simply moved or shifted relative to the new alignment of geodetic ascendant and midheaven degrees. (Note that my 14+ degree Virgo Sun has shifted from the 10th house to the geodetic 6th house.)

What additional information might I gain from this? A review of the geodetic chart shows that my Mercury-Saturn opposition (5th-11th houses in my natal chart) has been shifted to a prominent position of angularity, very close to the ascendant-descendant axis. This means that an important factor of my incarnation or embodiment at that spot on the globe, or what 'stuck' me there rather than somewhere else, is represented by those planets in that configuration! Other indicators can be seen from that chart as well. Perhaps the North Node-Mars conjunction, now in the 9th house for example, augers that I would be restless there and need to reach out to new cultures, perhaps by being pushed out of the nest to other world locations.

3. Let's continue with this theme and look at my geodetic chart for Scotland. I am often asked how I ended up living in Scotland. In truth I can only shrug my shoulders and say that events brought me here. Surely, I found vo-

Figure 79

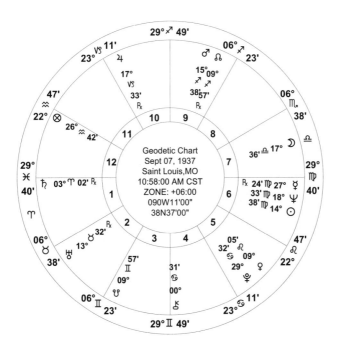

Figure 80

141

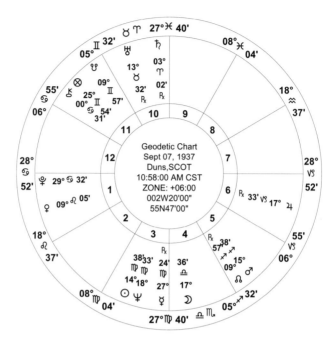

Figure 81

cational opportunities in Great Britain (first in Yorkshire and then in Scotland), which can be explained in part by the fact that my relocated chart for most of northern Britain has Jupiter rising[11]. But this doesn't explain the heart pull I felt to follow opportunities out of my home country. In fact I seemed to resonate with the land here as soon as I arrived. With this in mind, let's look at Figure 81, which is my geodetic chart for Duns, Scotland (a small town close to where I reside).

Please keep in mind that the ascendant, midheaven and house cusps are the earth's signature for Duns, and everyone born or residing there would have them. What is specific to me however, is that my natal planets are placed inside this wheel, in their usual zodiacal degrees but now orientated to Duns' geodetic signature.

Looking at Figure 81, we can see that the Mercury-Saturn opposition is once again brought to the chart angles, but this time geodetic power points of MC and IC. I have moved to another global location that activates those planets in angularity! Here too, once again, they are empowered and activated, now by the 'spirit' of this place.

Also it is noteworthy that intense and powerful Pluto is all but exactly rising on this chart. What might this mean in terms of my experience? We can assess this by using conventional astrological correspondences, this time from

142

the perspective of communal and cultural inputs, or what I see and refer to as one's resonance:

Mercury on the IC: Here, I was able to create an international software sales business from my home. It's as if the earth itself and especially the local culture support this and enable it to grow and flourish, sustained by friendly neighbours as well as efficient local services. Beam me down to Duns, Scottie!

Saturn on the MC: Here in Great Britain I became an authority on computer-related astrological matters and astrolocality astrology. My organisational abilities are appreciated. Growth in my business as well as my reputation in the field of astrolocality itself has come at a slow and steady pace, only unfolding as my steadiness of focus and understanding merit.

Pluto on the ascendant: As the only American within miles, I am noticed, whether I find this comfortable or not. I am listened to by the community, and this brings the responsibility of having to be earnest in my intentions. I believe I feel the pulse of life here both in the community and from the lovely natural surroundings.

Thus we can see how my geodetic chart for Duns, with its angular Mercury-Saturn opposition, adds a valuable piece to the puzzle of why I specifically settled or 'stuck' myself here. Not the only piece of the puzzle for sure, but a valuable one nevertheless.

Further Examples of Geodetic Charts

1. Krishnamurti finds his favourite place on Earth; the Resonant Chart defined

It's valuable to find a person who unequivocally states he/she has found their favourite place on earth. This affords an opportunity to correlate this earth location with astrolocality tools, seeing if any pick it out as a special place for the individual. The life of teacher and philosopher Jeddu Krishnamurti affords us this opportunity.

Krishnamurti settled in Ojai, California in the later years of his life and he declared that it was his true home on earth. Of course California and Ojai in particular are beautiful, with a fine climate and proximity to appreciative students, but Krishnamurti's love of this place seemed to go even beyond all that. In his diaries and lectures he talked about the beautiful quality of the earth there for him personally, which seemed to be like nowhere else[12]. So let's look at this situation in terms of Astrolocality techniques:

• Krishnamurti's relocated chart for Ojai would show Saturn near to the IC; therefore his ACG map would show Saturn on the IC as well. Though this grounds him there and shows the location is significant, it hardly leads to us expect it to be his favourite site. Jim Lewis, for example, says about a Saturn on the IC location, "One of the least desirable places... and while you are able to center yourself, it is only with bitterness and a sense of all you have missed in life"[13]

• His Local Space chart for Ojai would tell us much about his finding happiness there. It brings (empowers) his Venus and Jupiter to the east, opposed by his Moon in the west, adding beauty, bounty and companionship to the potentially barren Saturn in the north.

• Can geodetics add to our evaluation? Might it show us a resonance with his birth potential there? I believe it does. Figure 82 is his natal chart. Note his rising sign at 15 degrees of Aquarius and his midheaven in late Scorpio. Holding that information in mind, let us now look at Figure 83. Here we have his geodetic (earth) chart for Ojai. Note that geodetically the ascendant of 14 degrees Aquarius is aligned or resonates

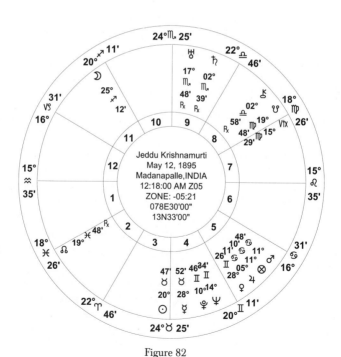

Figure 82

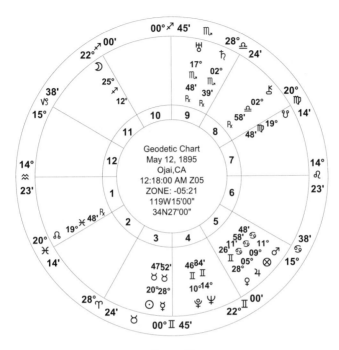

Figure 83

to his natal ascendant and that although the geodetic midheaven is 0 degrees Sagittarius, it is only about 5 degrees different from his natal placement. In other words, here in Ojai, Krishnamurti's geodetic chart resonates, practically duplicating his natal chart. The earth in Ojai, California is providing him with a vibratory input, a spirit of place, that is similar to the one he received at birth in India. No wonder he felt so at home there. From this point on we can define resonant charts as geodetic charts (at one location) that match the angles of regular natal or event charts at another location (or vice versa).

Fun for readers

Using the geodetic world map of Figure 78, find your own resonant world locations! These will be places where the geodetic chart angles (approximately) match those of your natal chart. The exact angular separation between your natal ascendant and MC can only be duplicated at an equivalent latitude, so I suggest you look for a similar ascendant first and let the MC be adjusted. Here's an example: I'm looking for a resonant location for myself (hopefully in a warm climate). I notice that western Australia is covered with Scorpio rising, my natal rising sign. A good start. A bit of Australia is also under the geodetic midheaven of Leo (my natal midheaven sign). I notice that in the north

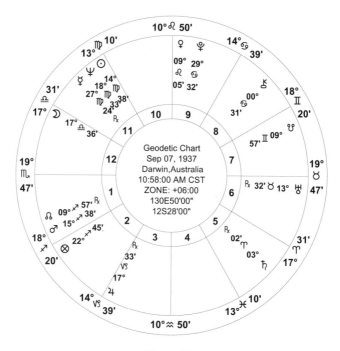

Figure 84

the city of Darwin may meet my requirements. Using my computer program to verify this, I run Darwin's geodetic chart. See Figure 84, my geodetic chart for Darwin Australia. Lo and behold it looks a lot like my natal one. Perhaps even better. The ascendant there is close, 19+ Scorpio degrees rather than 18+, but the midheaven has moved backwards in Leo to only 10+ degrees, now conjoining my natal Venus. Perhaps the locals would beg me to be a counselling astrologer there or I would be voted the sexiest over-60 in northern Australia!

2. Will the real USA chart please stand up? Geodetics and the Resonant Chart to the rescue.

It is widely known that there is disagreement among astrologers as to the 'best' birth chart for the USA. Most, but not all, choose July 4th 1776 as the birth day. Though I have pointed to the 11.00 AM chart from R. Howland's research and the astrolocality considerations, there are other proposed times and therefore charts for that day that vary considerably. With this diversity in mind, perhaps we can consider the USA chart as untimed for the moment and bring the geodetic technique into play. Figure 85 is the geodetic Chart for the USA using Philadelphia's earth signature near to a midday time (to get mean planetary positions).

It is striking to note that the transiting Sun that day was within one de-

146

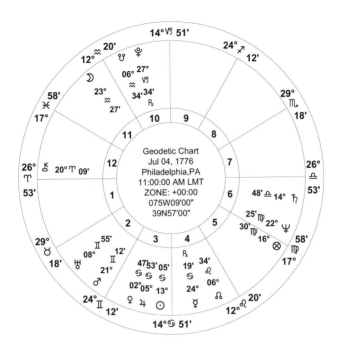

Figure 85

gree of exact conjunction with the foundation of the chart, the Cancer geodetic IC[14]. What might that mean? This perfect symbolism shows that the Founding Fathers would in fact be supported by the earth (the spirit of the place) and the prevailing culture in establishing their nation. Certainly the issues of their origins and family roots would be paramount to them, as would a possibly hidden but strong 'me first' attitude. We can also note that the chart angles themselves are all in the active cardinal signs, with martial Aries rising and powerful and effective Capricorn representing the face of the government itself. Students of Mundane astrology will note that Pluto in the 10th house adds much power to the activities of the government and that Uranus and Mars in the second house give some indication of the diverse nature and hard-driving effort for this nation to gain wealth. There are other observations that can be made; at the time of writing Neptune is transiting through the chart's 10th house, which I'll leave to the reader to ponder. The point I am making is that *in the absence of a truly known birth time, the geodetic chart makes a good starting point that can effectively be employed in astrological investigations.*

Now let us look at the transiting chart for that day in 1776 that would have resonated or have been equivalent with the geodetic one. It would match the angles of the geodetic chart. This is a reversal of approach compared with Krishnamurti example above. There we started with the natal and moved to the geodetic chart. Here we are starting with the geodetic and checking out

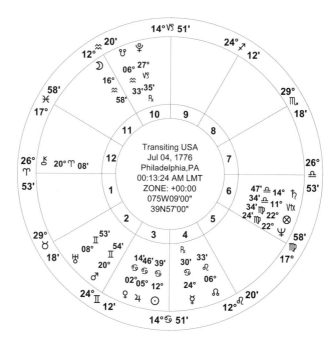

Figure 86

the matching transiting chart. No matter, as the issue is their equivalence or resonance. This transiting chart is shown in Figure 86. Here we see that just some minutes past midnight (at the start of July 4th) the transiting chart angles matched those of the geodetic chart. This might suggest that the Founding Fathers completed their work that night, past midnight, although there appears to be no historical evidence to support or refute it. They, of course, reconvened later the same day to recommend approval of the Declaration.

3. New Russia resonates, but what does it mean?

In the *Book of World Horoscopes*[15] Campion points out that the lowering of the Soviet and the raising of the Russian flag over the Kremlin represented the 'supreme and final symbolic' moment for the transfer of power to Russia. The time for this event has therefore been used as the birth moment for new Russia[16]. A comparative review of both the transiting chart for new Russia and the corresponding geodetic chart (for Moscow) shows an incredible matching or resonance between the two. Figure 87 is a chart for the birth moment of new Russia. Note the 24-degree Leo ascendant and 8-degree Taurus midheaven. Now let us look at Figure 88, Moscow's geodetic chart. The ascendant and midheaven are almost identical – in perfect resonance – with the birth chart!

What might this mean? We can hypothesise that to survive, Russia will continue to be very sensitive to its own cultural needs and communal stand-

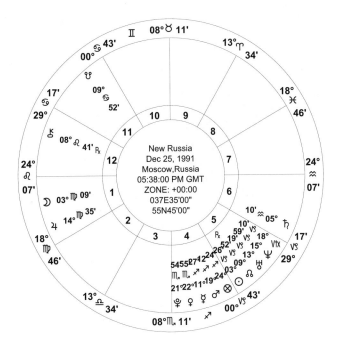

Figure 87

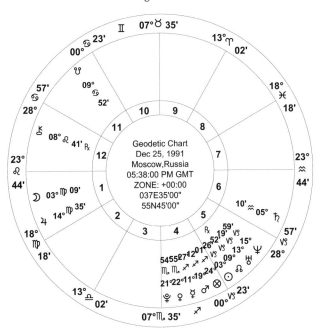

Figure 88

149

ards and, reinforced by this resonance, have to live according to its own models, its own signature (not necessarily those of the West). More important, we can see that time of day in Moscow as an opening where the spirit of the earth best matches activities that are culturally relevant and communal in nature.

4. The attack on Pearl Harbor

Called by President Roosevelt 'a date which will live in infamy', the attack on Pearl Harbor by the Japanese air force on 7 December, 1941, brought the United States into World War II. The attack united the American nation behind the President and ended its isolationist sentiments. Various times have been recorded for elements of the Japanese operation and the moments of the attack itself. Naval records record 7:53 am local time as the moment the first bombs fell on Hickam Air Force base, with bombs and torpedoes falling on ships some minutes later. Using the time of the first bombs, let's look at the charts for that moment and at the corresponding geodetic chart itself. Figure 89 is the chart of the moment. Note that it has Capricorn rising (with Saturn conjoining Uranus, the planet of surprises) and Libra on the midheaven (with Venus opposing Pluto and the Moon, possible violent, emotional upheaval). A prominent feature is transiting Mars exactly on the IC. What a great symbolism for an attack on one's home! Figure 90 is the equivalent geodetic chart

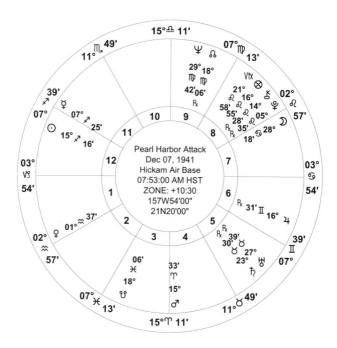

Figure 89

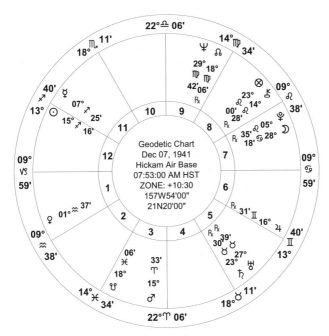

Figure 90

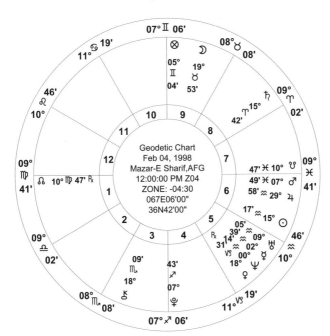

Figure 91

for Hickam. Note the resonance! The ascendant and midheaven signs are the same as those in the chart for the attack moment. By degree they are fairly close as well, being fewer than 7 degrees different for both ascendant and midheaven. If we use an attack time of some 28 minutes later, when the worst damage was being done to the US ships (the USS Arizona was lost with 1,104 men killed), we would have a strong – though melancholy – resonance between the two charts.

5. Earthquakes in Afghanistan; geodetics and calamities

Traditionally, geodetic charts have been used in astrological studies of earth calamities. Let's look at two recent earthquakes in Afghanistan. The first, on 4 February, 1998, measured 6.4 on the Richter scale. It killed about 4,000 people in the mountainous northern region of the country and left some 15,000 homeless. This quake was followed by aftershocks for a week. The second major quake occurred some 4 months later on 1 June. It too killed about 4,000 people outright and left an estimated further 45,000 homeless.

Figure 91 is the geodetic chart for the first quake on 4 February, 1998. We see that Pluto, the planet of the underworld, death and resurrection, is almost exactly on the IC or foundation of the chart. This is a perfect symbolism for a powerful earth purging from below. We can also observe that Mars is moving to the chart's descendant (and South Node), alerting us perhaps to a dangerous trigger point for the quake. Note that the Nodes are very close to the ascendant-descendant axis, having just crossed them in their retrograde mo-

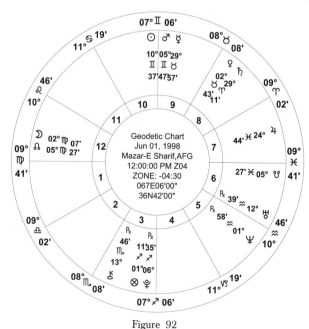

Figure 92

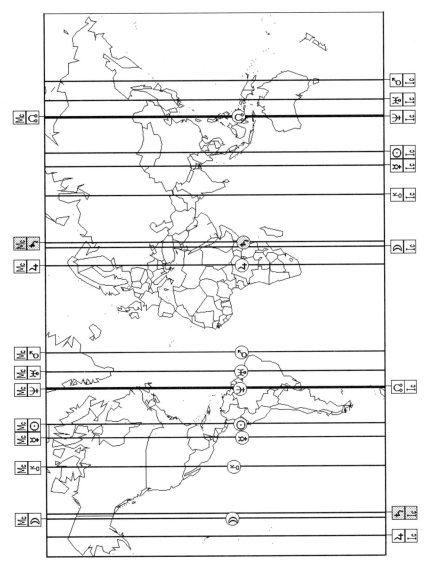

Figure 93

153

tion. The nodes often aspect chart angles in geodetic calamity charts. Figure 92 is the geodetic chart for the second quake to befall the suffering populace, this one even more violent then the first. Here we see that trigger planet Mars has now moved to the chart's midheaven (along with the Sun), that Pluto remains on the IC, and that the Nodes, now direct in motion, are still near the ascendant-descendant axis. Surely these geodetic charts offer us valuable insight into these events which where not specifically timed.

ACG maps can be created with a geodetic orientation (Greenwich meridian = 0 degrees Aries). Such maps can be employed to watch the earth for possible mundane events[17]. For example, since the geodetic Pluto on the IC has been moving across Afghanistan, not only have we seen the earthquakes, but the Taliban have brought about a thorough and brutal Plutonic-type purge of the culture there. In 1998 and 1999 with geodetic Neptune moving through the far east those economies have been going through a meltdown. With Saturn on the MC approaching Moscow the Russian economic system fell on hard times. Figure 93 is the geodetic world map for the new year, 01 January 2000 timed for London. I've only included MC and IC lines for clarity. I leave it to the reader to ponder the possible correspondences of geodetic positions and possible world events.

6. The Northridge California earthquake

California was hit by a quake, centred in Northridge on 17th January, 1994.

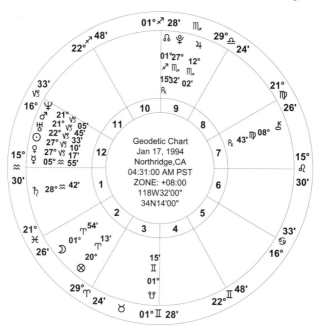

Figure 94

154

Figure 94 is the geodetic chart for the location at the timed moment of first tremor. Note that Pluto is moving to the chart's midheaven[18] and that the Nodes are involved yet again, this time all but perfectly aligned with the midheaven/IC axis! Trigger planet Mars is on the Uranus-Neptune conjunction of that time, which could be an indication of an instability or misdirected energy.

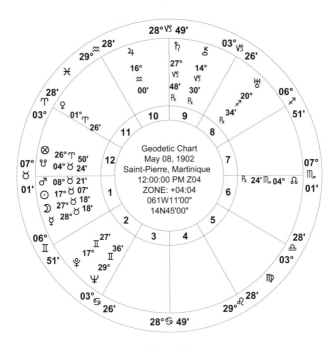

Figure 95

7. The volcanic eruption at Mt Pelee, West Indies

This deadly eruption occurred on 8th May, 1902, causing the most casualties of any such event during the entire 20th century. The city of St Pierre Martinique, nestled at the foot of the mountain, was completely destroyed by lava flow, and most all of its 30,000 inhabitants were killed outright. Since the event itself was untimed, we have a perfect candidate for a geodetic analysis. Figure 95 is the geodetic chart for that date and location. Note that Saturn, the planet of karmic pay-back, sits on the chart's most public point, the midheaven. And how can one help but notice that both trigger planet Mars and the Nodes (yet again) are conjoining the ascendant-descendant axis!

NOTES

1. For an account of Ptolemy's map and other earth zodiacs, see Appendix 9, *The Book of World Horoscopes*, by Nicholas Campion, Cinnabar Books, 1995.

2. The fullest historical exploration of earth zodiacs, including Sepharial's contribution, can be found in Chapter 11, *Mundane Astrology*, by Michael Baigent, Nicholas Campion and Charles Harvey, Aquarian Press, 1984. I would hope that every serious student of mundane astrology has both this book and Campion's work listed above. I can't recommend them too highly!

3. A big thank-you to Arielle Guttman who, on a visit here to Scotland, first showed me this diagram and alerted me to the value of geodetic charts.

4. This doesn't explain Gengis Kahn, who came from Mongolia, a Cancer-influenced region. Nor does it cover Japan's inclination for world conquest as part of the Axis alliance of WW II. But we should note that Japan is in the fiery geodetic sign of Leo, in harmonious trine to Aries.

5. This calculation of the geodetic chart can be found in computer programs such as WinStar and Solar Maps.

6. I believe that the first astrologer to calculate this world map was Chris McRae, who did her work in 1985 using Matrix Software's Blue*Star program and the new computers coming onto the market at that time. She published her work – and the map – in her book, *The Geodetic World Map*, AFA, 1988. Her map can also be found in *The Astrology of the Macrocosm*, edited by Joan McEvers, Llewellyn Publications, 1990, page 165. I used McRae's map approximations as the trial starting points of my hand drawn one.

7. When the map is drawn properly, Rome is just outside the geodetic Leo rising band, but most of Italy does in fact have a Leo rising signature.

8. Noting that the equatorial perspective is generally accepted for identifying earth location and for navigational activity, we see a symbolically powerful 'marriage' of the zodiac's 0 Aries point with the locational and navigational beacon, the Greenwich meridian. In terms of world time-keeping, the Greenwich meridian is also considered the prime meridian from which Universal Time (UT) is measured.

9. See Chapter 11, *Mundane Astrology*, Aquarian Press, 1984.

10. See 'The Mountain Astrologer', January 1996, Page 64: 'The modified Johndro Chart', by Marc Penfield.

11. This means I have a Jupiter rising line crossing northern Britain on my ACG map.

12. In spite of the intrinsic beauty of any place, some individuals would never feel

comfortable there, or at least they wouldn't describe it as their favourite spot on earth. I myself feel uneasy in California for any long period of time, perhaps due to the intensity of my Pluto on the MH line, which is nearby.

13. The ACG booklet accompanying official ACG maps, Jim Lewis, 1976.

14. If we were to use the Earth signature of Washington, DC for that day, as that location would later become the nation's capitol, the conjunction of Sun and IC becomes exact.

15. Page 318, 'The Lowering and Raising of the Flags'.

16. Campion also points out that "For such a major event the reporting (of the time) was surprisingly confused". Reports of the specific time ranges from 7:32 pm to 7:45 pm, a difference of only 13 minutes. For this study I have used the time of 7:38 pm as reported by Russian astrologer Y. Kuryakov. Any time selected in this range however would be in resonance with Moscow's geodetic signature. See *Book of World Horoscopes*, footnote 1173, page 689.

17. The Solar Maps computer program has this feature. Another possibility would be to use the geodetic world map (Figure 78) and estimate where a transiting planetary midheaven would be located on it.

18. Pluto is also at 27 degrees of Scorpio, a degree associated with calamity in geodetic astrology.

AFTERWORD

Thank you for joining me on this astrological journey through space and time. The purpose of this book has been to present a healthy cross-section of astrolocality astrology. I never, however, intended it to be an exhaustive survey of the field. With that in mind I'd like to acknowledge the astrologers and the computer mapping programs that haven't been specifically mentioned herein. They too are making significant contributions to the field, and I hope the reader will seek them out, utilising and applying what they have to offer.

The greatest problem of employing astrolocality astrology in our lives is a deeply personal one, rather than the issue of using one technique or the other. Essentially, whenever we arrive at a new place, the one thing that hasn't changed is ourselves![1] Will we allow the new energy and potential of a location to consciously influence us or, becoming fearful, will we put up psychological barriers and resist it? This personal responsibility, I believe, is the unspoken requirement for the successful use of astrolocality astrology.[2]

There is a concept in contemporary physics that is applicable here. It is called "active information". In systems that include active information, a form, having very little energy itself, enters into and directs (or "informs") a much greater energy[3]. An example of this might be the information carried in a relatively weak satellite radio signal which causes a huge oil tanker to change its course. I believe that astrolocality astrology offers us potent, active information. Armed with the information we get from its relatively modest and symbolic signals, we can make major locational decisions that are conscious and empowering. I can hardly conceive of anything more "active" for us then a thought or bit of information that changes our lives!

What of the future for astrolocality astrology? Certainly we can expect more tools and techniques both to widen our perspective and increase the information provided to us. That's in line with our expectations for most modern, computer-related systems. But what beyond that? Perhaps we can look to our experiencing a further archaic revival, this time from the realm of hermetic magic. Hermetic magicians agreed with astrologers that the stars influence our terrestrial domain. But to the magicians, astrologers were on a limited, one-way path, merely interpreting the stars for what would happen on earth. Behind the magical view was the belief that a link could be made to work in both directions, with individuals not only interpreting the celestial information but also feeding influences back to the stars to alter the course of their lives and history itself.

I believe this magical possibility is awaiting our rediscovery today, with astrolocality astrology as the stepping-stone to that achievement.

Martin Davis
Abbey Saint Bathans
Scotland

June 1999

NOTES

1. See Donna Cunningham's article, "Wherever you go, you take yourself along - Why moving won't solve all of your problems", The Mountain Astrologer, Issue # 84, April/ May 1999.

2. The specifics of how we truly learn at an earth location - or not - are mysterious and worthy of separate study. There is a quality of this learning process, however, which I can best describe as "courageous participation".
    A poetic description can be found in T S Eliot's Four Quartets:
    "... quick now, here, now, always -
    A condition of complete simplicity
    Costing not less than everything...".

3. *Science, Order and Creativity* by David Bohm and F. Peat, Routledge, 1989, page 93.

APPENDIX ONE

ASTRO*CARTO*GRAPHY INTERPRETATIONS

By Jeff Jawer

Jeff Jawer has been practicing astrology professionally for over 24 years. He is a highly respected teacher, regularly invited to leading conferences around the world. Jeff has written well over 100 articles and has co-authored four books. He is co-founder and CEO of StarIQ.com., the astrology portal site. For information on consultations you can also email him at Jawer@Bigfoot.com.

The most important consideration in interpreting a relocation chart or Astro*Carto*Graphy map is the condition of the planet in the natal chart. The following interpretations are just one way to combine the meaning of a planet and an angle. Adding information from the natal chart will enrich these interpretations.

The Ascendant, also called the Rising Sign or cusp of the 1st house, is the point rising in the East. It represents the beginning, the front, ones appearance or first impression. The Ascendant is where the turning Earth meets the sky. Any planet at this point takes on a position of prominence, it occupies the foreground, sometimes dominating the landscape. A planet at this point may be the first thing others see when they meet you. It can even be what you see when you look in the mirror. This is also about physical conditions, both of your body and your environment. Planets here influence health, energy levels and your general outlook on life for a given location.

The IC, or 4th house cusp, is the bottom of the chart, the northernmost point. It symbolizes one's roots, both physically and spiritually. It can be seen as the base or foundation, even as an entry point: the Ascendant is birth, the IC is conception. While this is a very important point, it is also quite hidden from the world, sometimes even from ourselves. But, from the perspective of relocation, it could be the most important angle in the chart. It is not so much about us, about how we appear, connect with others or the world. It is about how we connect with the *place.*

The Descendant, or 7th house cusp, is the primary point of partnership in the chart. It is the western point where the individual Sun sets to share the light with another. Planets here put the focus on relationships, both personal and public. A key to working with this point is to be the planet(s) that you find there. Projection, that is letting other people play these out for you, is a less desirable way to experience these. The influence you have on others and the quality of your relationships is revealed to a large degree by this point.

The MC or 10th house cusp is the uppermost point in the chart. It has to do with career, one's place in society and, to a certain degree, a place to which we are evolving. There is public notice here, but also public responsibility. Planets in this area often feel isolated as they carry a strong burden. It is not easy to share with planets here. This is a place where you are publicly accountable. Career is certainly emphasized, so planets in this area will bring professional issues to the surface.

THE SUN

Sun on the Ascendant - You're at the sunrise point. Confidence, courage and creativity rise to the surface. You can be generous or absorbed with yourself. In either case, you may feel like you're the center of the universe here. This is a good place to take risks and push the limits of self-expression. You can be a leader, not because you try to lead, but simply by the force of your personality. This is also an environment that can be physically invigorating for you. Vitality may be strengthened, the heart opened and your capacity to impose your will enhanced.

Sun on the IC - The Sun on the IC warms the home fires. There can be an inner confidence and feeling of creativity. But, this is primarily expressed in ones home. The need to shine or be noticed is not a public matter here. This is the place where you can be king or queen of your castle. Negatively, that could mean becoming the little dictator in your own little world. However, it is more likely to mean that you feel 'warmed' by this location, as it contributes to your physical well-being. You're connected to a powerful source of energy here, one that can fuel your creative endeavors. It can, too, be a place where the light is shined inward, where the greatest works are private. This is the midnight point of the chart, so the Sun's placement here emphasizes the night side of things. You can use this to illuminate issues of family, origins and early childhood.

Sun on the Descendant - You need partnership to shine in this location. The positive feedback of others is required to keep your creative juices flowing. Negatively, you can look for a hero to rescue you. But, positively, this can be the place where you're courageous in partnerships, able to create new and more dynamic forms of relationship. Your need for recognition by others is also strong here. But, if you're willing to come from the heart those needs can be met. Expect solar partners here. Ideally, that means individuals who are also creative and courageous. Negatively, this can be the egocentric partner. This is a place for you to be generous and expect the same in return from others.

Sun on the MC - This noon position of the Sun can be very good for your professional life. You bring confidence and creativity to the public arena. You can be a leader here, easily recognized for your courage and strong will. Others may regard you with more respect than they might in many other places. The spotlight is on you and the need to perform up to standards is very high. You can go far in fulfilling your 'destiny' here, but the challenges can also be great. You're not likely to able to just 'get by' - the full investment of your heart and spirit is expected. Fortunately, its also a place where it is easier for you to do so. The Sun is about risk, so this is a place to push the limits professionally, not an environment for just passing time. Public honors may await you here.

THE MOON

Moon on the Ascendant - Emotions come into the foreground here as your emotional antenna is up all of the time. This is a place in which you may be dominated by feelings. Self-nurturance is a major issue - concerns with your personal needs can take a great deal of your time and effort, and instinct and reactions are very powerful here. This is not likely to be a place that you feel neutral about. Either you belong or you clearly do not. Get in touch with your maternal instincts. You're a caretaker and need to make your own feelings your first priority.

Moon on the IC - This is home. It is where the Moon, the planet of home, is at the very roots of your chart. This can be a very familiar place, cocoon-like, and a security blanket that wraps you in its arms, cuddles and protects you. You should feel very comfortable here, like you've always known this place. Your roots can go deep, but that can also mean that the focus is on your inner, not outer life. Family matters count more than career here, unless you set up a cozy little business that feels like home. If you're interested in investigating your past lives, you should do it here.

Moon on the Descendant - Your sensitivity to others is very strong here. You may find partners who are caretakers or who need your caretaking. Relationship issues are rather emotional as your connections with others are dominated by feelings. This can be good for therapy as personal issues are more easily shared with others. You could wind up being 'married' to your family here and, at worst, lose touch with your own needs. Make sure that emotional support is reciprocal. In doing so, trust and intimacy are enhanced. Without these, dependency issues can become problematic.

Moon on the MC - You become the mother of the world. You can feel responsible for everyone and everything. If you like that role, this can be a very beneficial place. You're likely to be well-known here, perhaps a public figure.

163

But, beware of losing yourself in the demands of career and public activity. Nurturance is something you give others here, but don't easily get back in a personal way. Connected to everyone, you can nevertheless feel a bit isolated. Balance this with attention to your inner needs so that you don't lose touch with them.

MERCURY

Mercury on the Ascendant - Mental alertness and communication are the key influences here. Intellect may dominate your experiences. This can be a good place to be a writer. The minds activity tends to be very active. Curiosity is strong and you may be full of questions. Nervous energy or restlessness may be common in this location. It can be difficult to feel settled as there may be a great deal of coming and going. Ideally, this is a location when you may become more objective about yourself.

Mercury on the IC - This is the writer in her little garden of ideas. It's a place where you can connect to information without ever leaving home. Ideas move through you easily here, but perhaps can leave you feeling restless. Your home life is less marked by sentiment than by intellect. This can be a good place for you to study and advance your education. But, Mercury often raises more questions than it answers. Curiosity is piqued, yet coming to conclusions and resolving lifes larger issues may not be so easy.

Mercury on the Descendant - Intelligent conversation with bright partners is favored here. This is a place where relationships are dominated by the mind, not the emotions. If you need more rationality in your relationships you can be well served by this environment. Discussions may be lengthy, but they can provide the objective information you need. Of course, you could just feel like an outside observer of your own life. You may need to jump in from time to time to overcome this sense of distance.

Mercury on the MC - A profession that focuses on the intellect, communication and connections makes sense here. You may gain public recognition for your intelligence or communication skills. But, principles and big issues may have to yield to smaller details. Your ability to adapt in professional matters can be tested here. This environment should be good for education, a place where you gather information helpful to your career.

VENUS

Venus on the Ascendant - With the planet of beauty and attraction rising this can be an excellent place for relationships. Of course, your need for approval can also be very strong here. In fact, this placement is also about learning to please yourself, not just gaining appreciation from others. Natural grace and artistic skills are favored here. You'll have better instincts for making yourself look good. The pleasure principle is another aspect of Venus, so that fun and games may be more important than hard work and commitment.

Venus on the IC - Your home and family life can be graced by beauty and pleasure. This is a place where your connection with nature and the earth is favored. It is also a place where gifts come from your family. These can be in the form of talents and objects. Inner peace and the development of a loving relationship with your home are found here. Just look inside yourself and you'll find all the beauty you desire. You'll learn that love is something you have, not something given to you by others.

Venus on the Descendant - This may be the best place in the world to attract a loving partner. The likelihood of getting the approval of others is strengthened here. But, you could also connect with partners who are narcissistic or self-indulgent. Make sure that what you give is returned to you in equal portion. Your diplomatic and social skills can enhance all of your relationships. You've a better sense of what others need and how to give it to them. Just don't lose touch with the need to assert yourself as well.

Venus on the MC - Your professional life may be charmed here. Great pleasure and joy can come through your work and service to the community. Careers in the arts are supported here. This can also be a place where your social skills pay off professionally. One challenge may be that you feel the constant pressure to be nice to everyone, as if you are responsible for their collective happiness. Being clear about what you're willing to give (and what you need in return) can prevent this from becoming a problem.

MARS

Mars on the Ascendant - The warrior planet at this powerful personal point can push you to take the initiative. Physical activity and the pressure to act now are strong here. This can be very energizing and provides much needed motivation. But, there can also be a sense of struggle, the need to battle in your every day life. You need to choose your challenges, rather than sitting back and having to defend yourself on a regular basis. If you're willing to approach your life with a new attitude this can be a great location. But, if you're not ready for change the stress may be more than you desire.

Mars on the IC - This is a challenging placement as the battles of Mars work very deeply inside of you. The earth around you demands much work and attention. It's not an easy place to relax. Home and family life may be more stressed here. But, if you are interested in breaking ground, both psychologically and professionally, the forces here may help you do the job. This is a place to start all over. If you're ready, it can provide the juice you need.

Mars on the Descendant - Are you ready to push the limits of your relationships? You may have some serious battles with others on your hands with Mars placed here. Aggressive individuals and challenging situations keep you moving. It can be fatiguing unless you choose the time and place of your battles. You can break through old patterns in partnerships, but dont expect a lot of time to relax with others. You must be prepared to take initiative so you're not a fixed object of attack. Push forward and discover new levels of passion in your relationships.

Mars on the MC - There is a certain affinity for Mars and the MC. The MC is the cusp of the 10th house and Mars is exalted in Capricorn, the 10th sign of the Zodiac. Professional initiative and leadership can be displayed here. But, this is not a place to hold your ground. Rather it represents the need to push the limits professionally. You can be an innovator and pioneer here. It's possible that you may feel like all the responsibility falls on you in this place. If you are able to act independently and with courage you may be rewarded with a new career.

JUPITER

Jupiter on the Ascendant - Expansive Jupiter on the Ascendant often gives one a feeling of confidence in this location. You're able to express yourself with optimism, enabling your self-image to grow. This is a place where you are guided by vision, but may not have much patience for details. Jupiter needs to grow, so this is not a place to stand still. If you want to learn more about yourself and share your wisdom with others, there are few better places. But, it can be frustrating if your hopes are not attainable. You can feel like you're always falling short of your expectations.

Jupiter on the IC - This is the philosopher's home, a place where you can explore the world from the comfort of your own house. All the knowledge of the universe flows through you here. Understanding your origins is strong, and making connections with family patterns, even with past lives, is favored in this location. Your vision grows here, a positive step towards future professional expansion. The earth is welcoming and supports your growth.

Jupiter on the Descendant - Opportunities for partnership abound here. On personal and professional levels others are ready to welcome and support you. Your judgment is well respected by others. This is a place to give and receive wisdom. Your understanding of relationships grows here as you attract wise and generous partners. The ability to present your ideas is strong in this location.

Jupiter on the MC - This is one of the best possible situations for career and public recognition. Opportunities for professional success are strong. Take risks to expand the boundaries in your work life. You'll need to have something that pushes you to grow. This is not a place to stand still professionally. Your expectations of the outside world and of yourself are high. Teaching, travel, publishing, sales and promotion are possible career choices here.

SATURN

Saturn on the Ascendant - At first glance this looks like an unfavorable position. Saturn imposes limitations and the Ascendant is where we stand. This is a place where patience, discipline and persistence may be needed to overcome resistance. The rewards for such effort are self-respect and personal accomplishment. You can be master or your world if you have the necessary discipline. Life's challenges are right in front of you. This is your chance to master them.

Saturn on the IC - The inner world calls here. Serious matters are met at the depths of your being. Family issues, feelings of isolation and deeply felt insecurities can prove daunting. But, this is a place to build a solid foundation. It may take a long time to fit into this environment - it doesn't welcome you easily. You have the chance to manage your inner fears, overcome the past and reconstruct a new life based on dignity and self-respect.

Saturn on the Descendant - Serious work on relationships is likely here. You won't be given much without effort. If youre willing to take responsibility for building partnerships, and have the necessary discipline, you can be successful here. You could, though, attract partners who are older, fearful, limited or controlling. Positively, they could be mature, competent and reliable. Clarity serves you well here. You can earn respect and establish long-lasting relationships with focus and commitment.

Saturn on the MC - This is Saturn's natural position, generally good for career. But this doesn't guarantee professional success. In fact, struggle may be more likely, yet persistence will be rewarded. This can be a place where the weight of responsibility is heavy. You can be an organizer, manager or long-term builder. Career planning counts here, as Saturn likes structure. If you have a well defined goal and can manage your time and resources, you can accomplish a great deal.

URANUS

Uranus on the Ascendant - The planet of revolution at this personal point adds weirdness. You may feel a bit strange or different here. It's not easy to blend in and make yourself inconspicuous. This is, rather, a place to reinvent yourself. Originality is favored here. But, it can be difficult to feel comfortable with yourself. Flexibility and a willingness to break you old patterns can make this strange place feel more like home, even a place of great freedom.

Uranus on the IC - this is not an easy place to feel at home. It is a place for breaking free of the past, for letting go of old patterns and discovering new ways to live your life. You can move into new forms of living, not continue the old ones. You might feel disconnected, misunderstood and alone, but can also discover your genius here. This is your own little earthquake zone, great for shaking your old patterns, but not an easy place to settle down.

Uranus on the Descendant - Relationships can be volatile here. You can attract some very unusual partners and unusual forms of relationships. Movement and change are stronger than stability here. You can have a very strong effect on those you meet. They may find you magnetic and brilliant or weird and strange. Your job here is to wake up people, to shake their patterns. Expect change, look for it and create it. Dynamism is your ally, be ready to make break-throughs in partnerships.

Uranus on the MC - Careers can rise and fall quickly with this setup. This is about making radical changes in your professional life, perhaps taking on an unusual occupation. It can be very difficult to maintain stability in your work. Circumstances can change quickly. When they dont, you do. This can work well if youre very original and are willing to take risks. You may not appreciate authority figures here or accept your own responsibilities. Be a revolutionary and let your originality shine.

NEPTUNE

Neptune on the Ascendant - This is a place to cast yourself to the winds. It isn't you but destiny that calls the shots. You might as well relax and let go. It's not easy to see yourself clearly here, at least not on the personal level. Neptune leads you beyond this world to one of wondrous visions and holy truths, but also one of illusion. Life can become like a movie. You can use your imagination to create any image that you want. The risk, though, is to lose yourself in the process. Fantasy and faith are strong here. A good dose of reality provides balance.

Neptune on the IC - This can be like living in a dream world, a fantasyland of every day life. Life needs to be built on spiritual principles here. If so, this environment can support your ideals and dreams. Your home needs to be a very quiet place, a sanctuary from the world. The magic is behind closed doors here. This can be a challenging place for your professional life, as practicality is not supported by Neptune. If, though, you can live your life at a highly refined level of awareness, you can find yourself supported here.

Neptune on the Descendant - The place where you can marry God. It is the projection of the God principle on a partner. Neptune shows where we want to dissolve the individual and belong to something greater. Partnerships usually require clarity, communication, negotiation, contracts, conversations. Neptune requires only surrender and faith. You attract dreamers here. Good ones help you dream better. Bad ones help keep you in your illusions. There is, though, a beautiful marriage of body and soul possible here.

Neptune on the MC - Neptune is sensitive to everything and the MC is responsibility for everything. Be clear about your professional commitments so that you don't get worn out here. This may not an easy place for career. People can mislead you. You can wear yourself out for something that doesn't reward the effort equally. But, if spirituality is your business, or healing or music or anything else that inspires you, this is the place.

PLUTO

Pluto on the Ascendant - This is a place to focus the microscope on yourself. To closely observe yourself and carefully insert yourself into the environment. People may be frightened of you because you carry Pluto's power in your face. You can be very strong here, this is not a place for the weak. If you're interested in the psychology of self-mastery this can be a useful environment. Your body may be transformed, so healthy habits are very important.

Pluto on the IC - You have found a secret passageway to your own history. This dark place is full of mystery and memories. You'll meet your family karma here, that's for sure. If you want to go within yourself and discover your secrets, you have come to the right place. But, for mere mortals this can be a challenging location. The earth doesn't give easily of itself here. There may be great riches to be found, but your aim must be true to capture the prize.

Pluto on the Descendant - You may attract powerful partners here. Be powerful yourself and it can work to your advantage. You'll learn to measure what to give for what you want back. This is a place to see the exchanges taking place. Pluto is a furnace and here it is the furnace of partnership - if you are willing to face your inner demons and let go of fear a new depth in relationships is possible.

Pluto on the MH - Power struggles in your career or with authority figures are common here. This is the place to express your deepest desires through your profession, which can be totally transformed here. Ideally this is an environment in which your work enables you to be an agent of change, perhaps for doing research or managing the resources of others. If you're focused on your purpose you can be a powerful figure in this location. However, corruption can stick to you if your aims aren't pure.

APPENDIX TWO

LOCAL SPACE ANGULAR LOCATIONS

by Martin Davis

The nature of our experiences at specific angular locations in Local Space is similar to what we would find for angular lines in ACG (see Appendix 1). When we employ Local Space charts, however, the angular planetary qualities are seen as operating in a *practical* and *immediately substantial* manner. Evaluation of the lines in ACG can include the long-run implications of one's potential, growth and psychological development.

To illustrate this, a list of possibilities for Local Space planetary empowerment follows. Note that the east and west listings may represent new information for us. These angular locations are often different from the ascending and descending locations found in ACG maps or their corresponding relocated charts. Locations with angular north and south planets in LS, however, do directly correlate with ACG Midheaven or IC lines. I have included these north and south locations to further illustrate the gritty detail used for LS interpretations. Do note that for some locations (especially in the southern hemisphere), north and south readings should be switched:

THE SUN

East: Willpower, confidence, energy and enthusiasm seem to grow from the moment of arrival. It is fine now to push yourself forward and take advantage of the leadership roles and responsibility that are offered to you - here is a place, at last, where your potential can unfold. Whatever your profession, there is a high likelihood that it will be supported. Self-help and self-improvement courses, where you will be either the teacher or the student, are ideal. More spiritually directed endeavours of self-realisation will draw you to them as will projects in the creative arts.

Sounds good, doesn't it? Any catches? Well, yes. With all this creativity and energy buzzing around big-headedness is a distinct possibility; beware of becoming so self absorbed that you miss out on what is coming into your life from others and from great nature herself. Believe it or not, there are others in this world too! Don't stop *listening* to them. Be alert to the danger of becoming

171

arrogant or narcissistic and this location will work for you. Males or those in authority will be around to give support when it is needed.

West: Courage, self-expression and the ability to come from the heart are important themes when the Sun is placed in a cardinal direction, and at this location the focus will be on relationships. They will be successful if you show courage in creating new and inspired ones. Can you come from your heart in relationships? Can you shine forth? If you haven't been clear in the past about what that means, these issues will naturally emerge here. If successful, you should attract capable and loyal friends, an experience which will become a learning and heart-opening process. Overly egocentric partners or power struggles here may indicate that you are not respecting another's need for self-expression.

A natural flair for public relations could involve you working in sales or promotion.. Positions that require those skills will emerge as others sense your talent. A specific business partner should pop up when needed.

Marriage partner for a female? A real possibility. But whatever type of relationship develops, do listen to others, since they will be the channel and inspiration for ideas and growth for you at this location..

North: The expressions 'home is where the heart is' and 'keep the home fires burning' will become relevant for you at this location.

There will be a strong desire to set up a home and family, combined with the need to understand your roots - this may take the form of tracing your family genealogy for the first time ever. From the moment of arrival this place has felt like home and it will be a strong contender for a retirement spot. You may become known for your entertaining (perhaps of important people) and for the ability to create a beautiful environment.

On a practical level, if you are house or apartment hunting, a wonderful place is waiting for you to find it! The local society and culture won't hinder your private life-style. This location will support a career or interests in other houses, real estate, property management and land issues in general. It's a wonderful location for you to become involved in the causes of ecology and natural resources. You probably won't want to be a public crusader on these issues, but the location supports you in making important contributions, if behind the scenes.

What is the 'down' side of all this? The other side of solar locations is excessive pride, a tendency to dominate and the inability to listen when too full of yourself. If you are not getting along with your family and/or parents now, accept the fault as your own and turn to the bright side of your life. This 'bright side' is your natural potential at this location.

South: Hail to the chief! You will be looked upon as an authority here (whether it is deserved or not). People will feel that you came from a good family background, since you appear noble in your demeanour (enjoy their respect, as it may melt away in another location). Life events however will require that you perform at a high level - a minimal job really won't bring satisfaction - but the good news is that your will, courage, and general abilities are up to the tasks that this location presents to you. As the Hindu god Shiva says encouragingly to a recalcitrant Sun on the first day of creation, "You are the Sun, so why not shine?"[1] Here you'll gain influence with friends and colleagues through your career or profession. Your reputation for dependability and capability grows, and this prominence is deserved. One day you may come to see that your destiny unfolded at this location, especially if you enter into politics or another visible aspect of public life. Promotional work is supported here. Any job in your field that requires a manager or team leader should be yours, and you advance quickly in it as well.

So what's the problem? They say that every coin has two sides, so what's 'tails' for you at this location? Your public reputation can become one of notoriety if the yearning for fame and power causes you to use unscrupulous methods to gain it. This could lead to a nasty turn where you actually fall from power in public disgrace rather than a scenario where you gain public and professional adulation.

Are you shining forth at this location while respecting and listening to others as well? If so, enjoy your life's high noon here.

THE MOON

East: "Do you feel it, can you feel it?", the soul singers cry out to us in their songs. At this location you *will* feel it, ready or not! Blessed or cursed (the choice is yours), here you find the opportunity to experience emotional depths. Life events will show to just what extent you are in touch with your feelings. The Moon is about nurturing ourselves, and this golden opportunity will show how well you have been doing it. Lack of self-nurturing causes us to dry up both physically and psychologically, with very unpleasant effects.

It does seem as if women handle this location better than men. They have an easier time 'turning up the volume' on the intuitive, caring, loving, empathising side of themselves, making a good connection between their feelings and their consciousness. This, as a positive spin-off, increases their emotional stamina and the clarity of their memory or personal narrative[2]. The issues of home and family become heightened for them. For this reason motherhood becomes a possibility here.

Males may be relieved to have finally discovered their emotionally nurturing side. Like the rush of fresh air into a vacuum, males find they have the liberating experience of making the connection between their (formerly isolated) outer consciousness and (formerly suppressed) inner and unconscious sides. "Wow, what have I been missing?" they exclaim, as these sides merge, becoming a healing and healthful way for them.

Regardless of your own sex, issues relating to females will dominate at this location. Jobs that have to do with caring and sharing will be ideal and practically fall into your lap if you want them. Why? You really can handle them at this location, and here the cosmos will support you in getting them. Jobs connected with female beauty are also favoured, along with artistic endeavours where the expression of your unconscious is highlighted. In fact, if you are an artist, that's probably the only way to express yourself now. And finally, here at last you can talk to plants and they will even answer you!

So how do you keep a score card at this location? If the events coming to you and your responses to them are bringing a good flow of emotional deepening and self reflection, then you're getting a top grade! If your nerves are frazzled from over-sensitivity to people, issues and events, or the needs of others are swamping your own self-stewardship, you need a good rethink, a reflection on how you have structured your reality. The key is not to lessen your feelings or emotional responses but consciously to become clearer and more strategic as to what life issues you choose to connect with here. It is possible to balance a healthy inner, emotional life with all the other outer issues of your reality. The experience of that balance is the possible treasure of this location for you.

West: Has a partner ever complained that you are not particularly sensitive to their needs, that you left a lot to be desired, and you know deep down they may be right? That type of problem will become just a dim and irrelevant memory at this location. In fact, you'll find that here both your sensitivity to partners and your needs for warmth and nurturing from them, will swing to the 'turned on' side like a pendulum gone mad! Your emotional buttons are constantly activated and this includes close friends and even by members of a wider public circle.

How might this new sensitivity be put to good use? You will be a natural here for planning all sorts of public-relations campaigns. This location will offer support if you are in sales, especially of food, domestic and feminine products. Partnerships in the caring fields or the arts may be offered to you, but they are emotionally sensitive and less cool and strategic than you might wish for. Here at last you can open up to a therapist, as issues become clearer and you can share them with him (her).

Females will find they have an enhanced possibility of attracting a sensitive partner who will support them in establishing a home and family. Males will find they understand their female partners (at last!) and that they are better able to deal with females in general than ever before. For both sexes, this is simply a great place to take someone you love. The caring and sharing between you will flow as never before.

What should you be on the alert for at this location? Vacations may be fun here, but beware of becoming emotionally ragged and exhausted from long-term, intense relating. Feelings flow easily and frequently. Watch out too that you don't become a doormat to keep another happy.

As with other positions of the Moon, probably the worst thing to do is to try and shut down your feelings. That's just suppression and it won't work anyway, simply making you more prone to creating debilitating ego strategies for yourself, with resulting unhappiness. Of course you could move away, but that's missing the opportunities of this location. The best thing may be to dig deeper into yourself, striving to remain as conscious as possible, taking great care as to who you decide to relate with – or not – especially in those relationships of an intimate nature.

If you get it right at this location, you will not only come to truly understand works such as Shakespeare's Sonnets but you will be able to write your own, articulating your love for others authentically, from direct experience.

North: Home at last! Now you know how a triple Cancer might experience life. This can be a tough location to focus on career, as your attention is directed elsewhere to putting down roots, starting a family and buying a house. In time, everything should fall into place for you to be able to retire comfortably here. Happiness is an issue that has to be closely looked at with the Moon in the north. You may find that your happiness revolves around setting up a meaningful home life. If that doesn't happen right away, you might begin to feel incomplete as a person. This can result in the opposite of what you yearn for as you end up moving about, changing residences frequently. If this is happening, do ask yourself if the moves are coming from a need to seek new emotional experiences, a need which could be fulfilled in other, more direct, ways.

As with other Moon positions, women usually have an easier time integrating the requirements and pleasures of this location. It can be a great opportunity for a man, however, to become attuned to the joys of a cozy and secure home. And it's a great location for a man to learn how to cook – and really enjoy it. In fact, watch your diet, as both males and females will delight in preparing and eating food at this location. So much the better if this location affords the opportunity to be near lakes, rivers or even near an ocean. If it isn't, do create watery spaces like garden ponds for yourself.

You might as well keep a space in your home for parents or in-laws, since there is a high probability that they will enter your life here. Another thing to be aware of is that circumstances might lead you to an emotional reliance on your mother from this location. So do encourage her to visit, which might fulfil this energy in a positive way.

Gardening skills will come easily here and you may even want to become a farmer for the first time in your life. Business or career activities related to food, real estate and products used in the home should flourish for you as well.

South: Congratulations, you're the local hero! The problem is that the local folk believe they need you body and soul. You are their nurturer – at least for the time being. If you can handle the crowds - with their needs and demands – then this is the place where you will be asked (perhaps begged) to run for public office. In a similar vein, careers in acting or entertainment are also supported. Other careers that require public sensitivity will flourish here, such as in advertising, sales or in the caring field. It's a great location for a healer too. Assistance from a women of wealth or social standing is possible here, as is inheriting a family business or working with your family in a joint endeavour. As with other lunar locations, careers associated with food and items of domestic use are supported and should flourish.

What problems may face you? As you move into the public arena here, life situations may begin to test you. Intimate and personal details of your life may go on public display, and it becomes harder to hide specific facts about yourself. No skeletons in your personal closet? Fine. If some old bones are rattling about, get ready to have them be seen in the light of day. On a more personal note, you will be surprised at how easy it is to express your emotions in public now. This can take the form of anything from an argument with a loved one to a romantic embrace. I say, forget about arguments and use your increased sensitivity and empathy with people at this location to win their support, respect and their business too.

MERCURY

East: Speak out! I think, therefore I am! You will find the right words and others will listen. Like any good philosopher, you can now formulate the right questions and then answer them. You easily become identified with any endeavour requiring you to write, think or network. Want a job on the local transportation system? You'll get it here. Careers in writing, science, medicine, education, in libraries or as a secretary, should all be well supported by this locale.

On the plus side your thinking is as clear as it has ever been. You may find yourself taking on the newspaper's crossword puzzle for entertainment or borrowing books from the library on thinking skills. On the negative side you may become more restless and irritable, with your nerves getting frayed. It's from the need to talk, talk, talk or from rushing about too much. If you find this happening, do keep a serious side open in communicating and stay in touch with those you love or wish to learn from. At this location people think you look younger then you really are, something that is neither positive nor negative.

West: Do you feel tongue-tied and inarticulate in public situations? Fear not, as relief is in sight when you move to this location. There could be a shift now such that your own ideas, new opportunities and an appreciative audience all seem to manifest simultaneously, resulting in your becoming more effective in communicating with the public. This location is, therefore, an easy place to build bridges with others. Be a teacher here, as you are seen as a natural at it Specialist jobs, such as facilitator, dialogue leader, interviewer or even diplomat, are yours for the asking. This is a good location to take on cognitive studies and or to work with younger people. If you are accepting a position as a lawyer or negotiator or writer of business contracts, your career should flourish, as your mind is sharp and clear.

If you have longed for a brainy spouse or partner, this could be a good location to try and meet him or her, since it favours making contacts with intellectual and/or better-educated types. A good place to start looking might be at the work place, with a co-worker or employee coming into your life in this capacity.

What can go wrong here? Lots. The same strengths that this location offers can become a downfall. Communication with others can cause misunderstandings, both with partners and in business situations. Your task is to be careful of the agreements you make now (including marriage agreements) and then stick to them! Carefully ponder the meanings and consequences of these agreements and acknowledge your commitment to fulfilling them *before* signing on the dotted line. Also, your communication skills may disclose differences in opinion that others have on topics that you hold dear. Maturity of intellect will be required such that you can absorb these differences in a spirit of dialogue rather than in debilitating argument or debate.

North: Much to your surprise, you may find it convenient to invite a brother or sister to come and live and work with you now! Here, at this location you can finally bring together the library you have always wanted. And, it's simply a great place if you have always yearned to work from home. This is the perfect placement for tele-working. Set up your operation at home and sell from the Internet. The cosmos will support your efforts. If you have arrived already burnt out from a career or lifetime of hard work, this is a good place to take a sabbatical - to study and do research. Have a large room, as others will like meeting here. Expect lots of buzzy action around the home with your friends and family, but do keep aside some private time as this location encourages an inward assessment of personal goals and desires.

As with most all positions in the north, an interest in real estate may develop here. Specific to this location, however, you may find interests in ecological and environmental pursuits develop along with the ability to write about them for others. Or you could successfully go back to school and get that degree in geology.

Any dangers here? Sure: there is always the other side for us to deal with. At this location, problems can arise from becoming too subjective. Certainly it's important to have a location like this one for thinking about personal goals and desires, but we must take care that this doesn't cut us off from other people's points of view, in turn leaving us intellectually isolated and fragmented. This location, therefore, unlike other angular mercurial ones, is not so great for making contracts or conducting serious negotiations. Keep track of your self-development here by noting if you are merely restless, moving from home to home, which could leave you on a treadmill going nowhere. Also note if your family communication is really good and nurturing, rather than bringing many disputes or disagreements.

South: If you have been drawn to this location at a time when you must ponder long-term life goals (and determine if you are really fulfilling them), then be assured you are at the right place. If living the moment deeply has meant that long-range plans are cloudy , don't be surprised if you find the clarity here to begin seeing some as an unfolding possibility. Education is strongly favoured for you here and now. For this reason teachers will appear to guide you towards establishing a career or profession for yourself. Your organisational abilities are put to use as others begin to appreciate what you can do along those lines. Your ability to plan for the future and evolve strategies to gain objectives may become recognised, and you could become involved in political campaigns or even be asked to run for office yourself! In general you can communicate with people naturally and easily. An ability in writing speeches or dealing with communications, media, printing or publishing is indicated. It's a great location to become a teacher as well. All of these tasks will be fully supported for you by this location.

Don't be surprised if the local paper wants to do a story on you and if finally you even get on TV. And don't be surprised if your phone bills are astronomical here and the mailbox is stuffed with correspondence. Get ready not to shudder if your morning incoming e-mails number in the hundreds as well. In fact, you could become known as the Johnny Appleseed[3] of information bits and bytes. Go ahead and communicate; you do it so well here.

Let's have a look for some problem in all this: You may be tempted to turn to the dark side of the force, not squeamish about massaging the truth to gain your objectives. If this starts to happen, you run the risk of being exposed for untruthfulness. Warning bells should be going off if ambitions are overwhelming your principles. Stick to the truth and don't forget your heart in dealing with others, and this could be a very important location for you on the road of life itself.

VENUS

East: Moving to this location can bring sweetness into your life. The world looks good to you now and things seem more harmonious than before. Hi, good looking! It doesn't matter how you see yourself, others will find you attractive here and you discover how to create the look that appeals. A great location for nailing down that modelling job or to be an entertainer, artist or a (social) party organiser. The cosmos won't support this location for hard work so easily; look to other locations if your profession requires this. I mean, you'd like to balance your life now with some hard work, but there just are so many opportunities for fun parties and romantic interludes that it's hard to really buckle down. The strength of this location can also be the problem. On the plus side it's easy to see life now with a happy outlook, so practise happiness and express beauty! Beauty and happiness are said to be our personal birth-rights so this is a great location to experience them. On the other hand, do remain alert that you are not becoming infatuated with your own beauty. Remember it is the expression of the quality of beauty that makes you beautiful and not just your temporal form.

West: A great place to visit if you are looking for love and partnership. I hope it's not in the middle of the ocean for you, but if it is, buy a boat. If it's in the middle of the Sahara, rent a camel, but do check this location out. Jobs that require social skills and sensitive relating to others are yours for the asking here. Your new-found sense of tact and diplomacy might get you into the entertainment field or public relations. If you have been insensitive to others in the past, there may be a shift now as you become really concerned for their happiness. This in turn can become a healing situation for them and you too. Psychiatrist and shamanistic writer Olga Kharitidi[4] says "healing begets healing", and perhaps it all can start here for you, with happiness as the way. Any downsides to this location? Well, it's not a great place if you want to be a hermit for a while or to live alone. And do watch out for partners who may take more than they give.

North: If you are female this could be the best location to express your earth Goddess side. You find it so very natural to be at one with Gaia here. If you are male, stay alert, you may meet that same, new-born Goddess at this location and learn from her. Are you ready and capable of recognising her? Male or female, this is the location to taste the nectar of a sweet and beautiful home and family life. From your home environment the cosmos will be supportive in establishing activities that are artistic, creative and entertaining. You will be able to create a home that is beautiful and comfortable and will want to entertain close friends in it. This location is probably the best of any to support a situation of emotional closeness with your parents. Expect happiness to come through them and perhaps even an inheritance.
It's an ideal location to establish a small nature reserve and/or a meditative garden. It's difficult to imagine too many problems here, but you could find yourself overeating, especially rich and sweet foods. And the problem of laziness could crop up such that you avoid projects requiring hard work.

South: You are Mr Nice Guy here, or Ms Nice Gal. Change the world by loving humanity from this location, or at least tell someone you love them!

Relationships both professional and social all flow well and benefit you now. Venus-ruled jobs should fall into your lap: art, entertainment, counselling, crafts, and so on. Here, perhaps for the first time, you experience a social or artistic ambition, and it's in tune with your potential, since you do have a good opportunity to be recognised in these areas. Marriage to a partner who furthers your career is a possibility here. This is neither good nor bad by itself of course; it all depends on one's real intentions. Is it real love or might it be merely social climbing?

This is a great location to combine a holiday with contemplation of your next step in a career. Go and enjoy.

MARS

East: You'll want to be a warrior here, so do it correctly, like Castenada: be ever alert, choose your battlefields and learn what 'stalking' means in the sense of a Toltec sorcerer. This is a great location to see the other side of yourself if you think you're usually listless or lazy. Physical (and ego) energy is high and abundant. You may want to begin a program of jogging now or some other physical fitness regimen. It's a good place to compete in sports or to select as a training site. You will be asked to direct others in joint projects, and may be surprised at your self-motivation. Show the world what you can do and, at this location, the world might listen! Your ambitious side emerges and enables you to work harder now than others to achieve your aims.

Is there a downside here? You'd better believe it – a lot can go wrong when Mars is involved. The same energy that makes you feel so robust here can very easily turn, at worst, to aggressiveness or to your becoming rather egotistical and headstrong. Here, more so than at many earth locations, your energy must be focused by intelligence and self-discipline. Do it well and you will achieve. If you become involved in fights or disregard the rights of others, the worse side is manifesting and your potential to achieve at this location is in jeopardy.

West: "We want you on our team", others will plead. And do join in with them, as you will excel. The team can be of sports or business or social organisation. Jobs leading Outward Bound groups or in policing or in the military will be yours for the asking. At the same time be wary: this location, perhaps more so than any other, can be conflict-prone for you, bringing what Jeff Jawer calls "serious battles" and "challenging situations"[5]. This can be a great location to bring some sensual experience back into your life. as both males and females will find a surprising amount of passion emerging in relationships here as well as the desire to break the mould of any old patterns.

So, what can we make of all of our possibilities here? Do get in shape, appreciate your ambitious and hard-working side and enjoy the satisfaction of high energy surging through your body. However, the need to think before you act will be critically important now. And do remain vigilant that you are not running roughshod over the rights and feelings of others. This isn't a moral admonition as much as a way to ensure your happiness and growth at this location.

North: If you are moving here to take up a position in such fields as mining or construction, this location will be very helpful. It's ideal if you run a boxing or weight-training or physical-fitness gym from home; but whatever, if a home type business or pursuit requires a lot of energy, it should work well here. You'll want to build your own home now or at least to keep renovating a rented one non-stop.

That said, this place can entail problems that will require discipline and self understanding to avoid pitfalls. First of all, your professional life may become blocked, as your attention is really focused on your personal, not public, reality. Second, if you are not active and expressive enough, you may have to deal with your own anger and irritability. And lastly, with ego energies high, you could be involved in arguments with family members at home. Right here, at this location, you have the opportunity to examine and release pressures that have been a factor in your psychological makeup for some time. If these pressures seem to be building up and are causing you distress, perhaps this suggestion from the teaching traditions can help: try to contain the contradictions in your belly (the Hara), keep your heart loving and clear, and all the while use the dual energies as the fuel for self understanding.

South: Life is work! No, I've not gone crazy, and you may well come to agree with me if you settle here for a spell. At this location your desire for fame and success matches your drive, ambition and general energetic ability to pursue a career. Your unbroken flow of initiative is such that it may even be surprising to you too. This is a great location for an athletic competition. Your ego energies and competitive juices are at full throttle. In the text of this book I recount how I made an Olympic team when the event was held near this location for me and how energetic and youthful I felt.

Mars is less stressful here than on the other earth directions, but you will still be required to keep pushing your career to its limits to succeed. It's a great place, for example, to be a test pilot or racing driver. In a less dramatic mode you may pursue a career in the military or politics, engineering or management. This location is favoured for working with metals and, in general, most kinds of hard work. It's especially auspicious to undertake tasks that require innovation and the pioneering spirit. Jobs will be offered that call for leadership, otherwise it's best to work hard but alone. Yes, this is a great location to get ahead and therefore feel good about yourself in the world. This type of experience can bring both psychological and material rewards, but since we are dealing with Mars, the problem of proper focus comes into play. You must direct your new-found energy to the tasks at hand and resist the temptation to steam roll over others or to be unethical in getting to the top. Expressing the wrong side of your force here through wrongdoing will provoke resistance in others and could leave your reputation in tatters. Keep your balance at this location and you'll enjoy the rush and get ahead too.

JUPITER

East: Do the blues have you down? Are things a bit grim? Fear not, as your world will begin to change at this location. Events and the people you meet now will present a brighter side of life. This creates a warm and optimistic flow towards others and the world in general. This in turn attracts a response that is equal in warmth, optimism and good will. Your self confidence grows, as it is supported by this location like almost nowhere else. Jobs in teaching, preaching or self-promotion will be yours for the asking. You should find the school here that provides the vocational training you have been longing for. Work for self-knowledge and share your insights with others. It will be natural and beneficial to do this, since in this location you become more and more inclined toward following up interests in religion, philosophy, teaching and law.

In addition to your waistline growing, your circle of friends will also expand here. You might meet people you wouldn't ordinarily expect to encounter. Some of them may number among the rich or famous and powerful. Nice stuff, but do be alert that your new contacts really are part of a growth and learning process for yourself and that you aren't merely hob-nobbing.

If things are going well at this location, you will mature with the inputs of philosophy and religious ideas. Your world view should be broadening and with it you will be gaining a new tolerance to the differences we see in our 'global village'. If you guard against the negative possibilities of self-indulgence, exaggerated self-importance and promising more than you can deliver, this can be a wonderful location for self-development, as you imbibe a nectar of faith, optimism and expanded vision..

West: As the song goes, "I get by with a little help from my friends...". Tim Leary, nearing his death, said, "Whatever you do, do it with friends". On both professional and personal levels, partnerships will flourish and be supportive here. And I mean really supportive. Vacation here with a loved one and see how things get sweeter and problems can be worked out. Try out this location if you are longing to meet someone special. Perhaps not a guaranteed happening, but you are definitely increasing the odds in your favour. You pick out just the right counsellor or lawyer here too, if you need this type of help. The idea is that here you grow and develop *mutually* through your close contacts with other people. This makes the location ideal if you are a mediator, facilitator or negotiator. Other professions supported here will include law, sales and public relations.

Marriage can go well here with a likelihood of it being a fortunate and long-lasting partnership. You might marry someone of wealth or notable social standing. More important, you and your partner are honest with each other and perhaps share spiritual aspirations. You like and mutually support one another in addition to the love you feel.

Is this location a fairy-tale place where your romantic dreams come true? Well, perhaps. You may find yourself taking too much for granted and expecting too much from others at the same time. It's as if the possibilities in yourself and others for mutual growth never quite unfold to the full potential of the situation. You may be naive and exposed to grandiose ideas that don't have substance. I wouldn't fret too much over these difficulties, however. Bring your capacity to give and receive to this location and experience it in fullness. I think you'll be happy you did.

North: Oh, go ahead and put down roots! It felt like you belonged here right from the moment you arrived. Invest in property and watch its value rise. Don't be too surprised if you find a large house to live in, with family relationships better than they have ever been. If there have been problems relating to your parents, now is the time and this is the place for rapprochement with them. You'll come to see that within the limits of their understanding and abilities, they were simply doing their best in raising you; just as you may be doing for your children now. Keep open to the possibility of using your home for a centre of religious, philosophical, social or educational activities. In fact, now, be a philosopher yourself! It comes naturally, as Jeff Jawer declares, "All the knowledge of the universe flows through you here"[6].

This is a likely location to get the news that you have inherited land and propert from parents or family members. Careers in real estate, home construction or renovation are well supported. Farming or businesses related to growing food should also flourish. Remain alert to the need to make adjustments if outmoded religious beliefs are imposed on you by family members or if your home expenses are getting too heavy. But, overall, this should be a fine place for you, with the potential to get your act together, finally adopting a healthy lifestyle that expresses Truth, Love and Wholesomeness.

South: Astrological studies show that a prominent placement of Jupiter on the MC either natally or by transit is very favourable for election to public office. Here, you have moved to a location that brings this same possibility; as a transit in space rather than time, so to speak. With that in mind you can expect to be elected to office, especially if running your campaign from this location. In addition to offering the prospect of prominence in the public sphere, this is a great location in which to achieve a high standing in business, academic or religious activities. Jobs in the publishing or travel industries are also supported. You really want to be honest, reliable and benevolent now, and events (both inner and outer) allow it to happen. You are very willing to make the efforts necessary to achieve your aims; your ambition is strong, as is the thirst to study and learn. In other words, here, more likely than anywhere else, you have the opportunity to become a pillar of society! What an interesting experience that can be, especially if your past has included spells as a revolutionary or nihilist.

You'll want to expand your career or business now, which could mean travelling and meeting people from foreign cultures. That in itself is fine and even expected from this location, but the other side is that you must remain alert – perhaps cautious – to the possibility of over expansion, resulting in cash-flow or other types of 'overreach' problems. Do your homework and plan things carefully during expansion, mixing this with the sense of optimism and ultimate success you feel here. With things going so well in the public sphere, do keep an eye on your relationships at home. If they are suffering, you are being given a warning that a reassessment or rebalancing of your priorities of public vs. private activities and attitudes is in order.

Astrologer Rob Hand points out that Jupiter transits can represent either real growth or growth of fat[7]. At this location you have the opportunity to grow and mature both in your public persona as well as in the core of your being. Don't miss this opportunity.

SATURN

East: "Stop the world, I want to get off" might be the plaintive cry now, as this location may bring you some difficulties and hardships at first. You will be required to finish up incomplete tasks and to get serious about discovering what is truly necessary for the future. If you've been travelling about and living life with a superficial or frivolous attitude, you'll become aware of it here, and it can be a shock. The good news is that here and now you can simplify and strengthen your life in a way that is critical to future growth. There will be no significant expansion at other earth locations if your structures have not been properly developed first at a location like this one. Jeff Jawer (see Appendix 1) reminds us that patience, persistence and self discipline will be required here and will be rewarded with ultimate self-respect and achievement. It's an important learning experience to be able to achieve prominence through your own merit and to know you have done it. It's a confidence and soul-booster all in one.

Positions that require you to work seriously and hard with possible long hours will be supported. By 'supported', I mean that you find you have the will and endurance and focus to do them well. What a boon to have this background support when you have to perform this way!

I have much experience in living at or visiting easterly Saturn locations. This LS aspect is within 5 degrees for me in Moscow. Once I was invited to be a speaker at a Russian conference: Saturn's effects began immediately as I had to wait in line over 4 hours just to clear customs to get into the country. Then after my first talk I was stricken with a fever (I have Saturn in Aries, often associated with fevers) and was bed-ridden for 3 days. On the other hand, I was well cared for by loving folk and had the experience of living in a Russian flat in the heart of Moscow. Upon my recovery I returned to give my final talk and, as I heard later, was well appreciated by the audience. See the pattern?

At two major turning points in my life, unbeknown to me, I lived at easterly Saturn LS locations. The first one was in Ankara, Turkey, where I was unable to be the 'swinging single' I would have wished to be. Left with no option to follow those energies, I was forced inward to more serious activities of search and study – resulting in learning that was to become the backbone of my pursuits for the next two decades of my life. Later, for a period of some months, I lived in Jerusalem, a location that also has an easterly LS Saturn for me. Here, though short of money and comforts, I was able to focus on my pursuits, partaking of the three great traditions centred there of Judaism, Christianity and Islam, learning the power of ritual observance for the first time in my life. This experience was to prove invaluable to me when years later my gaze turned eastward to include India and its traditions.

Limitations at this location will bring a sense of realism concerning the discipline you need to master your world. The words of German philosopher Nietzche (1844-1900) sum up this location at its most difficult: "That which does not kill us makes us stronger". But don't worry, things shouldn't get that difficult, and the reward of personal accomplishment awaits you here if you can stay focused on the issues. Your personal affirmation for this location could be, "Regardless of my duties, I can and will lighten up and enjoy".

West: Have you escaped so far from relationships that carry responsibilities? Well, here you will have to pay much more attention to them and work carefully, avoiding shortcuts in your dealings with others. This is a great location if you are establishing a business partnership or need to experience what a serious commitment to another is all about. Expect to have to build on such partnerships, taking on responsibility and exercising discipline. This is great for character building but could leave you feeling short changed for warmth and love. Jobs or family situations that require you to care for others are ideal here, as you have the focus to get the job done. Partners who are mature and reliable can appear for you as well. Their help can be the beginning of the road to success, as the firm and reliable mutual support between you is just what is needed to get ahead. Professions such as law, business organisation, management and anything to do with formulating contracts will be highly supported here.

If you are of mature years and come to this location without a spouse, you may well marry the career-oriented partner you long for. Your ability to work hard and conscientiously will naturally match his or her ability. Moving here with a spouse can reveal lots of issues that will take the relationship one way or the other – strengthening it or breaking it up: just don't expect the relationship to remain the same.

If it all goes wrong you'll become negative in relationships. Immediate action will then be required, as the relationship dynamic, central to this location, must be dealt with before things spiral out of control. Your birthright here, however, is to find mature and stable partnerships. The long-haul is supported now, so do move in that direction and learn about the positive experience of commitment. Your personal affirmation for this location could be "I can and will radiate warmth and love in my relationships".

North: There is good news here if your career involves activities centred around real estate, building trades, contracting, farming and/or the manufacture of domestic products. The bad news? Most people don't find this an easy place to live. It often denotes that you will be required to shoulder heavy home or family responsibilities. But then again, this location supports you in successfully carrying those responsibilities through. This is an important dynamic to come to see about the earth's various locations for us. At a given location we are faced with issues demanding our involvement, and at the same time the local situation provides what we need to respond successfully. For example, one client found this location ideal to provide a proper home environment for her handicapped daughter. In addition to caring for her daughter she worked hard from home, building a good reputation as a journalist after years of effort. In fulfilling her life responsibilities here, she developed strength of character and a level of self-respect that brought inner peace. She told me she wouldn't have wanted to live anywhere else.

This is the best location to 'get away from it all' and have a serious rethink of what your life is all about, overcoming the past and planning to begin anew. It is the ideal place to be a hermit or take a secluded retreat. On the other hand, as already stated, family issues and deep felt insecurities can make day-to-day life difficult. Your personal affirmation for this location could be "I can and will radiate warmth and love in my home and family life".

South: There is no better location if your career requires focused effort, possible long hours and careful planning. This type of effort will be rewarded, whereas shortcuts or sloppy work will come back to haunt you. One client, for example, instinctively picked out this location to be a junior doctor at a hospital where long hours and responsibility were required. His efforts there were rewarded with solid professional growth and finally recognition. Employment in management or financial planning should be yours for the asking. And you will be appreciated, as a talent for farsighted managerial ability seems to manifest naturally here. You may even be able to attain high position and wealth at this location. You are seen as a leader who is able to provide stability to a situation and guide organisational growth along traditional lines.

Along with increased responsibility at this location, you will be able to make decisions and act upon them. This is no small matter, as you now have the opportunity to experience the magic of what the German philosopher Goethe (1749-1832) called "Decision Power". He wrote, "The moment one definitely commits oneself, then providence moves too. All sorts of things occur to help one that would not otherwise have occurred. A whole stream of events issues from the decision, raising in one's favour all manner of events and meetings and material assistance which no man would have dreamed would come his way."

A difficult consequence of this location is its 'karmic' implications. A steep fall from power awaits if you are tempted to compromise your principles for the sake of ambition. Transiting Saturn crossed President Nixon's south point (and Midheaven) within days of the Watergate break-in that he had authorised. At this location you are moving to this situation in space rather than in time! Another problem here could be the slow progress or obstacles faced in the rise to prominence. If you do feel this frustration, dig in deeper to accomplish your aims, as Saturn will support your patience and diligence. Your personal affirmation for this location could be "I can and will express the joyous elements of my public role."

URANUS

East: You've heard about it, you've read about it, you may have even felt its call, but, ready or not, here you can do it: reinvent yourself! If you have longed for more originality in your life, more excitement, and to break away from old patterns, this is the location to experience this. Of course, you should get ready for feeling weird and having life become more like a roller coaster. It will be easy to give yourself a new look and you may even wish to experiment with a more open sexuality here. You will meet and attract friends who are radically different from the ones you used to have. Yes, they will be more exciting and original, but don't expect rock-solid reliability from them, either. This location favours individuality which can make long-standing relationships problematical. You'll need freedom and your partner will have to understand this, hopefully allowing you to throw out many of the spoken or unspoken rules surrounding the relationship. This is a great location to study astrology or other systems that move you toward liberation and self-understanding. You will come into contact with groups that forward human rights in many forms. If any such groups need a spokesperson, the task is yours for the asking. Be aware that you will have quite a bit of restless energy here, so use it consciously. In an example in the text, I noted that feminist Simone de Beauvoir accomplished her radical ground-breaking work with this placement at her home in Paris, France.

West: Even though you may see yourself as a relatively logical and evenly balanced type of person, at this location you will have a dramatic impact on the people you meet. As Jeff Jawer writes, "...people may find you magnetic and brilliant or weird and strange"[8]. Suddenly you could be a reformer or what Tim Leary called a 'change agent'[9], waking folk up and challenging them to see their rigid patterns (others may simply see you as a troublemaker however). If your relationships have been 'ho-hum' and in a rut, get ready to have this part of your reality turned upside down. The good news? You will have personal break-throughs and fresh insights coming through and because of others. The bad news? Marriage or other committed relationships can suffer here and things can get hectic.

This is a great location to be an investigative reporter or gossip column-ist or even a social scientist studying the new order of things. Your insights about the new social combinations and permutations developing in the community are excellent because you are living them. In business matters this is a favour-able location to collaborate with others on unique telecommunications or IT projects. The more unique and far–out, the better. You and your colleagues might become very successful selling your product/idea for much money. Your personal affirmation at this location could be "I will remain centred in that which is permanent and eternal though I live in dynamic and creative change".

North: If you have ever felt uneasy that there are truths, patterns or ghosts of seasons past that you still haven't recognised consciously, you have come to the right location! Here is a place, as Jeff Jawer says[10], "..for breaking of the past, letting go of old patterns and discovering new ways to live your life". This augers well, but there are problems too. A home or family life will be difficult here, as family requirements seem to clash with your individual needs and attitudes. It's hard to put down roots and take on responsibilities, as events - and your own yearnings - require you to be free to express your new inner realisations. This is an advantageous location to take on unique, non-typical and non-traditional endeavours from your home base. This may be the best strategy for processing the restless and rebellious energy you feel here. Activities in telecommunications or Information Technology from your home would be ideal. Take care not to become addicted to long hours surfing the Net, alone and a seeming eccentric genius in the eyes of others. You really like the idea of being able to live life free of social pressure here. Finally, you will be able to establish yourself as a 'lifestyle pioneer', though don't be disap-pointed if others see you as merely eccentric. Whatever you do here, from working with computers to unisex haircutting, remain flexible to the onrush of events and situations in your life. Your personal affirmation for this loca-tion could be "I will remain as thoughtful as possible about the new inputs into my life, consciously integrating them to create a new and better me".

South: If you have been wishing to either kick-start or improve your career in science, technology, the occult or even in astrology, then this loca-tion is mother earth's helpful response. Additionally, being self-employed or somewhat independent in your career pursuits will also be favourable here. The point is, opportunities to establish yourself along these lines will seem to manifest miraculously, like a lightning bolt out of the blue[11]. On the other hand, clinging to a career that is locking you into an autocratic structure is going to become a big problem: it simply won't hold up. Inwardly you will begin to rebel against a professional environment that doesn't give you the freedom you now need, and outwardly others will begin to challenge your position. So be alert and ready for change. Expect the unexpected and be ready to flow with it – life as Tai Chi. Jobs at this location that require originality and some risk taking will be yours for the asking. If you are drawn to radical or revolutionary groups of any form (social or political or human change), others may ask you to lead them. And if you lead with originality as your personal beacon, you should be fine. Become the lightning bolt rather than the victim who is struck by it! Your personal affirmation for this location could be "In the midst of changing circumstances, I will remain conscious of what I am doing in the world, making the necessary changes in order to experience a new life".

NEPTUNE

East: Are you weary of everyday reality? Do you feel ground down by the burden of your practical problems? You've come to the right place, as here you can turn toward nurturing your life's dreams. There is a saying from the East that is pertinent for this location: "A knife is neither good nor bad, but he who grasps it by the blade is surely in error". The possibility of an erroneous grasping of situations and their meanings is a real issue at this location. Your strengths here can also become downfalls if maturity and conscious awareness are not maintained. What are some of these strengths, which also require you to remain master of your ship of self? Well, first of all, your sensitivity seems to increase dramatically at this location. Your psyche may be flooded with new impressions and sensations. This can help to draw you like a magnet to new creative aspects of yourself as well as to more spiritual or psychic influences, some of which may carry you to 'wondrous visions and holy truths'[12]. Another plus here is that your creative imagination becomes more active than you have experienced before. This can be ideal for creative projects of all kinds, with those in film, photography, theatre or the fine arts and crafts perhaps being most favoured. Ideas sensed or perceived here can become the stuff of significant creative projects either at this location or at another place and time. Whenever these ideas are brought to fruition, this location will have been the birthplace for the original creative insight.

A good strategy in using the energy of this location could be to become active helping others, perhaps in a caring organisation. And yes, you will enjoy films as never before. Their story lines now speak to you directly. Do take walks by the sea (if possible), allowing its vastness and beauty to inspire you. You have a real opportunity now to answer the famous question, "Who am I?" positively, as your spiritual world is ever present. If the sensitivities of this location begin to make you fearful, take the teaching of Sufi Sheikh Muzaffer of Istanbul[13] to heart. Questioning the validity of doubting itself, he taught his students, "Doubt your doubts!".

West: Have you ever felt baffled by your partner's changing attitudes toward you? Well, here is a location that will open many new doors to your perceptions about this. As with the other placements of Neptune in the earth's cardinal directions, you will find a rush of sensitivity to and in yourself. This time the sensitivity centres on the attitudes, intentions, desires and motivations of not only your partners but also the public at large. This is a wonderful placement if you have to judge artistic and creative trends in the literary field or in fashion or film or the TV industry. It might even make you a good psychic healer or even a karmic or intuitive astrologer[14].

Another strong possibility for you here is to meet and establish a spiritually based relationship either with a guru type or with someone you love. In Indian scriptures it is stated that one should consider one's marriage partner to be a physical manifestation of the divine. Some scriptures state that the love of one's spouse, when rightly comprehended, is an essential part of the process of enlightenment or moving toward the realisation of the Self[15]. In his corresponding Neptune interpretation for ACG, Jeff Jawer says it directly: "The place where you can marry God. It is the projection of the God principle on a partner". Alas, one must face the possibility of less happy outcomes at this location as well. The key to success here is discernment to a high degree. Without it, relationships don't become a source of spiritual uplift but rather cause great disappointment. Your trust in others becomes shattered as partnerships and legal situations become problems, with others taking advantage of you. You yearn for high standards from your partners here, and it's all too easy to refuse to see things as they really are. What to do? Perhaps it's best to surrender to Neptune's higher requirements for spiritual uplift at this location. This necessitates that you maintain a high quality in your true intentions and then to act in accordance with them. And remember that your partnerships will require clarity in communication, clear boundaries and most of all mutual respect, without undercurrents of manipulation. In summary, the positive side of this location is that the opportunity to experience "right relationship" may be offered to you here. Are you ready for it?

North: With a bit of luck, at this location you will find something you may not have ever experienced before; your spiritual home! This home might be a house or the wider environment of nature around you. The Neptunian sensitivities of this location give you a mystical attunement, a bonding link between your immediate environment of great nature and what seems to be the core of your being. At this place your body can sense, taste and feel, positively vibrating, the possibility of a rebirth to a higher level of refinement[16]. Once again with Neptune in a cardinal direction, your best strategy may be to surrender to its highest possibilities and to be vigilant to this placement's pitfalls. Ponder your spiritual ideals. Strive to create a home that is quiet, meditative and peaceful, respecting those ideals. Yes, moving to a monastery or ashram might tempt you and would be supported here. Pursuing artistic and creative endeavours from your home is very favourable. Photography in or of your environment is strongly supported. Psychic activities will be all too easy and only positive for you if balanced with the totality of your spiritual understanding. Keep in mind that spirit beings who contact you here also are evolving such that their limited vistas might not represent deep levels of cosmic understanding.

Thinking in terms of putting down roots at this location will be difficult because things seem so magical and ethereal that such considerations are unfocused and far from your immediate considerations. Your inner life will be so filled now that career concerns will also be difficult to keep in focus, unless perhaps you work in a caring profession, a very creative artistic job or at least in a work site located near the sea.

So, what are the indications that you are not achieving your best Neptunian possibilities at this location? You may live in a haunted house! Family relations may become confused and/or deceptive, with disturbing undertones that are causing you to suffer. Certainly don't ignore your mortgage or your partner's sexual needs. Always read the fine print of your lease or property deed and never succumb to the temptation of being a drug-dealer from your home, or you may end up in a secluded institution called jail! There is an old saying about our being naked when we are born into this world and also when we leave it. Therefore what we really have is what is inside us. At this location you can develop inner being, your real treasure and true security.

South: Have you usually thought that you had a clear idea of what you wanted to do or accomplish in life? If so, this location will cause you to become less than certain. And 'less than certain' will be experienced as an unexpected but urgent need to reassess your life goals. As with the other Neptunian placements, you will experience an onrush of sensitivity, this time about your public life and role. This sensitivity can cause confusion but can also put you in touch with spiritual intuitions of the highest degree. Yes, once again, when Neptune calls the shots, you must use it or lose it as far as your spiritual growth potential and very sanity are concerned! On the positive side you will meet people here and be given opportunities to establish yourself in new areas. Business itself is not excluded if it is creative and holds to humanitarian principals, but most directly favoured are opportunities for musicians, actors, painters, photographers, movie makers, psychologists, and various occult pastimes. You might become a guru type here, especially if you teach or exemplify an ego-emptying philosophy[17]. Work that you might do for others in hospitals or charities is strongly supported at this location as well. It is important to explore all of your new opportunities, having the courage to follow through on them even if they are uncertain for you. As with Neptune in the north discussed above, you must "doubt your doubts" if feelings of unworthiness arise. The point is that it will become critical for you at this location to feel right about your livelihood, no ifs, ands or buts. That's simply the way Neptune's influence works. If you try and buck this, then all those other Neptunian type things happen like scandal and erosion of your power and capacities at work. For example, Richard Nixon had Neptune exactly south of Washington, DC, and he paid the price there for his attempts at underhandedness[18].

Wherever we may reside, at this time we are all feeling the need to unfold a vision of a new self and a new world for ourselves. The good news is that your personal vision waits for you to reach out to it at this location. So make that special effort and connect with it, possibly leading to the biggest next step that you will experience for many years.

Though you may become inspired here, Neptune can leave you feeling sluggish when it comes to worldly action Therefore, great advice for this location can be found in one of Goethe's couplets: "Whatever you can do, or dream you can, begin it! Boldness has genius, magic, and power in it. Begin it now!"

PLUTO

East: Moving to or travelling through an earth location where you have Pluto angular (a cardinal direction on your relocated Local Space chart) is going to be profound. You will live life very fully and intensely now. That intensity can range from a sober assessment of your ability (or inability) to transform yourself, to the experience of a total upheaval and consequent change in your life. Events push you to the limit so you can see what really is true about yourself. The point to remember is that the things happening now, though possibly concentrated or extreme, are necessary for your growth, and that anything falling away in your life will clear the space for a new flower in the future. Jim Lewis said, "Pluto burns the fields for a new planting"[19].

With Pluto in the east you will be able to bring a new kind of microscopic focus into your life. You seem to be able to zoom in on yourself and others in a way that can make you and them quite uncomfortable. At its most powerful, you begin to see reality as energy! This ability is described as a developmental necessity by the Yaqui sorcerer Don Juan[20]. You now have a kind of x-ray vision of the subtle forces working around yourself and others. This perception is different than that found at locations with Uranus or Neptune on the east because you find that here, with Pluto, you can consciously use your x-ray type insights to, at best, regenerate yourself and at worst, to manipulate others. At this location you have the willpower and endurance to carry out your regeneration or manipulations. The key is to be aware of these powers, alert not to pursue selfish activities that fly in the face of your possible redemption and spiritual development. Your sensitivities may make you most comfortable away from others. Whatever you do, secretive or underground work is favoured. You'll be great as a private detective, a miner or a scientist specialising in atomic projects. The location is very supportive of self-empowerment work as in the teachings of Don Juan[21] or the "work on yourself" as proposed by the teacher Georg Gurdjieff (1872-1949)[22].

West: Here your x-ray vision turns to a profound intuitive ability to read the motivations and attitudes of others, both personal partners and society at large. As with Pluto in all positions, you will find a big range of possible outcomes. The choice is always ours to make. Here you have an opportunity to create a real and deep dynamic of constructive co-operation with others, or you will become involved in titanic and energy-draining struggles with them. What is for sure, however, is that you will meet powerful partners here, perhaps resulting in drastic changes in your life. If you are open to the possibilities of transformation – which means a give and take in complete honesty – things can go well, with new depths being realised. Otherwise you will suffer struggles of 'dominate or be dominated'. As Jeff Jawer says of this configuration, "Pluto is a furnace and here it's the furnace of partnership". Take care with business relationships, as power plays can result in lawsuits. Your intuitive insights will support you admirably here if you are a lawyer, judge or psychologist. Or you may find a psychiatrist or lawyer or another in a professional capacity who can really help you to see the blocks to living the way you would like. As Pluto is not completely comfortable in the west, you will have to make specific and positive efforts to achieve co-operative and transformative results. Or as Steve Cozzi advises, "Psychological preparation, like speaking softly and carrying a big stick, is very appropriate in this place"[23]. If you are strong and are able to face what can be painful truths in relationship, then new partnerships and understandings will be your reward at this location.

North: I find it useful to see Pluto's various positions in the cardinal Earth directions as synonymous with the Greek myth of the Hero's Journey. It goes like this: starting with Pluto in the east, extreme events cause a serious upheaval and subsequent loss for our hero. Shattered and without an idea of what to do, our hero seeks out a powerful counsellor for help and advice. This powerful partner is symbolised by Pluto in the west. The powerful ally lays out a plan of action and provides our hero with one or more magical devices to help in what will be a dangerous journey. Armed with nothing more than his (her) own wits and few magical boons from the ally, our hero embarks on nothing less than a journey to the underworld, where he (she) will confront dangerous archetypal elements representing both the devils of society and his (her) own repressed side. The goal seems to be to recover what was lost, but it's really about the redemption of our hero in the Plutonian furnace of his/her own psychological underworld. This underworld journey *is* Pluto in the north![24] If our hero is successful, using absolutely all of the skills and magical tricks available to reclaim that which was lost, he (she) returns to the world of daylight to inform and show others the possibility of redemption and the potentiality of rising again, reborn from the ashes of a formerly dead-end life. This return is Pluto in the south (the MH or top of the ecliptic chart), with the cycle of death and rebirth completed.

It is doubtful that your stay at this location will actually require you to descend into a Greek mythological underworld, so what might be expected? Events may require that you regenerate your family life, including relations with your parents. If you don't, you'll find yourself in challenges and battles with them. Skeletons in the family closet and any dark secrets about yourself are likely to be exposed, a painful but necessary process if you are ever to be freed from them. Watch out for property transactions here, as they may become a cause for a great power struggle. Any suppressed feelings will pop out at you as health issues, in the form of such things as skin rashes. This is one of the few locations where you can favourably express the energy with occult activity in your home. It's an absolutely marvellous location for home study in geology, ecology or conservation. If possible, mine Uranium ore! The location is thought to heighten abilities in dowsing and any activity that focuses on what is underground. So, if you are applying for the job of an undertaker, it's yours for the asking here.

South: Whether or not you have previously done any personal homework exploring your psychological basement and purifying your deepest desires (as described above), at this location those desires will be expressed through your profession. Suddenly you are able to bring the Plutonian x-ray vision, with its concomitant intuitive, occult powers, to bear, influencing people in power. The question and challenge here will now revolve around the issues of your life direction. Where are you going? What are you doing? How are you going about it?[25] If you are on the right track, you can become a powerful agent of change for the better of all. You might undertake a spiritual mission that could regenerate elements of society. You may make an impact by being good at politics or other forms of public work, research, financial management, physics and/or an intuitive type of astrology. More unusual talents such as healing, clairvoyance or prophes can come to the fore. The issue is really one of your integrity. As Cozzi states it, "In this locality (both) the transforming and corrupting influences of power await you"[26]. You will be able to judge which track you are taking (transformation or corruption) by the reactions you experience here. If you become engaged in power struggles, or are being exposed by others, if you seem to lurch from one professional upheaval to another, your warning bells must ring loudly and require an urgent assessment of your methods of achieving success. Pluto locations will simply not allow you to violate any rules about the misuse of power. It appears to give you that power here just for that reason, offering you the choice to use it or abuse it[27]. At this location, you'll feel the need to change and transform, taking control of things around you,. But doing this with dictatorial tendencies and selfish personal agendas may cause you lots of woe. Take care!

NOTES

1. Yoga Vasista.

2. "Narrative" is used here in the sense of the story we see as our personal history.

3. The story of Johnny Appleseed is from American folklore. He travelled the length and breadth of the eastern part of the USA, scattering apple seeds taken from his cloth sack. The story attributes the great number apple trees in that part of America to him.

4. *Entering the Circle*, by Olga Kharitidi, Thorsens, 1997.

5. See Jeff's deliniations in Appendix 1.

6. ibid.

7. *Planets in Transit*, by Rob Hand, Para Research, 1976.

8. See Jeff's deliniations in Appendix 1.

9. *Flashbacks*, by Timothy Leary, 1983, Tatcher/Putman Books.

10. See Jeff's deliniations in Appendix 1.

11. It is interesting to note that in a cosmological system based on the Samkhya philosophy, Uranus represents the (lightening) bolt of inspiration from spirit consciousness (Chaitanya) to one's intellect (Buddhi). Hopefully this can be integrated by one's ego (Ahamkar) to bring forth inspired action rather than merely unintegrated, cranky and restless behaviour.

12. See Jeff's deliniations in Appendix 1.

13. Halveti order. Their practice seems to centre on the use of "Zykr", a chanted mantra.

14. The great astrologer Dane Rudhyar felt that Neptune was a more apt ruler of astrology than Uranus.

15. Brihadaranyaka Upanishad: " Verily, it is not for the sake of the husband that the husband is dear, but for the sake of the Self. And it is not for the sake of the wife that the wife is dear, but for the sake of the Self..... And when the Self has been seen, when the Self has been heard, when the Self has been reflected upon, and when the Self has been known, then everything is known."

16. A Hassidic song, performed by the late Rabbi Shlomo Carlebach, sums up your highest possibilities here. It goes, "Return again, return again, return to the land of your soul. Return to who you are, return to what you are, return to where your born and be born again..... Return again, return again, return to the land of your soul...."

17. The Hassidic tradition has a very elegant way of approaching this. In it, one 'turns'. Turning is a process where the ego is neither suppressed or emptied. Rather, one's ego is turned away from the normal promptings of body and mind to those of a higher order as its guiding light.

18. Notice that would be the same as NE on the MH line of his ACG map. See page 164 of *The Astro*Carto*Graphy Book of Maps*, by Lewis and Guttman, Llewellyn Publications. US presidents Harry Truman and Dwight Eisenhower were much more fortunate with Jupiter exactly South for each of them at Washington, D.C.

19. ACG booklet that comes with 'official' ACG maps. Jim Lewis, 1976.

20. See the various works of Carlos Castanada about the technique of 'seeing'. For example, from "Uno Mismo", an Argentine magazine, Feb. 1997, Castanada states, "Shamans like Don Juan assert that all human beings have the capacity to see energy directly as it flows in the universe.... Shamans maintain that perception is assembled at this point (the assemblage point); that the energy that flows in the universe is transformed here into sensory data, and that the sensory data is later interpreted, giving as a result the world of everyday life....The pragmatic value of perceiving energy directly as it flows in the universe for a man of the 21st century or a man of the 1st century is the same. It allows him to enlarge the limits of his perception and to use this enhancement within his realm.."

21. Astrologers will note the Plutonian characteristics of Don Juan as described by Castanada also in the interview in "Uno Mismo", Feb. 1997. Castanada says, "Shamans like Don Juan are essentially practical. For them there only exists a predatory universe in which intelligence or awareness is the product of life and death challenges. ...(Don Juan) said that in order to navigate into the unknown like a shaman does, one needs unlimited pragmatism, boundless sobriety and guts of steel".

22. "One of the strongest motives for the wish to work on yourself is the realisation that you may die at any moment – only you must first realise this". Quote of a Gurdjieff aphorism taken from the wall of the study house at the Chateau du Prieure at Fontainebleau. Those wishing to explore where the contemporary Gurdjieff work has led via the inputs of John Bennett, Anthony Blake and physicist David Bohm (Dialogue) are referred to Blake's Web site, The DuVersity, http://duversity.org/

23. Steve Cozzi, *Planets in Locality*, 1988, Llewellyn Publications.

24. The Greeks called Pluto "Hades, the god of the Underworld". For a comprehensive introduction to mythological Pluto (and all the astrological parameters), see *Mythic Astrology*, by Guttman & Johnson, 1993, Llewellyn Publications.

25. These questions are a direct quote from the insights of noted astrologer Rob Hand. Refer to his classic work *Planets in Transit*, Para research, 1976, the section on Pluto conjunct Midheaven.

26. Steve Cozzi, *Planets in Locality*, 1988, Llewellyn Publications.

27. I believe that Jim Lewis was overly fearful of this position in his writings on ACG lines. His choice for you at this type of location isn't a very optimistic one: either "despotism or extreme antisociality". See the booklet accompanying official ACG maps, Astro*Carto*Graphy, 1976, page 27.

APPENDIX THREE

PLANETARY LINES IN YOUR HOUSE

by Angel Thompson

The Sun

The Sun is the light of the chart and here is where your ego is strongest - where vision, honor, and prestige are obvious. Objects placed on this line seem important or distinguished in some way: they are noticed and personalised. Colors associated with the Sun are gold, bright yellow and orange. Its shape is round.

In the house, the Sun line is a good place to display pictures of yourself, awards, trophies, certificates, or objects that are particularly significant for you. The temperature of the Sun is very hot and dry, making it an ideal line upon which to dry laundry or dehydrate herbs. It is also a good line for sun rooms, sportsrooms, playrooms, card rooms, ovens, fireplaces, rooms where tools, knives or chemicals are stored and for places holding coin collections, gold, jewelry, ornaments, or objects that give pleasure. The Sun also rules all the lights in the house. You will feel more powerful and 'at home' on your Sun line.

The Moon

The Moon rules sense perceptions, nurturing and mothering skills. Here is where you are most sensitive and vulnerable. Objects placed on the Moon line tend to be memorable, sentimental or in some way connected to home, family, or country. The Moon line is a popular place, racing with the pulse of humanity, good for placement of the family bulletin board. Things change and are impermanent on this line (like cut flowers). Its cool, watery nature is passive and gentle, making it a very positive place for plants and animals. Its shape is curved, waved or concave and its colors are silvery and pale blue.

In the house, it rules places where cleaning supplies or other fluids are stored as well as nurseries, both for plants and babies, cradles, gardens, alcoves, closets, cupboards, pools of water, the family room, bathroom, laundry room, the kitchen and the bedroom. If you want to be more sensitive, sleep on your Moon line and you'll have great dreams.

Mercury

Mercury is a neutral planet and is influenced by whatever it's near. It is a youthful line where events happen quickly. Communication is a major focus on a Mercury line, making it a good place to store your papers or records. However small worries can become big problems here with a tendency to over-exaggerate the mundane aspects of life, so don't put your bills on this line. It's a good place to do your mental work, as words have great power. Symbols and ideas flow easily along a Mercury line, making it an ideal place for your type-writer, telephone or computer. Mercury is associated with thin lines, clear objects and is fluid and flexible, like quicksilver. Its colors range from pale orange through violet, silvery blue and crystal.

In the house it rules the chimney, corridors, ducts, gutters, hallways, stairways, steps, pipes and conduits such as the electric, gas and water lines, as well as children's rooms, libraries and other places of communication. You are apt to feel young and lively on a Mercury line.

Venus

Venus represents affection, aesthetics and moods. Here is where sensations, values and indulgences are highlighted. A 'ladies line', Venus grants physical beauty and charm to objects and people. Memories give pleasure and objects are admired for their worth or attractiveness. A Venus line is a popular line, good for social activities, friendly feelings, sweet perfume and designer clothes. It is also a line that feeds addictions to sex, money, food or drugs. Venus lines are strictly Mae West curves, but they tend to be moist, damp or cloudy. Colors associated with Venus are bright green, emerald, aquamarine, yellow, copper and brass.

In the house, Venus rules places where money or other valuables are stored, flower gardens, dressing rooms, art studios, drawing rooms, window, rugs, cosmetics, costumes, fine art and basic food storage. A Venus line is where you indulge yourself, so be sure not to keep the Godiva chocolates there.

Mars

Mars represents physical strength and the ability to assert yourself. A Mars line energizes all of life's activities. Relationships seem competitive and life moves faster on this 'man's line', making it a good place for your stationary bike or that special calendar of 'hunks'. Mars is hot and dry and its color is red or fiery. It rules pointed objects like knives and swords and in the house it rules places where machines, tools and knives are kept. However Mars is an impulsive line, so even though Mars rules firearms it's not a good place to keep your Colt 45.

Mars in the house rules fireplaces, candles, stoves, ovens and other places where fire is used. A word of caution. Fires may start on a Mars line, so don't store chemicals, paints or other flammable materials unless there is good ventilation. You feel strong and 'manly' on a Mars line.

Jupiter

Jupiter is the planet of expansion and good luck and is said to bring success, social acceptance, rich and powerful people, status and conformity. It is associated with publishing, law, politics, religion, sports and gambling. Objects placed on the Jupiter line may appear larger than life, prestigious, or even a bit pretentious, making it a good place for your tiara, pictures of you and important people, or for displaying your Oscar. Jupiter rules large, full objects like flags and dressers. Its colors are purple, violet and deep blue, and its shape is tall, rectangular or columnar. Jupiter is windy and moist, a condition that will bring dry rot, blow the hardware off doors, and other wind-oriented problems.

In the house, Jupiter lines are suited to family altars, shrines, libraries, studies, stables, barns, balconies, attics, air conditioners, fans and forced-air heating units. You may feel lucky and more philosophical on a Jupiter line.

Saturn

Saturn is just the opposite of Jupiter. Objects may seem small and dense, limiting or restricting. This is a good line to display rules, regulations and official certificates. Saturn is dry, cold and brittle and rules heavy objects like pianos. A Saturn line is very stable and supportive, but things tend to age along this line (making it ideal for fake antiques). Just don't sit here for too long or you'll wither before your time. Saturn lines are thrifty, ideal for cutting the budget or coupons. It represents the foundations of your life and your home. Saturn shapes are square and box-like and its color is black.

In the house, Saturn rules the safe or strongbox, the foundation, the floors and basement, storage areas especially for vegetable, cold areas, formal rooms, offices in the home, brick walls, rock gardens and the roof. You feel safe (or old) on a Saturn line.

Uranus

Uranus is associated with electricity and extreme cold, making it ideal for the freezer or very cold storage. There is an inventive capability plus a certain restlessness, a longing to be free, to rebel, to be unique on a Uranus line. Objects placed here appear unusual, odd or of great antiquity. There may be disruptions or interruptions. Objects tend to break up, break down, or break through on this line. For example, the window on the Uranus line is the one the kids always break. Colors associated with Uranus are ultra-marine, brilliant or electric colors, plaids, checks, unusual patterns and extremely pointed or jagged shapes.

In the house, Uranus rules electrical appliances, electrical wiring, the fuse box, the formal living room and the sprinkler system. A Uranus line is a perfect line for trying something new.

Neptune

Neptune is associated with illusions of all kinds like photography, film, romantic idealism, religion or invisible things like X-rays and germs. A Neptune line is creative and imaginative; sacred objects find prominence; others are sensitized, subdued and idealized. Neptune dissolves anything it touches and tends to mystify or hide things; if you put something on a Neptune line it may disappear. Grey, purple, lavender or sea green colors are associated with Neptune, as are irregular shapes and glass. Neptune is watery or gaseous and rules poisons or other toxic liquid materials. Neptune lines often suffer insect damage or problems with leaks or wet areas that can debilitate what appears to be solid.

In the house, it rules hidden areas, behind walls, rear or side doors, drainage ditches, gutters and the fire escape. A Neptune line is good for dreaming or praying.

Pluto

Pluto represents the transformative process and a Pluto line puts you in touch with basic issues of survival. You may feel powerful and in control, or isolated and alone. On this line, objects appear to be dramatically good or evil and may even have a transformative effect on others. Pluto colors are crimson, dark brown, maroon, magenta and dark red. Its shape is hard and dense. Pluto lines are also secret places, and like Neptune, can make objects disappear. Pluto rules termites and other tiny insects, fungi and mold, and can eat away at what you thought was forever.

In the house, Pluto rules the compost pile, the toilets and waste disposal systems, the exhaust vents, the septic tank and sewer drains. Since Pluto isolates and alienates, don't put your telephone on a Pluto line or no-one will ever call you. A Pluto line is where you're continually tested and challenged. Use this line to eliminate rubbish, both real and psychological.

APPENDIX FOUR

Two Articles By Michael Erlewine

The following article was first published in 1977 in the 6th number of the Cosmecology Bulletin as published by Charles A. Jayne. Although astrologers had worked with the Horizon System before, Erlewine was the first to define the concept of Local Space as presented here. In particular, the combining of celestial positions (stars, planets, etc.) with directions on the globe (cities, places, etc.) and the concept of relocating towards a planet first appeared here. This was before the advent of the home computer, and Erlewine had worked out the tedious mathematics of Local Space first on a scientific calculator and later on one of the programmables. Today programs that calculate Local Space charts are available on many of the more popular computers.

The Astrology of Local Space
"There seem to be several distinct levels or dimensions to our life, and depending upon the clarity of the day, our awareness may be centered in a dimension ranging from the very mundane on up through an occasional sharing in some sort of more transpersonal or cosmic form of consciousness. It is becoming clear to many astrologers in these times that this multi-dimensionality of our life perhaps may best be represented and examined through a series of astrological charts; and that an attempt to extract all levels of our life - the many quite different dimensions - from the geocentric ecliptic chart alone is bound to be a frustrating experience. In a word it is unnecessary.

Astrologers make constant use of three very different systems of coordinates (whether they are aware of it or not) each time they erect a natal chart: namely (1) the Zodiac or ecliptic, (2) the Equatorial system (right ascension and declination) and (3) the Horizon system of coordinates. The actual distrinction between these different systems of coordinates are lost to most of us, and they are jumbled together to form some kind of Zodiac pie. It has become my realization that these basic physical planes of reference - the horizon, equator, ecliptic, and even the galactic and supergalactic planes - correspond symbolically to the various different dimensions or levels of our consciousness - as they exist now, in mutual interpenetration. These levels can be sorted out; and as astrologers we may learn to read these different levels as separate, yet related and whole dimension of our experience. Let me rephrase all of this. Our Universe, and therefore our Life, can be described or expressed in astrological terms using any one of several fundamental planes of reference: ecliptic, horizon, etc. These different planes and their respective coordinate systems are like different languages (or algebras), in that they each can express the same moment in time, the same planets - in fact, each can express the entire universe; and yet each orders these same objects and data *in a different way* so as to bring out and raise a particular dimension of reality above the general threshold of our life and awareness. Since our life and consciousness appear to flow through at least several quite distinct levels, it is our conviction that the most sensible method by which to express or map these different levels is through such fundamental orderings, or reference planes. Our almost exclusive concern for the plane of the Earth's orbit - the ecliptic or zodiac and the relation of all activity to this plane - results in a loss of contrast and dimensionality that the use of these alternative coordinate systems provide.

There are at least two basic factors to consider when examining these various coordinate systems; and they are summed up in the familiar axiom: "As above, so below; yet after another manner." The first factor is an indication that the various coordinate systems may be ordered to form a hierarchy in terms of a progressive "inclusivity," or greater comprehensiveness. In other words, the Galactic coordinate system includes the Heliocentric, which *includes* the Geocentric, which *includes* the Horizon, and so forth. This represents the "As above, so below" portion of the phrase: and this "wheels within wheels within wheels" concept is well understood, and a popular one through which to express the various dimensions of consciousness. In other words, a large frame of reference or coordinate system somehow involves information of a larger or more *meta*-physical kind when considered in relation to a more particular or less inclusive system.

The second factor to be illustrated in the phrase "As above, so below: *yet after another manner,"* while of equal importance, is less well understood. The great reference places and their respective systems of coordinates are not only inclusive of one another (that is larger and smaller in relation to each other), but they are also *inclined* at different angles or attitudes to one another. In other words, learning to use and understand the nature of a more inclusive system, such as the Ecliptic or Zodiac system, in relation to the Equatorial or "Right sphere" system is *not only* a matter of ordering the information along a different plane (taking a larger view or picture): it also involves a fundamental change in attitude, or inclination. This shift in attitude, or reorientation of attitude, is an important concept for astrologers to consider and to absorb.

Let me present an analogy which might relate to interpreting these various planes in our everyday life. We are becoming ever more aware on a social level of the Cosmic or transpersonal perspective as being associated with the idea of Expansion, with a more Whole-View: yet we have not understood on this same broad social level that such a change in scale or scope may also involve a basic change in attitude: a fundamental change in approach to life. We can no longer be inclined in directions we once were; and this must amount to a radical change - that is, change at "root" level - in our activity! Furthermore, a basic misunderstanding as to what is involved in spiritual growth has resulted from an attempt to view such growth exclusivity as some kind of "enlargement;" one wistfully looks forward to growing beyond the particular terms of his everyday existence. This is a result of ignorance of the *change of attitude* - the change in point of view, or vantage point - that accompanies true spiritual development: a change very difficult to imagine or assess for one not aware that such change is a natural and expected part of any deeper initiation.

So much for metaphysics. Much of my own research here in Ann Arbor has revolved around these various coordinate systems and the dimensions of life they describe. In particular, I have been concerned with the inclinations or attitudes of one system to another. I like to tell myself that the reason for this interest may be due to the fact that I was born with such a "bad" attitude towards some facets of life in this world, that vast changes in attitude on my part have been necessary simply for my survival. Let me repeat: these different coordinate systems are great Languages or Orderings of our total reality, and each one raises to our attention its characteristic gestalt of whole dimension of life.

To my knowledge, L Edward Johndro was the first modern astrologer to make a life-long concern the articulation of the difference between whole coordinate systems (Ecliptic and Equator). And in my opinion, a final assessment of Johndro's work may not deal so much in terms of his technical genius alone as with the scope and comprehension of his vision; and in particular, that focus of it relating to the essential differences between events as interpreted on the ecliptic or on the equator. In recent years, this research has been carried on and developed further by Charles Jayne, Theodor Landscheidt and others. Our research at the Heart Center School of Astrology has entered on the difference and relationship between the Geocentric and Heliocentric ecliptic systems and, in recent years, on questions of cosmic structure; in particular in an attempt to assess the meaning of the Galactic and Supergalactic planes as they stand in relation to one another, and to the zodiac. With these ideas in mind, we are ready to examine a most particular and fascinating system of coordinates: that of the Horizon. There is no intention here to document or "prove" the validity of this system in this very preliminary research. Our purpose is to present the impression we have formed regarding the dimension to provide those interested with the means to calculate such charts. We would very much appreciate feedback and comments from those of you who investigate this very interesting dimension.

In simple terms the Local Space (LS) chart is a map of the 360 degrees of horizon surrounding an event such as a birth...much as we might look around us toward the east, west, north and south. In this coordinate system, the fundamental plane to which all else is referred is the horizon of the observer; and the position of the various planets as they appear from this location are projected onto the horizon using the coordinates "azimuth" and "altitude".

Azimuth is the equivalent of zodiac longtitude in this system and is measured for our purposes, from the east direction, through the North and on around in a counter-clockwise direction, in the same way that we measure the traditional signs and houses.

Altitude, analogous to ecliptic latitude, is measured above and below the horizon to the poles from 0 degree to 90 degrees. It is worth the emphasis of repetition to stress that, from the standpoint of the Local Space chart, *the horizon is the whole azimuth circle* as it ranges around the wheel of the chart - not simply the line described by House cusps I and VII, as our astrological habituations tempt us to think. This, then, gives a sort of "flat earth" perspective, as it were, the visible horizon being much like a "Magical Circle". And as tradition teaches us regarding the nature of the Magical Circle: the Circle is realized to be the equator of a sphere which extends above and below the plane of the local horizon (apparent or rational horizon cuts the infinite sphere in coincident circles). Here is a map, in space, of an event from a topocentric perspective, or local center; and this, an astrology of Local Space.

Before we dive into the techniques useful in this new dimension of Local Space, here is our impression of "what it is all about": the general feeling of what portion of life is captured through this coordinate system. The most remarkable factor, and the key concept you may need in order to appreciate the particular quality of the Local Space chart, is that *every* object in the universe - whether Celestial or Mundane - has an equal and valid position in this chart. Not only the planets and stars, but on an equal basis, cities, countries and even the local water tower or the neighbor's house can be represented. All that concerns us here is the direction of any object in space - not the distance. In other words, the Celestial Sphere and the Mundane or Geographic Sphere exist side by side and are interchangeable! A star is a city is a neighbor. We can walk towards, write letters to, or get up and move into for instance - our Seventh House. Even more startling, we can travel into our natal planets, since they also represent a direction on the globe in the chart of Local Space.

Here, in a hopeless intermingling of various planes of reference and of objects, a strange and, I must confess, somewhat magical view of our world begins to emerge: one in which every city and friend becomes a radiating center of influence. Here for the first time the long history of Magic, witchcraft and sorcery take on a practical reality, where local deities and preferred directions become the rule, and we are thrust forever beyond the threshold of the just "slightly remarkable". The psychedelic character in Local Space charts is unmistakeable and appears to be intrinsic to the system. The world seems to appear as a kind of grand talisman and vast ritual ground through this perspective. The closest popular image of a similar nature in the modern consciousness is the remarkable world of Don Juan as generated by the author Carlos Castaneda. Here is no "subtle plane", but a personal landscape painted in bold and clear strokes, a world where the modern man is learning to move across the face of the Earth in an endless adjustment and tuning of his radix - of his self. Individuals driven in particular directions on a checkerboard world, unable to resist travelling to a goal that is no particular place on Earth as much as it is a direction within them: the direction of a force, or of a planet: "There! where Power hovers", to use Don Juan's expression. In a word, here is perhaps the most vulgar system, where the obvious is enthroned and the subtle unnecessary. Here then are some specific approaches we have found to be most useful in examining these charts.

Once you have mastered the mathematics involved in erecting these charts (programs that calculate Local Space charts are available from Matrix Software for most popular name computers) involved in erecting these charts, and have laid them out on 360 degree wheels similar to those pictured herein, a probable series of questions you want to investigate may arise. Let us consider some of them.

Compare the planets in the Local Space chart with your geocentric natal chart. As you will soon note, the individual aspects between two planets can be very different in the two kinds of charts; *also*, the larger Whole Chart Patterns may indicate a different quality. A planet may achieve great focus in the Local Space chart that is not brought out in the Geo chart; and yet you may have intuited and sensed the added importance of this planet or principle in the make-up of the individual involved, and yet had no physical basis for your intuition.

The single most important use of Local Space in the astrologer/client relationship in our experience has been in locality shifts. One of the most frequent questions asked the astrologer during a reading is; where would be a good place for me to live? I have made use of the quite valid and useful traditional technique of adjusting the RAMC of the radix to the new locality and coming up with a new Ascendant and so forth. The radix positions then are read in terms of these new angles. Local Space is by nature suited to express both celestial and geographic positions on one map or chart. Its special nature introduces several concepts not encountered in other techniques.

Radix Local Space Charts
Aside from the planetary aspects, there are two primary indicators of strong or high focus in the radix Local Space chart: (1) a planet is on or near the horizon (it has low altitude); and (2) a planet is conjunct to one of the four angles of cardinal directions. It is worth noting which of the planets is closest to the horizon, even if not conjunct. We use standard orbs for azimuth - although we haven't arrived at any "final rules" in this respect. It is also worth noting which planet is the most elevated (has the greatest altitude). And parallels and

contraparallels need investigation. The nature of parallel/contraparallel, as far as interpretation is concerned, may be somewhat different here since they do not describe coincident arcs (as time passes), as do parallels in declination.

We are now ready to examine a technique that gets to the heart of what these charts are all about. At this point we have in front of us our radix Local Space chart, with the various planets plotted on it. As we mentioned earlier, we can also plot the positions of cities and places on the Earth on this map; so, our next project then will be to translate all of the important cities in our lives into their equivalent positions on our radix map of Local Space.

We should be sure to include not only the places we ourselves have lived in or visited, but also the cities that we have always thought that we might like to visit - that bring a warm feeling to mind, and so forth; the positions of cities where friends and not-so-friendlies live, where there are business relationships, etc. We then examine these places in terms of their position (or direction) on the LS chart with these thoughts in mind: are these cities in aspect? In particular by conjunction or opposition? Are they in alignment with planets in the chart? In what quadrants and houses do these cities fall and are any on the angles? We have found that individuals tend to move towards cities that are also in the direction of planets that represents the particular kind of energy they may require at that time. An individul, for instance, needing to invoke the key to success, often obtained through Jupiter, may make one or several moves in that direction. Although its concept is so simple as to be almost embarrassing, this technique has shown itself to be of great value. In any case, its value seems to be *substantial* rather than hypothetical. Next to, for example, some of the cumbersome and ultra-traditional place rulerships, proposed national birth charts, etc - most of them very arbitrary, the complex and confusing juggling of all these factors seem a rather specious approach to the locality problem, and their results rather tentative. The LS chart, at least, can show a concrete, measurable reaction of the individual, even in the same locality, as much as their LS charts vary from one another, and whatever may be the intrinsic character of a place - and places undoubtedly have this, as a selection of people could react very differently to it from the point of view of each one's own make-up. Moreover, each one could react differently at times, under different astrological conditions. Although the mathematics involved in this system may seem a bit complex, the application of its technique is simple and direct; and this does much to recommend it.

Locality Shifts in Local Space

After the basic information in the radix chart has been taken in, we may want to construct secondary charts for the various localities where the individual has lived or travelled. These charts are equivalent to ones cast for this locality at the time of birth, as if one were born there. This involves a transformation of the radix planet's position, as well as a shift around the angles of these positions. Aside from the initial direction from the radix of the locality shift, there are other factors to note.

Through a shift in locality, a planet (or even a city) may be brought into (or away from) the horizon. We have found that a planet achieves high focus when on the horizon, in terms of its activity within the individual. In other words, we can adjust and tune our radix - and ourselves - through locality shifts, much as we might tune a musical instrument. Another objective that might be accomplished by a locality shift is to bring a yet farther away city to high focus - say, to an angle, or in aspect to a planet - allowing a *second* locality shift to be made in its direction. This alters or modifies the psychic interaction of person and place by altering the direction of approach to it. The effect achieved would be quite other than that invoked by approaching it directly. Some of the magical quality of the dimesnion can be seen in the checkerboard-like world concept that emerges, where individuals not only move in relation to a planetary energy they require but are ever adjusting and jockeying into position to achieve the most resonant move. Aside from the focus achieved through the angles and planets, we may compare aspects and Whole Chart Patterns with the radix chart; in particular by bringing one planet to a conjunction with another. As Charles Jayne has pointed out to me, this amounts to progression of the chart through space, rather than time (a very elegant concept) - for those of us, perhaps, who find it hard to wait! We have found that both the conjunction and oppositions (the alignments), as formed by this progression in space, are most significant.

There you have the fundamental ides with which we have worked thus far, the usefulness of these charts in the astrologer/client relationship should be clear. We have used these charts in our practice with success, and have found that many people are concerned with where they might live in order to bring the Self into some resonant and satisfying focus. Perhaps modern man is developing an intuitive sense for self-adjustment and focus through locality shifts - something that ancient man did very little of. It appears that one can enrich and complement various qualities of the radix through location adjustment - bringing our needed energies to one place and time, moving elsewhere for another life episode at another time. What we will need before this technique could ever achieve widespread use is a set of easy tables of azimuth and altitude to be designed and made available to astrologers, thus doing away with the somewhat complicated trigonometry. I hope some of you will brave the necessary calculations and take advantage of this opportunity to explore the astrology of Local Space."

This is taken from the 1978 edition of the Circle Books Astrological Calendar:

Local Space

"I want to relate to you a powerful new way (new to me) of coming to know ourselves through astrology. It involves another kind of map or chart of our birth moment: a map of the space surrounding the birthplace; and this form of topo-centric astrology we call the astrology of Local Space (LS). First I should tell you how I happened on to this fascinating approach.

I was involved in an attempt at understanding the many different House systems that astrologers use, trying to "decide" which, of all of them, might be the best for my purposes. For several years, I had not used any house system at all, but only the four angles of the chart, in a kind of protest or disgust at the lack of agreement among astrologers concerning systems of house division. It seemed rather strange to me that there were so many competing house systems. For many years of my astrological practice, I lacked the necessary mathematical background to decide for myself which of the many house systems made "sense" to me. I could only read about the merits of each house system and take the word of "those who knew". I came to use the Campanus system of houses because many of those astrologers that I respected most used this system. In recent years, I had been learning enough spherical trigonometry on my pocket calculator to make my first attempt at solving the mystery of House division.

I have always been a slow learner; so I had to sit down with an equatorial star-map of the constellations and attempt to draw out graphically the various ways of dividing space and time - in hope of being enlightened as to which house system had the most going for it. Of course, I wanted to draw out the House systems using my own natal chart. This was kind of complex, for I had to calculate, using spherical trigonometry, the 360 degrees of my radix horizon and plot this curving line on the star map (see Figure 59). All house systems agree on the validity of the horizon, and so I felt this was the place to start. This proved to be a most worthwhile exercise. I soon became aware that regardless of which House system was used, what was of interest to astrologers was not the horizon in its own right, but just those few places where it crossed or intersected our beloved Zodiac or ecliptic. In other words, House systems are concerned with different ways of sending meaningful lines to intersect the zodiac; and these intersecting points are then the cusps, or sensitive points, for that individual - a kind of astrologers' acupuncture point.

Laying these House systems out on a map helped me - a great deal - to understand what in fact the various House systems were. But I yearned for some simpler way to deal with it all. I reached a point where I took the problem into my own hands and said "OK Michael, let's suspend judgment on which of all these House systems is best and do something very simple, although perhaps unsophisticated, that will make sense to you". I started off by making the center of our House system the place where one is born, and I put the pole of the system overhead - the pole of the birthplace - and instead of using more complex methods of division, I divided the surrounding space into a simple pie of twelve divisions radiating out from the birthplace. This was represented on the Earth (geographically) and through space (astronomically). This, would be my very own House system! The points where the twelve radiating lines intersected the Zodiac place would be the House cusps or sensitive points in this system.

I was, at this point, as "bad" as the other astrologers who had developed their own systems. I did find that, although this method of House division was quite radical compared to the more familiar systems, the particular cusp degrees of the zodiac had already proved significant and were already "favorite" and previously noted points along the zodiac. My friend and fellow astrologer James Coats promptly termed this the Radiant House System, since the cusps radiated out from a central place on Earth. I had, in my own way, stumbled upon what I found out was already known as the Horizontal House System, which, along with the Campanus System represents one of two obvious and complementary ways to divide the space surrounding a birth into equal parts. The astrologer L. Edward Johndro calls the Campanus System "the Ferris wheel", and the Radiant or Horizontal System "the merry-go-round". Astrologer Charles Jayne has been pointing out the need to investigate this Horizontal System of House for many years.

I was still interested in those twelve little points where these radiating lines intersected the old familiar zodiac. Then something very important began to occur to me. I began to see that the Horizon System was a complete system in itself, just as the zodiac is, stretching a full 360 degrees around the heavens. Instead of considering the horizon as a necessary means to get at and define these zodiacal pressure points, I began to follow on the star map the line of my radix horizon through the heavens to the point where it intersected the plane or line of the Zodiac on this map. This point was, of course, my Ascendant and 7+ degrees of Sagittarius. But my eyes kept going past the Ascendant, following my horizon until it intersected another line: that of the plane of our galaxy; at which point the first shock rolled in. My horizon intersected the galactic plane constellation Cygnus, the Swan.

At this point, I must relate a more personal story to make clear what was happening. Over the past years, I had been assembling a book containing stellar points and planes: *Astrophysical Directions*, and in the process I had to calculate and plot quite a few maps of the heavens. In this way, I came to know and develop a sense of the major constellations in a much more intimate way than ever before. Throughout this work, I noted a "fixation" on a couple of constellations in particular. Above them all, I revered the constellation Cygnus; and on repeated occasions, for no reason I could determine, I felt such deep identification with this constellation and what it seemed to signify that tears came to my eyes. Now I find that Cygnus was one of the two constellations where my own particular horizon crossed the great plane of our galaxy - a kind of galactic Descendant and Ascendant; the other being the constellation Vela, the Sails, another constellations to which I had always been very sensitive. Well, I had to laugh at this point. What, I said to myself, if the entire 360 degrees of the horizon of my birth is as sensitive as the Node where it crosses the Zodiac, the Ascendant. What if there are other basic planes of importance to us, besides the Zodiac, to which we respond? Did I have a galactic and supergalactic Ascendant and new sets of constellations or "signs" to come to know?

At this point, I must shrink a long, and to me, a beautiful story and simply say that this discovery was the first of a great many such mini-enlightenments I was to have. I searched through my collection of horoscopes to see how my friends and acquaintances were oriented. I was discovering the strength and power of the local horizon. I had accepted and used the Ascendant and Vertex and other sensitive ecliptic points in my work, but always with the accent on the zodiac. I had never stopped to think that in each case it took another plane to bring these Nodes or points of intersection into existence - in this case, it was the plane of the horizon. And yet I had, in a subconscious way, used the horizon in all my work. I could now see that each individual had a kind of unique orientation or attitude to the whole cosmos and that in the horizon we had a plane capable of revealing much more about oneself than just those sensitive points which relate to the Zodiac.

At any rate, I began to explore the whole of the heavens from *my* point of view. For a time, I forgot the Zodiac and instead began to inquire, and thus to learn a great deal about my own attitude and orientation to my birth event, to my life. Somewhere during this time, another idea occurred to me that proved to be most compelling: the horion also traced a path on maps of the Earth, as well as the heavens. I had calculated by this time a complete chart of the planets' positions in the Horizon System using the system's equivalent to Zodiac longitude and latitude called - azimuth and altitude. How, I wondered, would the directions of the planets in my horizon chart relate to directions and cities on this Earth? I soon developed the trigonometry needed to answer these questions - quite a prodigious undertaking for me - and thus began a real "magical mystery tour" through my life history. Although I have lived in several different places, the one major move in my life has been from Lancaster, Pennsylvania (my birthplace) to Ann Arbor, Michigan. Of course, what I wanted to know was, what direction was Ann Arbor from Lancaster? That is what degree did Ann Arbor occupy on my radix or birth horizon?

And here rolled in the second great shock wave. Ann Arbor was right in the direction of my natal Jupiter position on the Local Space chart - within two degrees. In other words, a move to Ann Arbor was a move in the direction of my natal Jupiter. Jupiter rules my Ascendant and its position above the Seventh House cusp had made it very prominent in any analysis of my chart.

At any rate, I wondered at such a coincidence and set out to answer some of the other questions that now began to pop up in my mind. What about the other places I had lived, or to which I had travelled or thought of travelling to? The history of my travel came before my mind...some places of joy and learning, others of sorrow and pain. I plotted the directions and calculated the charts for all of these places, and what I found through reading these charts was overwhelming; it marked my initial surrender to what now appears to be - for me - a major discovery in my astrological life: that of Local Space. I erected different Local Space charts. These amounted to maps of the space surrounding each place as if I had been born there, rather than at Lancaster. The story of my life and self, interpreted and confirmed through my reading of these Local Space charts, was moving - to say the least.

Let me cite an example of the sort of thing I found. I am well known to my friends as being a homebody. It is very difficult for anything to induce me to leave Ann Arbor. At one point in my life however, I sold everything I owned. My wife and I moved north to go into the green plant business, to manage our own greenhouses. I actually left Ann Arbor and moved away! It so happened that we were a couple of years ahead of our time in offering fine greenhouse plants to people; the demand for these plants and the plant store craze did not appear until later. We lost everything in this venture. On the material or investment plane, it was a disaster. Now, in my Local Space chart I have triple conjunction of the Moon, Uranus and Saturn to the same degree; in anybody's astrology, this has accounted for quite a strong focus. The move into the greenhouse business was a move precisely - to the degree - into (or towards) this triple conjunction! I had actually *moved into* my Moon-Uranus-Saturn conjunction! It was is if we had gone there to wrestle and come to terms with my Saturn (or with Satan, you might say) - and come out the wiser for it. For this experience, as hard as it was, ended many more superficial fears on my part concerning loss. We lost what to us at the time was everything, and still our life went on.

What had impressed me through this voyage of discovery was the potency of the *entire* horizon, and of more than just a couple of its points; and the fact that somehow the orientation of an individual to the cosmos made a difference, or was reflected in behaviour and activity at the supramundane level. It took me quite a while to "develop the faith", or to let myself believe that God was so thorough in his/her influence as to be all-pervading down to the finest details. It was a while later before I could entertain with grace the idea that this same orientation or attitude was reflected *as much upon the map of the Earth* as upon the map of the heavens. Another way of putting this (and this is, to me, the beauty of Local Space astrology), is that Heaven and Earth are interchangeable, or are in the last analysis one living entity - a single whole. This is made ever so clear in the LS chart, where every object in the universe, celestial and mundane, has an equal and valid position. Not only the planets

213

and the stars, but on an equal basis, cities, countries, and even the local water tower or friends' houses can be represented. All that concerns us is the direction in space: the orientation, not the distance. In Local Space the Heavens and Earth, the Celestial and Mundane (or Geographic) spheres exist side by side and are interchangeable.

In drawing this year's article to a close, I would like to share a few experiences and thoughts with you concerning some of the structure in space beyond the Zodiac and how it can be of value in individual development and growth. Let me relate a personal story as to how I first got interested in the deeper regions of space. Our research, as some of you will know, has centered on the difference and relationship between the geocentric and heliocentric ecliptic systems. My interest in the space surrounding our solar system was minimal. I was put off by the billions of stellar objects out there and, on a more basic level, by the ideas of Coldness and Blackness I had been programmed to associate with outer space. Distant space somehow represented the epitome of "otherness" and foreignness" to me. I was embarrassed, in terms of astrological usage, by all of the books I had read on the fixed stars, with the exception of L.E.Johndro's book *The Stars.* How was I to determine the significance of these billions of stars and use them in my practice, when I had enough difficulty, as it was, using nine planets?

And then the unexpected happened. I had a dream. It was not an ordinary dream but one of those dreams that are more real than waking consciousness - that take months to understand and absorb. In my dream an "astrologer" appeared to me whose eyes were filled with light. There were rays or stalks of light coming out of his eyes. This strange being said but one word: "LOOK!" and with his arm turned and pointed to the night sky. I looked. The sky was filled with brilliant points of light. The stars and all of this starry material was clustered together to form the great glowing arch of the Milky Way or galactic plane. It was wondrous beyond description and in that instant my heart went out from me and filled this bright space. Never again have I had the feeling of being here on Earth, warm and trembling before the Cold and Black of space. I became the space and light and reversed my polarity or attitude. I was a living representative of this mother galaxy. I was the spaceman!

From that night forward I began to venture beyond the zodiac in an inquiry as to the nature and structure of this universe. Here, in brief form, is what I found for myself: We are nodes or information aggregates. The Universe is in intimate contact with itself through us. The manyfold nature of the cosmic events is represented through our self and lives. There is not only a correlation between these seemingly remote cosmic events and our person, but an identity as well. Information coming from the Galactic Center, carried by electromagnetic and gravitational radiation from every last star and cosmic plane and event passes through us at all times. We are, in some way, a node or information complex caught in a matrix or web of manifestation.

The overpowering idea that occurs when we make some acquaintance with the universe and its structure is that there is no difference between out there and in here. We are out there! Our world and our self and relationships are a perfect reflection of what is and what is happening out there. Not an analogy, but an identity. Black holes, supernovae, quasars and the like are not remote cosmic events, but this identical story is represented, reflected, lived and acted out each day in our lives.

Information circulates through the universe and our identity or sense of our self in this very process of circulation. Identity is not a substance, but a relationship, in fact, a circulation and a process of communion or communication. Not only is there a connection between our life and that of our galaxy and universe, but *we are* the connection. A study of the structure of the universe, at any level, is a study of ourselves. In summary, the idea that I am elaborating here is: Astrology is not only a symbolic system of psychological discussion. The symbol is also, in fact, real. If we say it is an analogy, then the analogy is complete down to the limits of any specific example we might choose.

We are all time and space travellers. There are no better words that I know of than these of Emerson in his *Essay on History* : 'All inquiry into antiquity is the desire to do away with this wild, savage and preposterous There or Then, and introduce in its place the Here and the Now. Belzoni (an archaeologist) digs and measures in the mummy-pits and pyramids of Thebes until he can see the end of the difference between the monstrous work and himself. When he has satisfied himself, in general and in detail, that it was made by such a person as he, so armed and so motivated, and to ends which he, himself, should also have worked, the problem is solved; his thought lives along the whole line of temples and sphinxes and catacombs, passes through them all with satisfaction, and they live again to the mind, or are now'."

APPENDIX FIVE

THE LOCAL SPACE CHART

by Sean Lovatt

This is an excerpt from an article called 'The Local Space Chart' by Sean Lovatt. The article in its entirety can be found in the Autumn 1992 edition of the Astrology Quarterly Volume 64 no. 4.

Using the Local Space Chart[1]
The LSC is most interesting when it differs a great deal from the natal, as it often does. Sometimes it will offer clues as to which area of the natal chart is likely to be felt most strongly at the birth location, information that does not readily exist elsewhere. This side of LS can be very useful when looking at childhood and other experiences and may explain why obviously hard aspects in the ecliptic chart are sometimes modified.

Relocating the Local Space chart
Relocating the LSC offers advantages over relocating the ecliptic chart because of the greater number of variables. When considering a local space chart, it is important to first understand the natal chart. Naturally since we are using the planets in both systems the natal chart's planetary patterns give clues as to how the Local Space energies will manifest. To know, for instance, 'what sort of Uranus' is brought into focus in the Local Space chart we must firstly look to the natal chart. Having understood both the natal ecliptic and the natal local space chart we are then ready to relocate.

Planets that are not aspecting each other in the natal chart are especially important when they form a meaningful aspect in LS; at these locations people tend to be affected by intense emotions that are outside their usual experience. Local Space offers us a more transpersonal view. A specific place can bring into focus certain planetary patterns that are not in the natal chart, which is how we can analyse our geographical experiences: in Local Space we have a profound method for enhancing our understanding of ourselves and our place in the world. Each point on the map has a unique planetary pattern for each individual. With Local Space charts it is truly possible to find healing spots,

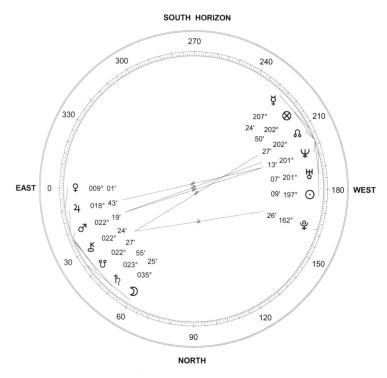

Figure 96

places to retreat to and, of course, places to retreat from. The ability to divine the experience that someone might have in any given region provides astrology with an extremely powerful tool, and as such the versatility of Local Space is virtually unlimited.

Local Space charts can be uncannily apt. The planetary symbolism often shouts extremely loudly, sometimes so obviously that it is hard to credit. The charts can express themselves in very physical ways, allowing us to clearly predict what sort of energies and events are to be experienced in a given place.

The chart shown in Figure 96 above is extremely instructive. 'Mark's' local space chart (data from his mother to the author & withheld by request) is relocated from the birth place in the U.K to Mombassa Kenya and tells us not only why he might go there but also what might happen on arrival.

Venus and Jupiter in the east strongly suggest that this is a holiday destination. The easterly position of Mars hints at sports and its aspect to Neptune suggests activities of an aquatic nature - Mark was in fact proposing to go on a scuba diving holiday! With the Sun in the west he felt this trip was very important as it offered the chance to spend time with his father, something he had not done since his parents' divorce. We can see from the Uranus/Sun conjunction that the break from routine he was looking for was on offer in this

218

part of East Africa. Uranus/Sun in the west is very apt as Mark was technically too young to dive according to international regulations: never-the-less his father had found a way to circumvent the rules. What is not immediately obvious is that Mars and Neptune are the real key - not only are they are in opposition to each other and quite close to the east-west axis, but they share similar altitude close to the horizon at -2 degrees 55 minutes and -8 degrees 6 minutes respectively. Three factors that when combined offer very powerful indicators. Although Uranus is involved in the Mars-Neptune opposition, its altitude is vastly different, and its influence therefore is secondary. I was worried about Mark's health if he were to actually go to Mombassa. Mars-Neptune equalled infection, drowning, or some other terrible fate (in my mind), and I went to great pains to advise Mark to be particularly careful about his diet whilst on holiday. I had images of him eagerly devouring suspicious looking sausages at a beach side barbecue and suffering the consequences.

Mark did in fact go to Mombassa for two weeks. The first week he spent diving, and by all accounts had a great time, however, during the second he became ill after cutting himself. The wound became infected and would not heal (very Mars-Neptune). On his return to the UK, Mark's GP referred him to a specialist, and after some extensive tests he was diagnosed as having caught a rare and unpleasant, but not fatal, blood infection. I am glad to say that Mark has now made a full recovery, but his convalescence took three months.

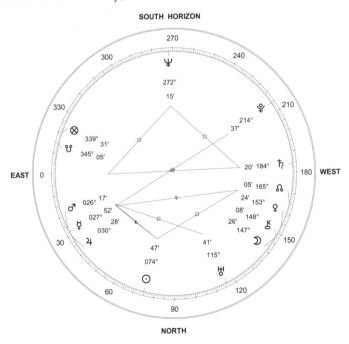

Figure 97

219

Figure 97 shows Richard Nixon's [2] local space relocated from his birth place in Yorba Linda, CA to Washington DC, the seat of his infamous presidency. With Neptune in the south (which is equivalent to the MC for charts cast north of the planet's declination) we are given a suitably apt symbol for a man who was known firstly for his idealistic Quaker inspired policy that lead to the US withdrawal from Vietnam and secondly for the political and criminal deceptions that caused his downfall. With the Moon conjunct Venus trine that prominent Neptune we can see why the public gave him such a landslide victory in the elections for his second term. It is no surprise with these aspects strong that Nixon was given a free pardon by his successor Gerald Ford, fully rehabilitated as a public figure and a very popular after dinner speaker before his death.

Saturn in the west indicates clearly why Nixon became so suspicious and confrontational in his dealings with the Washington establishment, and its square to the southerly Neptune more than hints at the scandal which Watergate was to become. Mercury/Mars opposite Pluto is yet another powerful symbol that bears witness to the skulduggery, misuse of intelligence and information that led Nixon to be the only US President ever to resign whilst in office.

In this aspect we can see Nixon's refusal to produce evidence that was required of him by the Judiciary at the Watergate enquiry. Mars and Mercury are conjunct both in conventional terms and by the fact that they share the same altitude; being square to Uranus is it any surprise that electronic bugging devices featured so prominently in a scandal that rocked the world's most powerful nation?

Local space charts are not always so obvious, but with a little practice they can be a very effective tool for the astrologer to draw on when the question of geographical changes are to be considered.

NOTES

1. Calculation of the LSC can be performed by most astrological software, and can be requested from most calculation services. Tables do exist designed for navigation aids, such as the British Admiralty Nautical Almanac - but they require skills not usually possessed by astrologers and are expensive.

2. 9th January 1913; 09:35 PM PST, Yorba Linda, CA. Source: AA/T. Pat Davis.

BIBLIOGRAPHY
Local Space - A Guide to What it is and How to use it, by Martin Davis.
    Astro*Centre Publications 1989.
Planets in Locality, by Steve Cozzi, Llewellyn 1988.
Astro-Physical Directions, by Michael Erlewine, Ann Arbor MI. USA 1977.

APPENDIX SIX

PLUTO'S POSITION ON ACG MAPS

by Martin Davis

When we view and employ ACG as a technique in its own right we have a relatively simple and straightforward situation; the map's lines are derived from the planetary positions in angularity to the earth. These alignments are astronomical fact. An issue arises however when we see ACG as an overview of planetary angularity in natal or relocated charts. The problem is that the usual ecliptic charts introduce an astronomical approximation. They are calculated assuming that all of the planets are on the ecliptic. In fact, at any time, some planets may be above or below the exact ecliptic plane, as measured in celestial latitude. This means that a discrepancy is introduced (in our charts) such that an ACG map may portray planetary lines of 'true' angularity which don't exactly match the planets on the angles of a corresponding chart at a specific earth location.

The situation for our era (c. 2000) is that Pluto is 11 degrees of celestial latitude above the ecliptic, Saturn is 2 degrees below, Venus 2 degrees above, while the Moon zips about monthly moving anywhere from a position on the ecliptic (0 degrees of latitude) to a maximum of about plus or minus 5 degrees above or below it. The other planets are close enough to the ecliptic (including the Sun, which is on the ecliptic by definition) such that there are no noticeable discrepancies between the angular lines of an ACG map and the planetary angularity in a corresponding chart.

Let's look at some examples to make this clearer. Alex was born on 17 July 1965 at 4:22 PM in London. His birth chart is shown in Figure 98. Note that zodiacal Pluto (at 14 degrees, 23 minutes of Virgo) is in almost perfect conjunction with his midheaven (at 14 degrees, 20 minutes). We might therefore expect that the Pluto MC line on his ACG map would run right through London, a location on his natal MC meridian. As we see in Figure 99, Alex's ACG map in European detail, this is not exactly the situation. We have two possible Pluto MC positions for him, with the astronomically true or so-called 'in mundo' position not over London at all but through Western Belgium some 250 miles away! Why? At Alex's birth moment, Pluto's latitude was 14 degrees

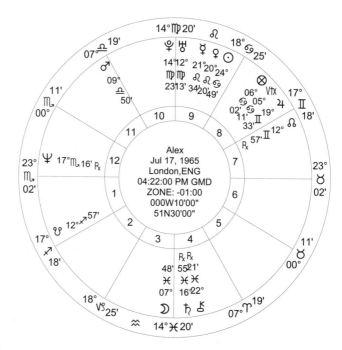

Figure 98

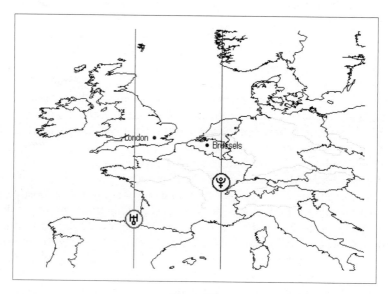

Figure 99

above the ecliptic with its projection onto the ecliptic (not its actual position) bringing it to London's MC meridian. This London ACG position for Pluto would then be called its zodiacal placement[1].

Which position to use? Fortunately, for most planets the differences are negligible. What to do if there is an occasional but significant difference? Jim Lewis had no doubts about this as he felt that the 'true' or in mundo position was what ACG was all about. I tend to agree with this or at least feel that the difference for an MC or IC line of even 250 miles is still within the orb of effectiveness that he recommended. I would see Alex's Pluto MC line as being centred over the Netherlands and Western Belgium (see Figure 99) but would also view him as being a Pluto-on-the-MC type of personality (see Figure 98).

Neat and tidy? Case closed? No way! There has been commentary from people of Alex's age (the so-called Generation-X era) stating that the zodiacal position for their Pluto (on either the MC or the IC) makes as much sense to them as the 'true' or in mundo placement, if and when they take their life experience into account. That is, the projected placement of an angular Pluto (zodiacal) seems to manifest as (or even more) strongly then the 'true' one (in mundo) some few hundred miles away.

Pluto's rising and setting lines at extreme latitudes can result in the differences between in mundo and zodiacal positioning becoming even larger. In experimenting with various charts proposed for Czar Nicholas II, I found one example that yielded a difference of 1000 miles! For this one set of proposed birth data[2], dangerous Pluto was placed on the ascendant of the chart relocated to the site of his assassination - the northern city of Ekateringburg (56 degrees, 51 minutes north) - yet his in mundo ACG ascending line was 1000 miles away from there! The issue of whether I had the best data for him or not does not change the fact of possible large differences between zodiacal and in mundo placements, especially at extreme latitudes.

NOTES

1. Thanks to Graham Dawson of Esoteric Technologies Ltd (Australia) for including an 'in mundo' vs. zodiacal switch option in Solar Maps.

2. Various times and birth dates have been proposed for Nicholas II and used in studies by astrologers. The one that highlighted the great difference to me was: 31 May 1868 [new style], 00:30 AM, St Petersburg, source unknown. The data set that I have the most confidence in however is listed in Rodden's Astro Databank program: 18 May 1868 [new style], 00:30 AM, St Petersburg. Source: W. Bruce Lincoln's book, "*Nicholas II*", page 603.

APPENDIX SEVEN

JIM LEWIS

5th June 1941 - 21st February 1995

At Washington D.C. in 1992, to the applause of his fellow astrologers, Jim Lewis marched up to the rostrum to receive astrology's nearest equivalent to the Oscars. Voted by his colleagues, he was awarded the Regulus Prize for astrological research and innovation. This was final confirmation of what the public had recognised for years, that Jim Lewis was an exceptional and original astrologer.

Astro*Carto*Graphy, (A*C*G) - the system of mapping out lines where the planets were angular for a particular time onto a terrestrial map - was Jim's baby. Locational astrology was not new - perhaps originating long before the Three Wise Men converted stellar observations onto maps to locate a special birth. Imitators argued that 'Right Ascension' could not be copyrighted. But Jim was the first to develop detailed world maps, a complete technique, a systematically-written 'cook-book' analysis, a trade-mark, software, a commercial service, lectures, courses, articles and a certified examination in the field. He made what was an obscure technique, accessible. On that no one could touch him.

Jim's astrology used only the most basic and established theories. In working with angular planets, he followed the tradition of the Chaldeans. Ptolemy later defined the technique. More recently Michel and Francoise Gauquelin refined, scientifically proved and replicated this planetary effect. With the notable exception of Carl Jung, Jim seemed to bypass most Arabic, Roman and recent western astrological developments. As well as the IC and the distant outer planets, his work focused on visible celestial bodies in visible locations: planets rising, setting and at the midheaven. Although he accepted the recent addition of lines for Chiron, the Node and the ecliptic, he rejected lines displaying planetary aspects despite their commercial possibilities. Throughout he retained this clarity, integrity and purity of his theory. In this sense Jim was a scientific astrologer, living out the potential of Saturn conjunct Uranus in Taurus in his 10th house.

Astro*Carto*Graphy was an evolving technique. Jim built up his knowledge with real examples based on feedback from grateful clients all over the world. He studied and wrote about the A*C*G of current affairs and the charts of prominent individuals of the day. His observations were acute, radical and persuasive. I remember his comments on the Queen's A*C*G, with her natal Saturn MH line running along the British Isles and the essentially conservative nature of a country that makes one person superior to another by virtue of their birth. And he had equally sharp observations for the country of his birth, where he found it difficult to express his strong Pluto, without feeling alienated. This was a love - hate - love relationship.

As a lecturer, Jim was undoubtedly a 'class act', a star attraction on the international circuit. He worked with his own excellent material: original, solid, tried and tested astrology backed up by amusing anecdotes. True to Pluto rising in Leo, his height and manner gave him a strong, dramatic presence and with the Sun and two planets in Gemini a coherent and flowing delivery.

Jim Lewis, born James Slayden on 5th June 1941 at 9:30 am EDT in Yonkers, NY, had an intriguing life outside astrology. He recounted tales of hunting deer and other wild animals whilst living in a commune at Big Sur in the redwood forests of California. Later he spent a year on a sparsely populated Caribbean island. He was also a significant, though discreet, member of the San Franciscan gay community.

But it was Astro*Carto*Graphy that made Jim Lewis renowned around the world. It was his greatest success and yet he was also a victim of the work. Jim was strongly litigious and considerable resources and intense emotion, were directed into protecting his trade-mark. And he was not immune to the negative potential on A*C*G's 'planetary power lines'. In the mid '80's he was struck by a vehicle while crossing Military Road, in Sydney, Australia on his Mars Ascending line. In a strange way he felt that his illness was brought on by the pressures of the A*C*G business. Behind the tragedy, there is a cruel irony that someone so cerebral (Sun and Moon in Air) should have been afflicted by a brain tumour at the age of 54 years.

His work will live on. It is a little known fact that his Astro*Carto* Graphy handbook that accompanies the world A*C*G maps has been the most successful astrological publication outside sun-sign titles and the ephemerides. Besides the continuing operation of his three A*C*G licensees in Oregon, London and Zurich and his many certified A*C*G interpreters, he has been published posthumously. His friend and certified Astro* Carto*Grapher, Erin Sullivan has published his final work "The Psychology of Astro*Carto*Graphy" as part of the Penguin Arkana series.

God, we astrologers were lucky to have a mind like his among us and by heaven, we will miss him.

Robert Currey
Cert. A*C*G Interpreter Equinox, London

BIBLIOGRAPHY

Allen, Peter. *The 91 Before Lindbergh.* UK: Airlife Books, 1984.

Baigent, Michael, N. Campion and C.Harvey. *Mundane Astrology.* UK: Aquarian Press, 1984.

Barker, Stan. *The Sign of the Times.* Minnesota: Llewellyn Publications, 1986

Blake, A.G.E. *The Intelligent Enneagram.* London: Shambhala, 1996.

Bohm, David and F. Peat. *Science, Order and Creativity.* London: Routledge, 1989.

Campion, Nicholas. *The Book of World Horoscopes.* Bristol: Cinnabar Books, 1995.

Cozzi, Steve. *Planets in Locality.* Arizona: AFA publications, 1997.

Erlewine, Michael and Margaret. *Astrophysical Directions.* Michigan: Heart Centre, 1977.

Ebertin, Reinhold. *The Combination of Stellar Influences.* Arizona: AFA, 1972.

Fenton, Sasha. *Astrology on the Move.* London: Zambesi Publishing, 1998.

Guttman, Ariel and Kenneth Johnson. *Mythic Astrology.* Minnesota: Llewellyn Publications, 1993.

Hamaker-Zondag, Karen. *De Astrologische Windroos.* Amsterdam: Symbolon, 1993

Hand, Robert. *Planets in Transit.* Pennsylvania: Whitford Press, 1976.

Hand, Robert. *Horoscope Symbols.* Massachusetts: Para Research, 1981.

Hand, Robert. *Essays on Astrology.* Massachusetts: Para Research, 1982.

Harding, Michael and Charles Harvey. *Working With Astrology.* London: Arkana, 1990.

Hathaway, Edith. *Navigating by the Stars.* Minnesota: Llewellyn Publications, 1991.

Hill, Lynda and Richard. *The Sabian Symbols as an Oracle.* Australia: Hill & Hill P/L, 1995.

Howland, Ronald. *A Chronology of American Charts.* UK: Poz Publications, 1998.

Kharitidi, Olga. *Entering the Circle.* San Francisco: Harper, 1996.

Lavoie, Alphee and Lorraine Welsh. *Essentials of Intermediate Astrology.* USA: NCGR, 1995.

Lewis, Jim and Ariel Guttman. *The Astro*Carto*Graphy Book of Maps.* Minnesota: Llewellyn Publications, 1989.

Lewis, Jim and Kenneth Irving. *The Psychology of Astro*Carto*Graphy.* London: Arkana, 1997.

Lovell, Mary. S. *The Sound of Wings.* London: Hutchinson, 1991

Mayo, Jeff. *The Astrologer's Astronomical Handbook.* U.K.: L.N.Fowler & Co., 1982.

McEvers, Joan. (ed). *Astrology of the Macrocosm.* Minnesota: Llewellyn Publications, 1990.

Mckenna, Terence. *The Archaic Revival.* New York: Harper, 1992.

McRae, Chris. *The Geodetic World Map.* Arizona: AFA, 1988.

Meadows, David. *Where in the World with Astro*Carto*Graphy.* Arizona: AFA Publications, due 1999.

Morell, Virginia. *Amelia Earhart* . National Geographic, January 1998.

Morse, Eric. *The Living Stars*. New York: Amethyst Books, 1988.

Pottinger, Maritha and Zipporah Dobyns. *Planets on the Move*. San Diego: ACS Publications, 1995.

Rudhyar, Dane. *An Astrological Mandala*. New York: Random House, Inc., 1973

Rudhyar, Dane. *The Lunation Cycle*. New York: Aurora Press, 1986.

Sakoian, Frances and Louis Acker. *The Astrologer's Handbook*. London: Penguin, 1974.

Wertheim, Margaret. *Pythagoras' Trousers*. London: Fourth Estate, 1996.